9780918024060
AF574493

ST. DUNSTAN'S
COLLEGE
LIBRARY

Selective Bibliography *of* AMERICAN LITERATURE

Selective Bibliography of AMERICAN LITERATURE 1775-1900

A BRIEF ESTIMATE OF THE MORE IMPORTANT AMERICAN AUTHORS AND A DESCRIPTION OF THEIR REPRESENTATIVE WORKS

By B. M. FULLERTON

WITH AN INTRODUCTION

BY *Carl Van Doren*

WILLIAM FARQUHAR PAYSON

NEW YORK 1932

PRINTED IN THE UNITED STATES OF AMERICA
BY THE STRATFORD PRESS, INC., NEW YORK

To

CHARLES P. EVERITT

whose friendly encouragement has been an invaluable stimulus

PREFACE

THIS book is designed to serve as a guide to noteworthy achievements in American letters between the years 1775 and 1900, rather than in any way as a complete check list or bibliography. As such it selects from among the many writers who have graced that period only those who have to greater or lesser degree made a definite contribution to the form, trend or substance of American literature, or to the Nation's true intellectual development, and from among their works to choose only such as are representative of them at their best.

To the usual method of handling such subject matter is added a treatment of each author as an individual, which makes it possible to bring the lesser ones into a true and just perspective and substitutes for the generalizations with which they are commonly dismissed a careful bibliographical identification of their best work. It is this aspect which the author hopes will prove of especial value, for, though we have many excellent reference books on the subject, up to the present time not one of them has included carefully compiled bibliographical data.

In the selection of the earlier authors it has been impossible to apply modern critical standards. Our earlier novelists particularly must be viewed in their historical setting. If we fail to consider them as pioneers we miss much of their true, and in many cases their chief significance. Not until the appearance of the "Sketch Book" can American literature be said to have matured, and even after its appearance occasional allowances have to be made.

For their assistance in compiling the bibliographical information in this book I am deeply indebted to Mr. Parma of the Library of Congress, Mr. Blackburn and others of the staff of the New York Public Library, Mr. Brigham and Mr. Vail of the American Antiquarian Society, Prof. Damon of Brown University, Mr. Winship of the Harvard College Library, Mr. Whitman Bennett, Mr. Merle Johnson and Mr. Oscar Wegelin.

I owe especial thanks to my father. His collaboration has been invaluable. If he had permitted me to have my way his name would have appeared on the title page with mine.

B. M. F.

INTRODUCTION

MOST historians of American literature will have to wince when they read Mr. Fullerton's *Selective Bibliography*. No matter how careful they may have been about, for instance, their dates, they are almost certain to have been occasionally reckless. When, assigning the year of publication to some book, they came upon a conflict among authorities, they have too often been content to guess and let it go at that. Mr. Fullerton has not guessed. He has hunted for an actual copy of the first edition of every book he was describing, and has either found it and given its date correctly or else has admitted that no copy was available to him—or, so far as he could learn, to anybody. Dates are the true stepping-stones across the flood of literary history. If they are insecure or slippery the crossing is dangerous. To be lax about them is to slip into errors and to flounder on to false conclusions. There is an almost living energy in a wrong date when it has once been printed. Unquestioned because it looks precise, it is passed along like gossip. When it has been a few times repeated it acquires a stubborn momentum which only original research can check, and it may still continue to have its false authority in all but the most exacting quarters of scholarship. The first duty of every living historian of American literature, now that this *Selective Bibliography* has been published, is to look again at his own work, checking every date he has set down. The scrupulous hand of Mr. Fullerton will appear, however hidden, in many new editions of such works. His stepping-stones are corner-stones.

Nor is it only for the accuracy of his dates that Mr. Fullerton must prove useful. Selecting the books to be described, he has gone back to the sources. That is, he has studied what was actually written and printed in America between 1775 and 1900 rather than what has ordinarily been stressed by literary historians. In the history of literature, as all experts and many amateurs have observed, the successive chroniclers have a way of following one another like elephants in a parade, each of them with his trunk firmly gripping the tail of his predecessor in the obedient file. The earliest historians, chopping what path they can through the wilderness of books, establish a canon. The writers they have chosen to discuss, and the books by those writers, have thereafter a presumptive claim upon subsequent historians, who must either support it or else give space to challenges. Rarely does a new historian have the bravery and power to survey and map the field as if he were the first in it. Even when he does, he is likely to be self-conscious, and for that reason bumptious, cutting down reputations and setting reputations up with evident pride in his audacity. Mr. Fullerton has not betrayed the pride which he is justified in feeling. His method has been, with that humility which makes pride seem a little absurd in comparison, to discover what books were published, when and where, and how the first editions may be recognized. His descriptions are based upon the books as issued, not upon them as enlarged by the fame or belittled by the obscurity which has affected them since then. Here are the bare facts which will make it necessary to test all kinds of generalizations previously made about the course of American literature.

Mr. Fullerton has, of course, the bias which shows itself in every authority who is also a human being. This *Selective Bibliography* has been compiled by a book-seller who has specialized in American books and who has, further, an antiquarian disposition. He is generous towards the older books he has to deal with, and with certain books which belong up dim blind alleys, not on the highroad of his subject. This gives his work a particular value for book-lovers as well as for book-sellers. They both know that the historians of literature, perhaps unavoidably, deal for the most part with the books which have been successes in their world: which have seemed representative of general thoughts or sentiments, which have shown in which direction the greater winds were blowing, which have left landmarks behind them, and so may have a standing in history which they have nowhere else. But book-sellers and book-lovers also know that there are many books, never quite successful, which continue to delight inquiring readers. Overlooking them is like studying only the tallest trees in a forest, with no attention to the underwoods which may contribute much to the forest's character and which at least have characteristics of their own. To such minor works of art, to such often engaging documents, Mr. Fullerton has given the room and care usually reserved for masterpieces. His *Selective Bibliography* is a bibliography of the American Apocrypha.

And yet he has not, by snubbing masterpieces, made himself a mere collector of literary curiosities. Big books and little are ranged side by side in his conscientious retrospect. If he has been a scientist in his search for his materials, he has been an artist—or at any rate an anthologist—in his choice of what he should include. He has not put in all the writers he knows about, nor all the books of all the writers he has put in. With the courage of his taste, the taste of a book-seller who is a book-lover, Mr. Fullerton has chosen those titles which he thought important, interesting, deserving. At some points he may well seem, to some rival specialists, wilful, if not capricious. Why did he include this writer or exclude that book? Questions of the sort must begin as soon as his work has come under calculating eyes, and will go on for years. The *Selective Bibliography* is, within its punctilious scope, something which promises to last. It will not be less permanent because it rouses controversies as frequently as it settles them.

CARL VAN DOREN

Selective Bibliography *of* AMERICAN LITERATURE

CERTAIN ANONYMOUS AND MISCELLANEOUS BOOKS

ADSONVILLE: OR MARRYING OUT. A Narrative Tale. Albany, 1824.

Errata note at the bottom of page VIII.

A SIMPLE story of the trials and difficulties attending the courtship of a Quaker maiden and a youth of different faith. Rigidly conventional from a modern point of view, yet highly significant as perhaps the first American novel dealing even indifferently well with this vexing problem.

AMELIA; OR, THE FAITHLESS BRITON, an Original American Novel, founded upon recent facts. To which is added, Amelia, or Malevolence; and, Miss Seward's Monody on Major André. Boston, 1798.

WITHOUT disparagement of "Constantius and Pulchera" and "Mis Mac Rea," both of which preceded it—though the latter is doubtfully American—"Amelia" was the first truly American novel of the Revolution. Even so, its Revolutionary interest is subordinated to a story of discreet seduction, so characteristic of contemporary fiction.

AMERICAN POEMS, SELECTED AND ORIGINAL. Volume I, Litchfield, Collier and Buel, (1793).

THE first anthology of American verse. It contained selections from Barlow, Dwight, Trumbull and other of the more important figures, as well as from the lesser known poets. Volume I was all that was published. (Errata note at end.)

THE ANARCHIAD. A New England Poem . . . by David Humphreys, Joel Barlow, John Trumbull and D.

Lemuel Hopkins. . . . Edited by Luther G. Riggs. New Haven, 1861.

THIS poem first appeared in the *New Haven and the Connecticut Magazine* for October 19, 1786. The above is its first printing in book form. It was written by the famous group of Yale men known as the "Hartford Wits," to combat the influence of various forces then attempting to undermine Federalism.

THE ATLANTIC SOUVENIR. A Christmas and New Year's offering. Philadelphia, (1826). The first of the Annuals.

THESE gift books, for years almost universally read, played a leading rôle in the earlier development of the short story, indeed, were essential factors of the progress of our literature as a whole. Prior to the general appearance of the magazine, inadequate copyright protection and a persistent reverence for English models made the annual the only available general medium of expression open to the aspiring writer.

THE HAPLESS ORPHAN; OR, INNOCENT VICTIM OF REVENGE. A Novel. Founded on Incidents in Real Life: In a Series of Letters from Caroline Francis to Maria B——. In Two Volumes . . . By an American Lady. Boston, 1793.

DIDACTIC in tone, and full of absurd and incongruous situations, this book is significant as the true forerunner of an almost endless sequence of romantic, sentimental novels later to be produced by American women writers.

THE HERO, OR THE ADVENTURES OF A NIGHT. A Romance translated from the Arabic into Iroquese; from the Iroquese into Hottentot, from the Hottentot into French, and from the French into English . . . Two volumes in one. Philadelphia, 1817.

PROBABLY the first American attempt to satirize the Gothic novel. An ingenious and amusing dovetailing of phrases literally lifted from the most popular Gothic novels of the day. Of itself a work of art, and in its ingenuity a masterpiece.

ABBOTT, JACOB and JOHN S. C.
1803–1879 1805–1877

BOTH typical New Englanders, both educated for the ministry, and later associated in educational work at the Abbott Institute of New York City, the brothers Abbott, under the inspiration and guiding hand of Jacob, were in a measure collaborators in the most famous "series" juveniles of their day. As such, they were essentially the founders of that large and prolific school of American juvenile writers whose works have since enjoyed an undiminished popularity.

The outstanding characteristics of the Abbotts' work, of which the Rollo series is perhaps the best known example, were its qualities of sustained interest and the vast fund of information which it gave to the inquiring, youthful mind.

ROLLO. LEARNING TO TALK. Boston. (1835?)
This is the correct title of the first of the Rollo Books. The date, however, is approximate. No copy which can truly be identified as the first edition has so far been located by the compiler.

ROLLO. LEARNING TO READ; OR EASY STORIES FOR YOUNG CHILDREN. Boston, 1835.
The first of the Rollo Books of which the first edition has so far been identified.

ADAMS, CHARLES FOLLEN
1842–1918

ADAMS was in some respects an imitator of Leland, although not his equal as a creator of character. He wrote ostensibly for the young, but whatever genuine appeal he made was chiefly to the older reader. He was born in Dorchester, Mass., served in the Union army during the Civil War, and was seriously wounded. Later he engaged in mercantile business in Boston, Mass. The "Yawcob Strauss" verses first appeared in the *Detroit Free Press*. Whatever their limitations in literary merit and enduring quality may be, they were immensely popular in their day.

LEEDLE YAWCOB STRAUSS AND OTHER POEMS. Boston, 1878.

ADAMS, ABIGAIL
1744–1818

MRS. ADAMS, the wife of one President and the mother of another, was born in Weymouth, Mass. She spent much of her girlhood with her grandparents and was educated by her grandmother. In 1764 she married John Adams, and it can truthfully be said that she became the distinguished wife of a distinguished citizen. Mrs. Adams was a woman of much wit, charm and high ideals, and her "Letters," published some time after her death, are among the most vivacious and human documents of their time.

LETTERS OF MRS. ADAMS, THE WIFE OF JOHN ADAMS, WITH AN INTRODUCTORY MEMOIR BY HER GRANDSON, CHARLES FRANCIS ADAMS. Boston, 1840.

A two volume second edition appeared the same year.

ADAMS, HENRY (BROOKE)
1838–1918

ADAMS, a worthy descendant of the distinguished historic Adams line, was a Bostonian by birth, for a few years a professor at Harvard and later editor of the *North American Review*.

His great and enduring contributions to American letters were his philosophical and historical writings. Yet he was a good novelist as well, and in "Democracy," a pessimistic but accurate picture of Washington society, produced one of the few really notable stories of American political life. "Esther" is also an excellent bit of work.

DEMOCRACY. An American Novel. Boston, 1880.
The end paper advertisements should make no mention of this book.

ESTHER: A NOVEL by Francis Snow Compton. New York, 1884.
"American Novel Series, No. 3."

ADAMS, WILLIAM TAYLOR
(Oliver Optic)

1822–1897

"OLIVER OPTIC," the author of one hundred and twenty-six boys' books and nearly eleven hundred boys' stories, was the most popular writer of juveniles who has yet appeared in America.

At the time of his birth his father was proprietor of the Lion Tavern in Boston, but, when William was sixteen, the family took up its residence on a Roxbury farm. After securing an education as best he could, he traveled for a year in the South, but eventually returned home to engage in teaching, in which profession he continued until 1865. He then retired to devote himself to writing, at the same time editing *Oliver Optic's Magazine,* the *Student and Schoolmaster* and *Our Little Ones.*

Adams' style was slovenly, and he has been condemned—with measurable justice—on that account. Yet he knew unerringly the sort of story that his youthful readers wanted, and his books were always clean. He had, moreover, a gift of fascinating narrative. His most popular work, "The Boat Club," ran into at least sixty editions.

THE BOAT CLUB; OR THE BUNKERS OF RIPPLETON. A Tale for Boys. Boston, 1855.

ALCOTT, AMOS BRONSON
1799–1888

AFTER a rather sketchy education in his native Wolcott, Conn., Alcott, went to Virginia with the intention of teaching. Pressing necessity compelled him to take up peddling, and while so occupied he apparently became deeply impressed with certain Quaker religious views. He later removed to Boston and eked out a precarious existence as a teacher, developing meanwhile, with some success, certain radical educational theories of his own.

In 1840 he moved to Concord and presently engaged in an abortive Utopian farming experiment nearby, from the embarrassments of which he was finally relieved by the success of his daughter's "Little Women." His later years were passed serenely in Concord as the presiding genius of the Concord School of Philosophy.

Alcott was a radical in education, a mystic in temperament and thoroughly unpractical, but his personality was lovable in the extreme. He was perhaps the most ardent of the Transcendentalists, and the figure most typical of their ideals. His friendship with Emerson was intimate. It is arguable that the "Sage of Concord" was greatly in his debt.

CONCORD DAYS. Boston, 1872.

ALCOTT, LOUISA MAY
1832–1886

THOUGH of New England stock and all but lifelong Massachusetts residence, Miss Alcott was born in Germantown, Pa. She received her early education in part from Thoreau, but chiefly from her father, Amos Bronson Alcott.

Her first book, "Flower Fables" (1855), was written primarily for the amusement of Ellen, daughter of Ralph Waldo Emerson. Her early literary work was undertaken under pressure of necessity, and for a time she struggled against heavy odds. Her success was immediate, however, following the appearance of the first series of "Little Women," in which, ignoring the moralizing manner of her predecessors, she gave full play to her quick perceptions and unfailing humor, in a simple, fresh and lifelike tale of childhood, the appeal and charm of which survive. "Little Women" is her masterpiece, but some of her later juveniles, for example, "Little Men," "Old-Fashioned Girl" and "Eight Cousins" are only slightly less meritorious.

LITTLE WOMEN; OR MEG, JOE, BETH AND AMY. 2 volumes. Boston, 1868–69.

Copies of Part I are dated 1868 and must not announce "Little Women, Part Second" at the foot of the last page of text.

AN OLD-FASHIONED GIRL. Boston, 1870.

Measures 1⅛ inches across the top of covers.

LITTLE MEN: LIFE AT PLUMFIELD WITH JO'S BOYS. Boston, 1871.

First printings have four pages of advertisements in front, the last announcing "Pink and White Tyranny" as "Nearly Ready."

EIGHT COUSINS; OR, THE AUNT-HILL. Boston, 1875.

ROSE IN BLOOM: A SEQUEL TO EIGHT COUSINS. Boston, 1876.

UNDER THE LILACS. Boston, 1878.

ALDRICH, ANNE REEVE
1866–1892

MISS ALDRICH was a native of New York. She commenced to write when she was fifteen years old and soon became a regular contributor of poems and stories to *Scribner's, The Century* and other magazines. A greater freedom and insistence on reality place her poetry on a somewhat higher plane than that attained by the uninspired though polished verse of many of her feminine contemporaries.

THE ROSE OF FLAME AND OTHER POEMS OF LOVE. New York, 1889.

SONGS ABOUT LIFE, LOVE AND DEATH. New York, 1892.

ALDRICH, THOMAS BAILEY
1836–1907

THOUGH born in Portsmouth, N. H., and resident as a lad in New Orleans, Aldrich began his literary work in New York, where he was associated editorially and otherwise with various publications. His successes during this valuable literary apprenticeship led to an invitation to join the editorial staff of the *Atlantic Monthly* of which, upon the retirement of Howells, he became the editor-in-chief.

When Aldrich spoke of "fine writing" as a fault he was "inclined to," he uttered what many consider the final critique of his own work. His poetic craftsmanship was faultless. Yet, save in a few collections like his "Songs and Sonnets," (1906), he suffered from the subordination of substance to form.

He influenced the American short story profoundly when he perfected its surprise ending, and few volumes of short stories have had greater significance than his "Marjorie Daw." He wrote, also, one of the first modern detective stories, "The Stillwater Tragedy," to say nothing of one of America's best known and most popular juveniles, the human and confessedly autobiographical "Story of a Bad Boy."

POEMS. New York, 1863.

THE STORY OF A BAD BOY. Boston, 1870.
This story first appeared serially in *Our Young Folks* for 1869.

MARJORIE DAW AND OTHER PEOPLE. Boston, 1873.

THE STILLWATER TRAGEDY. Boston, 1880.

ALGER, HORATIO
1834–1899

ALGER, one of the most successful writers of juveniles in the history of American literature, was born in Revere, Mass. He was the son of a clergyman, and was honored by his boyhood acquaintances with the pleasing nickname of "Holy Horatio." After graduating from Harvard, he taught for three years, attended divinity school, spent a wild year in Paris—perhaps as an antidote—was ordained in 1864, retired at the end of two years and presently removed to New York, where he remained until 1896.

Alger was a bosom friend of all New York street gamins, which accounts for the type of hero he usually selected for his tales. He wrote in all one hundred and nineteen stories in which virtue, aided by appropriate good fortune, always won its just reward. His methods, like those of "Oliver Optic," were slipshod, but he told a story effectively and in so doing gained far greater popularity than many a more deserving author.

RAGGED DICK OR STREET LIFE IN NEW YORK WITH THE BOOTBLACKS. Boston, 1868.

(ALLEN), MRS. ELIZABETH ANN AKERS (CHASE) (Florence Percy)

1832–1911

MRS. ALLEN, one of the most popular of the "household poets" of her generation, was, up to the time of her first marriage in 1851, a resident of her native town of Farmington, Me. Pressing circumstances, following an early divorce, caused her to secure a position on the *Portland Transcript*. The proceeds of the sale of her first book, "Forest Buds from the Woods of Maine. By Florence Percy," enabled her in 1856 to make a trip to Europe, where she met and in 1860 married the sculptor Benjamin Chase. Mr. Chase lived only a year. She was again married in 1865 to E. Y. Allen, and moved to Richmond, Va., where she remained until 1874. She then returned to Portland as literary editor of *The Advertiser*.

Mrs. Allen is now best known for a single poem. It is doubtful whether any two lines in American literature are more often quoted than the first two verses of "Rock Me to Sleep":

> "Backward, turn backward, O Time in your flight,
> Make me a child again just for tonight!"

POEMS. By Elizabeth Akers. (Florence Percy). Boston, 1866.

In the "Blue and Gold Series."

The poem "Rock Me to Sleep" was first printed in the *Saturday Evening Post.*

ALLEN, JAMES LANE
1849–1925

AFTER serving for several years as a teacher of languages in his native state, Kentucky, Allen, who was born on a farm near Lexington, became head master of his own private school. Later he moved to New York City to pursue a literary career.

He began writing as a disciple of the local color school, adding to it a new conception of the interdependence between man and nature. This sympathetic treatment, already in evidence in "Flute and Violin," his first important published work, became even more marked in "A Kentucky Cardinal," perhaps his most charming story. In "The Choir Invisible," his first full length and most popular novel, he still further enlarged his canvas, assigning to Nature an even more important rôle. Meanwhile, throughout, though openly contemptuous of the niceties of literature, he is essentially a stylist and craftsman. Even his earliest work shows little that is immature.

FLUTE AND VIOLIN, AND OTHER KENTUCKY TALES AND ROMANCES. New York, 1891.

Copies measuring one and one sixteenth

inches, plus, across the tops of covers are presumably the earlier printing.

A Kentucky Cardinal. A Story. New York, 1895.

The advertisements should contain no mention of "Aftermath."

Aftermath. Part Second of "A Kentucky Cardinal." New York, 1896.

Contains no advertisements of "Aftermath."

Summer in Arcady; A Tale of Nature. New York, 1896.

The Choir Invisible. New York, 1897.

ALLEN, PAUL
1775–1826

Though far more widely known as co-editor of what is generally considered to be the best narrative of the Lewis and Clarke expedition, Allen was in reality of greater literary interest as one of our better early imitative poets.

He was born in Providence, R. I., and after graduation from Brown University became a notable contributor to the Philadelphia *Port Folio* and other journals. His verse is elegant and easy, but lacking in originality.

Original Poems, Serious and Entertaining. Salem, 1801.

ALLSTON, WASHINGTON
1779–1845

Allston was born in Waccamaw, South Carolina, educated at Harvard, and resided in Europe as art student and painter, save for two years, from 1801 to 1818. The remainder of his life was spent in Massachusetts.

His intimate friend Coleridge said of him that he was surpassed by no man of his day in artistic and poetic genius. In the light of time's verdict this is too high praise, yet he was certainly one of the first, if not the first American to bring more than mediocre talent to the poetic field. Nearly all of Allston's literary output was in verse. Once, however, in "Monaldi," a tragic romance of Italy, he ventured into prose, —with indifferent success.

THE SYLPHS OF THE SEASONS, WITH OTHER POEMS. . . . First American from the London edition. Boston, 1813.

ANDREWS, JANE
1835–1887

AS A child Miss Andrews showed evidence of a studious disposition and a genius for teaching. Following her graduation from Normal School she was invited to join the staff of the recently established Antioch College by its founder, Horace Mann. Unfortunately, failing health forced her retirement shortly after undertaking her new duties. Following her recovery, she established a school for young children at Newburyport, Mass., which she conducted until her death.

Miss Andrews loved and understood children, for whom she wrote simple, little stories as an equal and a friend. She was a pioneer in the field of sympathetic nature studies. Two of her works, "Seven Little Sisters" and "Stories Mother Nature Told Her Children," are ranked as classics in their field.

(Anonymous) THE SEVEN LITTLE SISTERS WHO LIVE ON THE ROUND BALL THAT FLOATS IN THE AIR. . . . Boston, 1861.

THE STORIES MOTHER NATURE TOLD HER CHILDREN. Illustrated. Boston, 1889.

This book was published posthumously. A school edition was also issued the same year—not illustrated.

ARTHUR, TIMOTHY SHAY
1809–1855

ARTHUR, a native of Orange County, New York, but nearly all of his life a resident of Philadelphia, was a prolific and extremely popular writer in his day. Of his voluminous output,—his histories, his moral novels, his "Advice to Young Men," etc.,—only "Ten Nights in a Bar Room" endures. It has no literary merit. Yet it exerted a tremendous influence and still remains an interesting specimen of the moral novel of its time. It is for this, and probably in a measure because of its dramatic title, that it is remembered.

TEN NIGHTS IN A BAR ROOM. Philadelphia, 1854.

The book appears with several different imprints on the title. In view of Arthur's residence in Philadelphia it seems logical to prefer the Philadelphia Lippincott Bradley imprint. The Bradley name appears on all copies. The frontispiece appears in two forms—priority undetermined.

AUSTIN, JANE (GOODWIN)

1831–1894

Miss Austin, daughter of a New England antiquarian, was born in Plymouth, Mass. She was married at the age of nineteen to Loring H. Andrews and shortly thereafter moved to Concord, where she gained the friendship of Louisa Alcott, Emerson and Hawthorne. Her summers she continued to spend in Plymouth.

Miss Austin's first work of consequence was published in 1860, but her best and best known stories are undoubtedly her "Plymouth Books," a series of remarkably accurate and charming historical novels dealing with life and scenes in the Plymouth Colony. Read in their proper chronological order they are "Standish of Standish," "Betty Alden," "A Nameless Nobleman" and "Doctor LeBaron and His Daughter." A fifth novel of the series remained unfinished at her death.

(Anonymous) A Nameless Nobleman. Boston, 1881.

In the "Round Robin Series."

Standish of Standish: A Story of the Pilgrims. Boston, 1889.

Doctor LeBaron and His Daughter: A Story of the Old Colony. Boston, 1890.

Betty Alden: The First-Born Daughter of the Pilgrims. Boston, 1891.

AUSTIN, WILLIAM

1778–1841

Austin was born in Lunenburg, Mass., was educated at Harvard, and later studied law while teaching school. Following a short term as a chaplain in the Navy and a visit to England, he began the practice of his profession, and soon became interested in politics. His subsequent years were made turbulent by the frequent and serious disputes into which his violent and outspoken prejudices frequently led him.

With Austin writing was a casual pastime incident to his political activities. Yet, with the exception of Irving, he was the best of the early American short story writers. "Peter Rugg the Missing Man," the story of a wandering chaise driver vainly searching for the town of Boston, is one of the most original and imaginative tales written before the advent of Poe and Hawthorne, and foreshadows the manner of the latter in its psychological approach. Other tales of his, also, evidence a genuine ability.

(BUCKINGHAM'S) NEW ENGLAND GALAXY FOR 1824, 1826 AND 1827. The Boston Book for 1841.

The issue of the *Galaxy* for September 10, 1824 contains the story of "Peter Rugg the Missing Man" which was continued in the issues of September 1, 1826 and January 19, 1827 and first published in book form in the "Boston Book" for 1841, its first complete appearance.

THE NEW ENGLAND MAGAZINE. Boston, 1831.

The July issue contains "The Late Joseph Natterstrom."

AMERICAN MONTHLY MAGAZINE. New York, 1836 and 1837.

The January 1836 number contains "The Man with the Cloaks."

The December 1837 issue contains "Martha Gardner or a Moral Reaction."

Note: "The Literary Papers of William Austin" was published in Boston in 1890.

BAKER, WILLIAM MUMFORD
1825–1883

HISTORICALLY one of the most interesting accounts of the Civil War was written by William Mumford Baker, a native of Washington, D. C., but a resident of Austin, Texas, during the conflict.

"Inside, a Chronicle of Secession," though purporting to be a novel, is in reality a compilation of the author's notes—in which, without literary pretension, he presents an undoubtedly faithful picture of Southern society in wartime. His other works are of negligible interest.

INSIDE, A CHRONICLE OF SECESSION. by George F. Harrington. New York, 1866.

BALDWIN, JOSEPH GLOVER
1815–1864

BALDWIN was born in Winchester, Va., of a fine old Southern family. He went to work as a law clerk at the age of twelve, and at seventeen was editing a newspaper. Hard self-imposed study made up his scholastic deficiencies, and in 1836 he was admitted to the bar. Shortly thereafter he saddled his horse and started South. For a time he sojourned in Tennessee, but 1839 found him in Gainesville, Ala., where he married and entered politics. Disappointed at his lack of success in this vocation, he removed to California in 1854, where he joined the forces of "law and order," and eventually became a justice of the State Supreme Court.

"The Flush Times of Alabama and Mississippi," Baldwin's

masterpiece, is usually referred to as a work of humor. It is more than that. Baldwin kept notes on the eccentric charactors whom he met. These jottings he expanded into "Flush Times." The book is humorous because the characters themselves were humorous and were drawn from life. The accuracy with which they are portrayed prevents that degeneracy into horseplay so common in books written primarily in jest. "Flush Times" is perhaps the best work of its kind to come out of the South before the Civil War.

THE FLUSH TIMES OF ALABAMA AND MISSISSIPPI. A Series of Sketches. New York, 1853. In lines nine and ten of page 107 the word "said" is repeated.

BANGS, JOHN KENDRICK
1862–1922

BANGS was born in Yonkers, N. Y., and attended the Columbia Law School. Later he was for varying periods editor of *Life, Harper's* and *Munsey's,* a candidate for Mayor of New York, and a popular playwright, lecturer, humorist and poet. He was not a great creative artist, but his original conceptions, possibly best exemplified in the "House-Boat on the Styx," occasionally struck a responsive chord.

A HOUSE-BOAT ON THE STYX. New York, 1896.

BARLOW, JOEL
1754–1812

BARLOW was born in Redding, Conn., educated at Yale and later admitted to the bar. After serving three years as a chaplain during the Revolution, he returned to Hartford and became a member of the celebrated group of five Yale men known as "The Hartford Wits." Though he wrote many satirico-political papers, Barlow was known chiefly as a poet, and as such did not hesitate to rank himself with Virgil. His last years were spent in public service abroad.

In common with most of his contemporaries, Barlow lacked any marked poetic talent, yet an occasional line of his possesses more than ordinary merit. He was one of the true prophets of Nationalism, as may be seen in his "Vision of Columbus," later expanded into "The Columbiad." This, despite its tediousness and imitative quality, helped to bridge the gap between the Revolution and the true national flowering of the early nineteenth century. From a literary standpoint his best work was "The Hasty Pudding," one of the first poems of which the humor can with any justice be considered essentially American.

THE VISION OF COLUMBUS. . . . Hartford, 1787.
The second edition is so marked.

(Anonymous) THE HASTY PUDDING. A Poem in three Cantos. . . . (New Haven, 1796). 15 pp.
There is also a New Haven (1796) edition containing 12 pages, and a New York 1796 edition.

THE COLUMBIAD. A Poem. Philadelphia, 1807.
One of the earliest pieces of fine printing done in America.

(BARNUM), FRANCES COURTENAY BAYLOR
1848–1920

MRS. BARNUM was born in Fort Smith, Ark., and as a child lived in New Orleans, San Antonio and Virginia. After the Civil War she traveled for a year, returned home, married, and settled in Savannah, Ga., where she remained until her husband's death. She subsequently lived in Lexington, Ky.

Mrs. Barnum was the author of certain novels of minor importance, and of a worth-while juvenile, the story of two young Mexicans captured by Comanches, and of their ultimate escape. In it she evidences a passing knowledge of natural history, a real acquaintance with Indian customs and a sufficient sense of thrilling narrative to captivate the not too sophisticated youthful reader.

JUAN AND JUANITA. Boston, 1888.

BARR, AMELIA E.
1831–1919

IN 1849, Mrs. Barr, a native of Huddleston, England, emigrated with her husband to the United States and settled eventually in Texas. After the Civil War, following the death of her husband and four sons from yellow fever, she moved with her three daughters to New York City, where she found employment as a private tutor.

On the advice of Henry Ward Beecher, she became a contributor to various magazines, notably to *Harper's*. After being confined to her chair by illness, she wrote "Jan Vedder's Wife," the first of an interesting series of historical novels, the best of which, perhaps, is "The Bow of Orange Ribbon," an entertaining story of pre-Revolutionary New York. Other works of hers have Scotch and English settings, reminiscent of her girlhood days. Mrs. Barr was a cultured and careful writer, whose upbringing in an atmosphere of refinement is reflected in her work.

THE BOW OF ORANGE RIBBON. A Romance of New York. New York, 1886.

On page 215, fifth line from bottom, the "s"

in "some" should be present. (There are other instances calling for perfect type.)

BATES, ARLO
1850–1918

Bates, the author of an occasional good sonnet and certain rather indifferent novels, was born in Machias, Me., and graduated from Bowdoin in 1876. He went to Boston shortly to establish himself in literature, took a room in a garret and for a time supported himself by teaching. He later became prominent in politics, was editor of the *Sunday Courier* and eventually served as a professor at the Massachusetts Institute of Technology. His essays on literary style and form are probably the most valuable part of his work.

Told in the Gate. Boston, 1892.

Talks on Writing English. Boston, 1896. Second Series 1901.

BEECHER, HENRY WARD
1813–1887

Beecher, the son of a distinguished clergyman, and for years Pastor of the famous Plymouth Church of Brooklyn, N. Y., was born like his famous sister, Harriet Beecher Stowe, in Litchfield, Conn.

Throughout his busy life as preacher, lecturer and writer, Beecher's vigor, intellectual power and oratorical ability made him one of the greatest molders of national opinion of his day. From a strictly literary point of view his "Star Papers," a collection of short essays on a broad range of subjects, undoubtedly exhibit him at play and at his best.

In his single novel, "Norwood," he clearly stepped outside his proper field.

STAR PAPERS; OR EXPERIENCES OF ART AND NATURE. New York, 1855.

BEERS, ETHEL LYNN
(Ethelinda Beers)
1827–1879

MRS. BEERS, daughter of Horace W. Eliot of Goshen, N. Y., and a lineal descendant of John Eliot, Apostle to the Indians, is now conceded to have been the author of one of the more famous Civil War poems, "The Picket Guard," better known as "All Quiet Along the Potomac,"—a tender and somewhat over-sentimental tribute to an unknown soldier. Both Thaddeus Stevens and Lamar Fontaine, however, claimed authorship after its appearance in *Harper's Magazine* for November, 1861. The poem was first printed in book form under Mrs. Beers' name in an edition of her poems published just one day before her death.

ALL QUIET ALONG THE POTOMAC, AND OTHER POEMS. Philadelphia, Porter and Coates. (1879).

BELKNAP, JEREMY
1744–1798

BELKNAP was born and educated in Boston, but later removed to Dover, N. H., where he served as a clergyman for twenty years. He returned to Boston in 1787, continuing in his profession, and subsequently founded the Massachusetts Historical Society.

Belknap's real place is among the historians, where he ranks with the elect. His most noted historical works are his "History of New Hampshire," (1784–92), and his "American Biography," (1792–4). His one important work of fiction was "The Foresters," an "allegory of the clearing out of John Bull's wilderness, and incidentally of John Bull himself." It was the third American novel published, in a very tenuous sense the first American historical novel, and, except for Hopkinson's "Pretty Story," the first bit of American fiction of even modest literary merit.

THE FORESTERS, AN AMERICAN TALE: BEING A SEQUEL TO THE HISTORY OF JOHN BULL THE CLOTHIER. . . . Boston, 1792.

The 1792 edition contains a frontispiece which is omitted from the 1796 re-issue.

BELLAMY, EDWARD
1850–1898

BELLAMY was born in Chicopee Falls, Mass., and was educated abroad. Though a lawyer by profession, he engaged in newspaper work, in the course of which he published three pleasing novelettes of no great merit.

He was the author of only one novel of distinction, "Looking Backward," a story of cooperative and semi-social community life, which, though originally accepted as a romance, was quickly recognized as a confession of the author's social and economic faith. This novel is probably the outstanding American "Utopia." Its profounder significance was political rather than literary and it ranks as one of the very few works of American fiction to have exerted a definite influence upon our national life.

LOOKING BACKWARD. 2000–1887. Boston, 1888.

Cloth copies usually have the imprint of the

printer on the verso of the title, which does not so far as observed appear in copies bound in wrappers.

BENNETT, JOHN
1865–

Bennett was born in Chillicothe, Ohio. He studied for a time at the Art Students' League in New York City, but returned to Chillicothe as editor of the *Daily News*. In 1890 he moved to Charleston, S. C., where he now resides.

Bennett has written some excellent studies of negro folklore and dialect, but his masterpiece is "Master Skylark," one of the best historical novels for boys yet written in America.

Master Skylark, a Story of Shakspere's Time. New York, 1897.

BIERCE, AMBROSE (GWINETT)
1842–1914

Bierce was born in Meigs County, Ohio. He served in the Civil War, and later, after its close, went to San Francisco where he became editor of the *News Letter*. He subsequently went to England, returned to California where he won national fame as a columnist on *The Examiner* and finally settled in Washington, D. C. His end was in complete keeping with the high lights of his extraordinary and sensational career. He is assumed to have perished at the age of seventy-two in Mexico while serving in some capacity with Villa's revolutionary bandits.

Like Poe, Bierce appealed to the intellect; like Poe, too, he was a superb technician. He was a fierce individualist, a bitter satirist, enigmatic and eccentric in the extreme. Admitting his lack of sincerity, he was, nevertheless, one of the most amazingly brilliant figures yet to have appeared in American literature.

Tales of Soldiers and Civilians. San Francisco, 1891.
Later title "In the Midst of Life."

Can Such Things Be? New York, Cassell. (1893).

BIRD, ROBERT MONTGOMERY
1806–1854

Bird, the first novelist seriously to attempt to interest the American reader in a non-national subject, was a Philadelphia physician. He was born in Newcastle, Del., was educated at the University of Pennsylvania and began his practice in the Quaker City. His first ventures into literature were in drama, and several of his plays were staged with marked success.

In 1834 he published a tale of the conquest of Mexico, "Calavar," which won high praise for its accuracy from Prescott, and he followed it the next year with a sequel, "The Infidel." His best and best known work is "Nick of the Woods," a vigorous but melodramatic tale of frontier Kentucky in 1782, in which his realistic treatment of the Indian is in marked contrast to Cooper's idealistic conception.

(Anonymous) Calavar: or, the Knight of the Conquest: a Romance of Mexico. 2 volumes. Philadelphia, 1834.

The Infidel; or, the Fall of Mexico: a Romance. (Sequel to Calavar). 2 volumes. Philadelphia, 1835.

The Hawks of Hawk-Hollow. A Tradition of Pennsylvania. 2 volumes. Philadelphia, 1835.

Nick of the Woods; or the Jibbenainosay. A Tale of Kentucky. 2 volumes. Philadelphia, 1837.

The Adventures of Robin Day. 2 volumes. Philadelphia, 1839.

Pages VIII to 12 inclusive are omitted from Volume I.

BLEECKER, ANN ELIZA (SCHUYLER)

1752–1783

Facts regarding the life of Mrs. Bleecker are relatively meager. It is, perhaps, enough to know that her most intimate associations were Knickerbocker, and that, after her marriage, she moved from New York City, her birthplace, to New Rochelle, and was for a time, also, resident near Albany, N. Y.

Her works, including some of her poems, were published posthumously in 1793, and later with a life sketch by her daughter in 1809. Copies of either book, however, seem almost unprocurable.

It would appear that, while not a poetic genius, Mrs. Bleecker yet wrote with a refined taste and talent, which, to quote Mrs. Sarah J. Hale in the *Woman's Record,* "might have been cultivated to higher effort, if the circumstances surrounding the author had been more propitious."

Mrs. Bleecker's most important work, separately published, was her "History of Maria Kittle," a story of the French and Indian Wars, remarkable for its time in its unusual knowledge of Indian manners and customs, and evidencing at least a nice discrimination.

THE POSTHUMOUS WORKS OF ANN ELIZA BLEECKER, IN PROSE AND VERSE, TO WHICH IS ADDED, A COLLECTION OF ESSAYS, PROSE AND POETICAL, by Margaretta V. Faugeres. Portrait. New York, 1793.

THE HISTORY OF MARIA KITTLE. By Ann Eliza Bleecker. In a Letter to Miss Ten Eyck. Hartford, 1797.

A later edition was published in Hartford in 1802.

This story was originally published in Volumes I and II of the *New York Magazine; or, Literary Repository*, 1790–91.

BOKER, GEORGE HENRY
1823–1890

GEORGE HENRY BOKER, one of the larger figures in American literature, was the son of a Philadelphia banker. He began to write immediately following his graduation from Princeton. His first volume, a book of poems, appeared in 1847. "Calaynos," his first play, followed shortly, opened in London and had a highly successful run. Thereafter, he devoted himself chiefly to playwriting, with occasional ventures into verse.

Boker's poems, particularly his sonnets, are strong and for the most part well written. But it is as a playwright that he stands essentially alone among nineteenth century American writers. "Francesca da Rimini," the scene of which is laid in thirteenth century Italy, is regarded as one of the finest pieces of dramatic poetry written in the English language between the years eighteen and nineteen hundred.

PLAYS AND POEMS. 2 volumes. Boston, 1856.

There are two known fragmentary copies of

"Francesca da Rimini," published separately in 1853.

BOYESEN, HJALMAR HJORTH
1848–1895

BOYESEN, one of a number of foreigners who have come to America to grace her literature, was born in Norway. Immediately after completing his education at Christiania and Leipsic he emigrated to the United States and settled in Chicago as editor of a Scandinavian paper. Later, in 1874, he accepted a professorship of German at Cornell, and later still, in 1880, a chair at Columbia.

Boyesen, an exceptionally talented linguist, acquired such remarkable facility in English that within six years of his immigration he had achieved great popularity as a writer of both prose and verse in that language. He had been resident in the United States only two years when "Gunnar," his first and perhaps his best known work of fiction, appeared. Without denying the vigor of some of his Norse tales, his powers were overestimated by his generation, and his final place in American letters does not appear to be one of great importance.

GUNNAR. A Tale of Norse Life. Boston, 1874.

BRACKENRIDGE, HUGH HENRY
1748–1816

BRACKENRIDGE, a Scotchman by birth, a resident of the United States after his fifth year and a classmate of Philip Freneau, at Princeton, was at different times a divinity student, teacher and editor, before becoming a distinguished lawyer.

He eventually served for a number of years as a justice of the Supreme Court of Pennsylvania.

Brackenridge was the merriest of our eighteenth century writers. Though he produced in his younger years a few more or less popular dramas, his literary recognition now rests upon "Modern Chivalry," a spicy and rollicking satire on homespun politics, that is at once the first important American novel and the first to treat of the frontier. He wrote with vigor and in a more modern spirit than any of his contemporaries. Part III of "Modern Chivalry" has the distinction of being the first novel printed west of the Alleghenies.

MODERN CHIVALRY: CONTAINING THE ADVENTURES OF CAPTAIN JOHN FARRAGO, AND TEAGUE O. REGAN, HIS SERVANT. (4 volumes.) Volume I, Philadelphia, MDCCXCII; Volume II, Philadelphia, MDCCXII; Volume III, Pittsburgh, MDCCXIII; Volume IV, Philadelphia, MDCCXCVII. . . . Also Part II, Carlisle, 1804.

The errors in the datings of Volumes II and III are still unexplained.

BRADFORD, EBENEZER

Dates Unknown

THOUGH Bradford was unquestionably the true name of the author of "The Art of Courting," biographical facts regarding him are apparently non-existent. The book is a good example of the educational didacticism of the early American novel. No true understanding of the early struggles of our literature to come into its own is possible without at least a passing acquaintance with this didactic tendency and an appreciation of its persistence,—a die-hard survival of earlier Puritan clerical dominance.

(Anonymous) The Art of Courting, Displayed in Eight Different Scenes; the Principal of which are taken from Actual Life, and published for the Amusement of The American Youth. Newburyport, 1795.

BRAINARD, JOHN GARDNER (CALKINS)
1796–1828

Brainard was born in New London, Conn., attended Yale and studied law, but gave up the profession because of an inherent shyness and a dislike of controversy and became editor of the *Connecticut Mirror*. Poor health and melancholia eventually forced his resignation. He died of consumption just a month before becoming thirty-two.

It is possible that Brainard's greatest literary virtues may have been the result of the brooding mood attendant on his illness. His verse shows traces of a real sensitiveness to beauty.

Occasional Pieces of Verse. New York, 1825.

BRIGGS, CHARLES FREDERICK
1804–1877

Briggs was born in Nantucket, but spent his entire literary life in New York City, first as the founder and leading spirit of the *Broadway Journal* and later as editor-in-chief of *Putnam's Monthly Magazine*. He was a friend of James Russell Lowell, a keen observer and one of the best known critics of contemporary men and affairs.

His one worth-while novel is "Harry Franco," an entertaining tale of New York land speculation in the early thirties and of the general economic extravagances culminating in the panic of 1837. As a story it lacks sustained interest, but is frequently relieved by touches of genuine humor and by illuminating pictures of the manners, customs and foibles of the day.

(Anonymous) THE ADVENTURES OF HARRY FRANCO. A Tale of the Great Panic. 2 volumes. New York, 1839.

BROOKS, MARIA GOWEN
1795–1845

MISS GOWEN was the daughter of a Boston merchant. On the death of her father she was educated by her brother-in-law, a Mr. Brooks, whom she afterwards married. When her husband died in 1823 she lived for a time with a brother in Cuba, and later went to England, where she visited Southey.

Southey's oft quoted tribute to her as "the most impassioned and most imaginative of all poetesses" is undeniably unjustified. Even the occasional intense passage in "Zophiel," the work which inspired Southey's laudatory outburst, is but the inevitable temporary lucidity of incoherence.

ZOPHIEL; OR THE BRIDE OF SEVEN. By Maria del Occidente. London and Boston, 1833.

A Boston edition appeared in 1834. The first canto with other poems was published in Boston in 1825.

BROOKS, NOAH
1830–1903

Brooks, though educated to be an artist, began his active life as a newspaper man in California, then, in 1854, a far cry from his native town of Castine, Me. His work there gained him an appointment to the staff of the *New York Tribune,* which he joined in 1871, and from which he went to the editorial staff of the *New York Times* in 1874. After remaining with *The Times* for ten years he became editor-in-chief of the *Newark Daily Advertiser,* with which he remained until his retirement in 1892.

Brooks was a natural writer, who fortunately had an opportunity during his Western experience to gather the materials necessary to his success. His boys' stories of frontier life are singularly accurate, and are written in an entertaining manner and with a fair degree of literary skill.

The Boy Emigrants. New York, 1877.

BROWN, ALICE
1857–

To one familiar with the departed glories of an earlier New England, Miss Brown's birth, education and years of residence in and near Hampton Falls, N. H., are facts of deeper significance than the debt she is alleged to owe to her close study of Stevenson and other writers for her mastery of short story technique.

With Sarah Orne Jewett and Mary Wilkins Freeman she maintains the earlier New England literary tradition, in the short story field. In "Meadow-Grass" and "Tiverton Tales" she pictures passing phases of life in her native environment with fidelity and moving pathos. Her stories of desires thwarted and happiness denied show occasional traces of sentimentalism, but her workmanship is admirable.

MEADOW-GRASS. Tales of New England Life. Boston, 1895.

TIVERTON TALES. Boston, 1899.

BROWN, CHARLES BROCKDEN

1771–1810

HOWEVER much of his inspiration Brown may have owed to the radicalism of William Godwin, he was himself the first truly significant figure of American fiction, the first professional American man of letters, the first to bring to the American novel a studied shape and form.

He was a Philadelphia Quaker, studious and retiring, but a man of feverish intellectual energy. His first constructive effort was devoted to the study of ideal architectural design,—a study quickly abandoned for the pursuit of elaborate projects for the development of Utopian commonwealths,—his conception of which he embodied in a youthful romance, "Carsol," first published posthumously.

His first published work, "Alcuin," a rather daring essay on women's rights and liberties, was followed by a series of four novels produced with an amazing rapidity,—"Wieland," the first American masterpiece, a tale of mystery resolved into a case of ventriloquism, intense in feeling and invention, —"Arthur Mervyn," and "Ormond," studies in villainy, both of which contain remarkable descriptions of the yellow fever epidemic in Philadelphia,—and "Edgar Huntley," a less important local color romance dealing with somnambulism. "Clara Howard" and "Jane Talbot," though good analyses of contemporary womanhood, met with but indifferent recognition when published.

(Anonymous) ALCUIN: A DIALOGUE ON THE RIGHTS OF WOMEN. New York, 1798.

(Anonymous) WIELAND; OR THE TRANSFORMATION. An American Tale. New York, 1798.

ORMOND; OR, THE SECRET WITNESS. New York, 1799.

ARTHUR MERVYN; OR, MEMOIRS OF THE YEAR 1793. Philadelphia, 1799. Second Part. New York, 1800.

EDGAR HUNTLEY; OR, MEMOIRS OF A SLEEP-WALKER. 3 volumes. Philadelphia, 1799.

CLARA HOWARD, IN A SERIES OF LETTERS. Philadelphia, 1801.

JANE TALBOT, A Novel. Philadelphia, 1801. Plate.

BROWNE, CHARLES FARRAR
(Artemus Ward)
1834–1867

BROWNE, the most important of the Northern humorists before the appearance of Mark Twain, was born near Waterford, Me. When a young man he drifted to Ohio as a journeyman printer and eventually began contributing articles to the *Cleveland Plain Dealer* under the name of "A. Ward, Showman."

After wandering further westward and lecturing widely to enthusiastic audiences, he visited England in 1866, and there met the first cordial reception accorded to an American humorist. His career was cut short by consumption in 1867.

It is not too much to say that Browne deserved his popularity. He was the first to add cacophony to the stock in trade of his profession, and he used the unexpected effectively and in a manner all his own. Only an occasional reader now chuckles over the incongruous whimsicality of his sketches, but Browne deserves a better fate. His talents were genuine and the appeal of his plaintive personality remains.

ARTEMUS WARD; HIS BOOK WITH MANY COMIC ILLUSTRATIONS. New York, 1862.

It seems probable that copies containing a half title preceding the advertisements at the back, headed "A List of Books Issued by Carleton, Publisher," were printed first.

ARTEMUS WARD; HIS TRAVELS. New York, 1865.

ARTEMUS WARD IN LONDON, AND OTHER PAPERS. New York, 1867.

BROWNELL, HENRY HOWELL
1820–1872

BROWNELL was born in Providence, R. I., was educated at Trinity College, Hartford, and after studying law became a teacher. He published his first book of "Poems" in 1847, but the full measure of his poetic inspiration waited on a short but dramatic experience in the Civil War. He was present at the battle of New Orleans, and later, as Admiral Farragut's secretary, at the Battle of Mobile Bay. His two best poems, "The River Fight" and "The Bay Fight," describe these engagements.

Though his work is occasionally uneven and at times, perhaps, undignified, he undoubtedly produced the best Northern poetry of the Civil War, a fact which Oliver Wendell Holmes gracefully recognized in styling him "Our Battle Laureate."

LYRICS OF A DAY: OR NEWSPAPER-POETRY. By a Volunteer in the U. S. Service. New York, 1864.

The first edition of this book contains only one hundred and sixty pages and does not contain his two best poems, "The River Fight" and "The Bay Fight." These poems were first published in the second edition, so marked, containing one hundred and ninety-two pages.

WAR-LYRICS AND OTHER POEMS. Boston, 1866.

BRYANT, WILLIAM CULLEN
1794–1878

BRYANT, historically the first among the masters of American poetry, acquired his early education under great difficulties, among the rugged Berkshire Hills. He was born in Cummington, Mass., and began composing verse at the age of eight; his "Embargo," necessarily immature, yet withal a lively political satire, was written at thirteen. "Thanatopsis," his masterpiece, was finished when he was eighteen, though not published until six years later in the *North American Review*.

At his best Bryant depicts life with a fine austerity and stoicism and with a purity and conciseness unsurpassed, if indeed matched, by any other American poet. His first volume of poems appeared in 1821. His subsequent failure to rise to greater heights seems satisfactorily accounted for by the fact that his literary work became incident to a long and distinguished career as editor of the *New York Evening Post*.

Even so, these journalistic years were far from sterile. To them we owe the "Forest Hymn" ("Poems," 1832), and his superb lines "Truth, crushed to earth, shall rise again" in "The Battlefield" ("Poems," 1839). Later when relieved of editorial cares, he displayed a renewed vigor in "Thirty

Poems" and his classic of childhood, "The Little People of the Snow"; and his solemn requiem, "The Flood of Years," constitutes a fitting climax to a career which began with "Thanatopsis."

THE EMBARGO; OR, SKETCHES OF THE TIMES; A SATIRE. By a Youth of Thirteen. Boston, 1808.

Republished in 1809, in an edition which, itself scarce, is practically the only one procurable.

POEMS. Cambridge, 1821.

POEMS. New York, 1832.

Also Boston, 1832.

POEMS. Fifth edition. New York, 1839.

Contains the first printing of "The Battle-field."

THE FOUNTAIN AND OTHER POEMS. New York, 1842.

THIRTY POEMS. New York, 1864.

Some copies are on laid paper and some on plain. There seems to be no preference.

THE LITTLE PEOPLE OF THE SNOW. New York, 1873.

A HAPPY NEW YEAR. Carriers' Address. No place, imprint or date. (New York, 1877.)

Contains "The Flood of Years."

Also issued in an illustrated edition. New York, 1877.

BUNNER, HENRY CUYLER
1855–1896

BUNNER was born in Oswego, N. Y. As a nephew of Henry Theodore Tuckerman he had an almost unequaled opportunity to acquaint himself with the best in fiction. He prepared for Columbia, but instead of matriculating joined the staff of *Puck,* then the foremost American humorous paper. In the years during which he remained with this magazine he contributed to it and to other papers a series of clever stories, lyrics, editorials and cartoons.

To quote from Professor Pattee's "American Literature Since 1870," Bunner's verse is "trivial (but) . . . restrained, refined, faultless"—his short stories "humorous, artistic, effective, and in addition he touches at times the deeper strata of human life and becomes an interpreter and leader."

AIRS FROM ARCADY AND ELSEWHERE. New York, 1884.

Also thirty-six copies on large paper for private distribution.

"SHORT SIXES." Stories to be read while the candle burns. New York, 1891.

Page 47 must be numbered. It is interesting to note that the copyright copy filed in the Library of Congress is bound in light blue boards.

ZADOC PINE, AND OTHER STORIES. New York, 1891.

THE RUNAWAY BROWNS. A Story of Small Stories. New York, 1892.

BURNETT, FRANCES HODGSON
1849–1924

Mrs. Burnett was born in England, but her long American residence dating from the age of sixteen when she emigrated with her family to Memphis, Tenn., and her subsequent marriage here would seem to qualify her as an American author.

A few of her books, notably her first, "That Lass o' Lowrie's," published four years after her marriage, have an English setting. Most of her work, however, treats of American themes, and her most popular novel, "Little Lord Fauntleroy," combines both scenes. Probably no American juvenile has been more irritating to the host of boys who have read it than the latter, but as a book for adults it possesses a definite wistfulness and charm.

Little Lord Fauntleroy. New York, 1886. It would appear that the first published copies bear the De Vinne imprint.

BURROUGHS, JOHN
1837–1921

Burroughs spent his early years upon his father's Roxbury, N. Y., farm, amid natural surroundings. After his marriage at the age of twenty he taught school for a while. He then worked in the Treasury Department for nine years and served another eleven as a national bank examiner.

As a popular essayist on Nature Burroughs was the successor of Thoreau,—less imbued than the latter with a sense of its ethical significance, yet equally sympathetic and far exceeding him in scientific spirit.

His first book, "Notes on Walt Whitman," is something of a literary anomaly, being possibly written in part by

Whitman himself. In his second, he steps into his proper field. Though not published until he was nearly forty, "Wake-Robin" is a book of youthful ardor. Its freshness is unquestioned, its philosophy charming and its manner that of distinguished literature.

NOTES ON WALT WHITMAN AS POET AND PERSON. New York, 1867.

The earliest copies have trimmed edges.

WAKE-ROBIN. New York, 1871.

Some copies have no pictorial designs on the covers. No priority has been demonstrated.

WINTER SUNSHINE. New York, 1876.

BIRDS AND POETS WITH OTHER PAPERS. New York, 1877.

LOCUSTS AND WILD HONEY. Boston, 1879.

PEPACTON. Boston, 1881.

BUTLER, JAMES

Dates Unknown

FACTS regarding Butler's life, save that he was a native and resident of Pennsylvania, seem elusive to the vanishing point. It is known, however, that he was the author of "Fortune's Football," probably the first original tale of foreign adventure written in America. Like Tyler's "Algerine Captive" it deals with the Algerian slave trade; unlike the latter it treats the subject in a romantic rather than a realistic manner.

FORTUNE'S FOOTBALL; OR THE ADVENTURES OF MERCUTIO. 2 volumes. Harrisburg, Pennsylvania, 1797–8.

BUTLER, WILLIAM ALLEN
1825–1902

Butler, the son of B. F. Butler, was born in Albany, N. Y. He was educated at N. Y. University and after his admission to the bar, became one of the most famous lawyers in New York City. His writings, which consisted of novels, poetry and biography, were wholly incident to his legal activities, but he became one of the most popular authors of satirical society verse of his time.

Nothing to Wear: An Episode of City Life. New York, 1857.
There is a leaf of "Recent Publications by Rudd and Carleton" tipped in between the front end papers of some copies.

BYNNER, EDWIN LASSETTER
1842—1893

Bynner was a Bostonian, a Harvard graduate, a practicing attorney in his native town, and later in St. Louis and New York. He was intensely interested in New England colonial history, and in 1886 gave up his profession in order to devote his entire time to research and literature.

His novels reveal his studious habits. From the literary standpoint they are lacking in distinction, but their historical aspects are ably handled and their style is agreeable.

Agnes Surriage. Boston, 1887.

The Begum's Daughter. Boston, 1890.

CABLE, GEORGE WASHINGTON
1844–1925

CABLE, a native of New Orleans, served in the Confederate army during the Civil War and after its close secured a position on a newspaper in his home city. Later he was employed as an accountant by a firm of cotton factors. When success as a writer was achieved he moved North and settled in Massachusetts.

"Old Creole Days," his first book, brought Cable national recognition. It was immediately hailed as a masterpiece and has since been recognized as one of America's notable books. Its handling of the kaleidoscopic Louisiana character is subtle, its finish brilliant, its charm exotic. But "Old Creole Days," his novel "The Grandissimes," and "Madame Delphine" marked the high tide of his achievement. Success brought in its train a too great consciousness of literary art, in the pursuit of which he lost the inspiration of his early days.

OLD CREOLE DAYS. New York, 1879.

THE GRANDISSIMES. A Story of Creole Life. New York, 1880.

MADAME DELPHINE. New York, 1881.

THE CREOLES OF LOUISIANA. New York, 1884.

STRANGE TRUE STORIES FROM LOUISIANA. New York, 1889.

CAREY, MATTHEW
1760–1839

CAREY was a highly educated Irishman of distinguished family. During a short exile in France, occasioned by his political activities at home, he made the acquaintance of Dr.

Franklin, and after an imprisonment following his return to Ireland, emigrated to Philadelphia at the age of twenty-three.

Immediately after his arrival he founded the *Pennsylvania Herald.* He followed this shortly with the *American Museum,* and within a few years, outstripping all competitors, became the leading publisher in America.

Carey was a vigorous, sound and finished writer on economic, political and sociological subjects. His personal views, as expressed in his own works, and his broad and public spirited attitude as a publisher made him, perhaps, the chief molder of the public opinion of his day. His first work published in the United States was "The Plagi-Scurrilliad"; his best known work of any literary flavor "The Porcupiniad."

THE PLAGI-SCURILLIAD; A HUDIBRASTIC POEM. Dedicated to Colonel Eleazer Oswald. Philadelphia, 1786.

THE PORCUPINIAD: A HUDIBRASTIC POEM. In Three Cantos. Addressed to William Cobbett, by Matthew Carey. Printed for and sold by the Author. Philadelphia, 1799.

This was originally published in three cantos in two parts—part I, Canto I, March 2, 1799; part 2, Cantos II and III, April 15, 1799.

CARLETON, WILL
1845–1912

CARLETON, the most popular "People's Poet" of his immediate day, was born in a log cabin near Hudson, Mich. He earned his way through college as a reader of his own verse, and later entered upon a journalistic career which eventually led him to New York.

Carleton offered little that was of distinction, and his work was crude and conventional, appealing only to the simpler emotions. But his sympathies were kindly and in his heyday he could boast of a wide circle of admirers.

Farm Ballads. New York, 1873.

CARMAN, (WILLIAM) BLISS
1861–1929

Canada and the United States may each rightly claim Carman as its own. He was born in Frederickton, New Brunswick, and "Low Tide on Grand Pré," was inspired by his earlier Canadian days. Yet the major part of his output was written after his removal to the United States, in 1890, to take up editorial work.

Carman's association with Hovey in the "Vagabondia" series was both a stimulus and a benefit to his art. He was never a great poet, but he was always a charming singer of sweet lyrics.

Low Tide on Grand Pré. Toronto. (1889.)
The first American edition, "Low Tide on Grand Pré: A Book of Lyrics," was published in New York in 1893.

CARRUTHERS, WILLIAM ALEXANDER
1806–1872?

Contradictory life dates are variously given for Carruthers —the year of his birth from 1800 to 1806 and that of his death from 1846 to 1872. Altogether very little seems definitely to be known about him, save that he was a practicing physician in Savannah, Ga., and was the author of certain novels.

Carruthers' most telling piece of work was a thrilling sketch on "Climbing the Natural Bridge of Virginia," printed in the *Knickerbocker Magazine* in July 1848. As a novelist he was neither a real success nor yet a failure. His stories of the old Dominion are rather illogical in plot, and his characters, save in the case of three or four of his major male figures, are ill-defined. Yet his action is at times spirited and the historical interest of his work is real.

THE CAVALIERS OF VIRGINIA, OR THE RECLUSE OF JAMESTOWN, AN HISTORICAL ROMANCE OF THE OLD DOMINION. 2 volumes. New York, 1834–5.

THE KNIGHTS OF THE HORSE-SHOE; A TRADITIONARY TALE OF THE COCKED HAT GENTRY OF THE OLD DOMINION. Wetumpka, Alabama, 1845.

CARRYL, CHARLES EDWARD
1842–1920

AMONG the numerous earlier imitators of Lewis Carroll in the production of nonsense books, Charles Carryl, a New York stock broker, railroad director and father of Guy Wetmore Carryl alone deserves especial mention.

Though lively and entertaining, "Davy and the Goblin" is not the equal of "Alice in Wonderland." Yet if the child's reaction is to be considered it has vitality. Probably no other book has won so many popularity contests conducted among youthful readers.

DAVY AND THE GOBLIN; OR WHAT FOLLOWED READING "ALICE'S ADVENTURES IN WONDERLAND." Boston, 1886.

CARY OR CAREY, ALICE AND PHOEBE
1820–1871 1824–1871

THE Cary sisters were born on a farm, near Cincinnati, Ohio, and as children suffered together the privations of frontier life. They visited Whittier as young women, and when Alice moved to New York Phoebe quickly followed.

Both were poets—Alice the more prolific writer and better known, and Phoebe the more versatile, spirited and witty. The well known poem, "Nearer Home" ("One Sweetly Solemn Thought") was the work of Phoebe. Alice, on the other hand, was the better prose writer. Her sketches of girlhood still have charm.

POEMS, by Alice and Phoebe Carey. Philadelphia, 1850.

CLOVERNOOK; OR RECOLLECTIONS OF OUR NEIGHBORHOOD IN THE WEST. (Alice Carey). New York, 1852.
Second Series, 1853.

POEMS AND PARODIES, by Phoebe Carey. Boston, 1854.
Contains "Nearer Home" ("One Sweetly Solemn Thought").

CATHERWOOD, MARY HARTWELL
1847–1902

OF THE several novelists who about 1890 sensed the natural reaction setting in against the prevalence of local color and who found its antidote in a return to the historical romance, Mrs. Catherwood may properly be called the pioneer.

She was born in Luray, Ohio, but went with her parents to Illinois when she was only three. On the death of her father and mother her training devolved upon near relatives. After reaching maturity she became a teacher, and almost immediately began her writing. A subsequent marriage to an Indianapolis confectioner turned out unhappily, and following their separation she spent most of her summers on the Great Lakes and her later years in Chicago.

In 1889 Mrs. Catherwood published the first of the "new" historical novels, "The Romance of Dollard." She chose as her scene the early French settlements of Canada, the Lake Region and the Mississippi, and the approval of Parkman is ample evidence of her careful research and accurate knowledge. She possessed, moreover, a well defined sympathy with the past and an excellent sense of the picturesque, but with them also an unfortunate tendency toward melodrama.

Mrs. Catherwood is best known for her series of historical romances, yet it is at least arguable that she did her finest work in her volume of short stories, "The Chase of St. Castin."

THE ROMANCE OF DOLLARD. With a Preface by Francis Parkman. New York, The Century Co. (1889.)

THE STORY OF TONTY. Chicago, 1890.

THE LADY OF FORT ST. JOHN. Boston, 1891.

THE CHASE OF ST. CASTIN AND OTHER STORIES OF THE FRENCH IN THE NEW WORLD. Boston, 1894.

CAWEIN, MADISON JULIUS
1865–1914

CAWEIN was born in Louisville, Ky., but early moved to Indiana where he secured a job as cashier in a poolroom. Encouraged by Howells' praise of his first book he turned to stocks and real estate as giving him more time for writing. Thereafter, he devoted his mornings to business and his afternoons to composition in the woods and fields.

Cawein's great crime against himself was his over-production. Certain of his descriptive nature poems are delicate, sincere and colorful, but his insistence upon another poem tomorrow forbade all spontaneity. He and Robert Burns Wilson are commonly considered the most important of the later nineteenth century Southern poets. He is not, however, Wilson's equal.

BLOOMS OF THE BERRY. Louisville, 1887.

CHANNING, WILLIAM ELLERY (The Elder)
1780–1842

CHANNING was unquestionably one of the great minds of his generation. He was born in Newport, R. I., and matriculated at Harvard at the age of fourteen. Following his graduation, he tutored in Richmond, Va., until 1802, when he returned to Harvard as Regent. He was ordained as minister of the Federal Street Church in Boston in 1803, and remained there as pastor until his death.

During his lifetime Channing was a center of intellectual turmoil. His opinions left a profound impress upon American life and thought. He was one of the leading figures in the "Unitarian Controversy," and it was largely through his instrumentality that Unitarianism became an important force. His interest, however, was more than sectarian. He saw clearly the changes which were coming in American life and he warned the nation to prepare.

In literature he sounded the first clear call for Nationalism. We need a "reformation," he said. "We cannot admit the thought that this country is to be only a repetition of the old world." His essay on "Self-Culture" is a model of brilliant thinking.

THE IMPORTANCE AND MEANS OF A NATIONAL LITERATURE. London, 1830.

This discourse appeared in the *Christian Examiner* for January, 1830. It was reprinted in his "Discourses," Boston, 1834. Its later title was "Remarks on a National Literature."

SELF-CULTURE. An Address Introductory to the Franklin Lectures, Delivered at Boston, September, 1838. Boston, 1838.

CHESEBROUGH (CHESEBRO') CAROLINE
1825–1873

MISS CHESEBRO', a native of Canandaigua, N. Y., and later a teacher at The Packer Institute in Brooklyn, began writing in earnest after winning two prizes in literary contests. Thereafter, she became a considerable contributor to leading periodicals, gradually enlarging her field until it included the novel and the juvenile.

Miss Chesebro' has found little general favor with the critics, who, though admitting the excellence of her descriptions, condemn her work as heavy with emotional moralizing, slow in action and lacking in strength and finish. Yet Oscar

Fay Adams pronounced "The Foe in the Household"—"one of the best of American novels."

THE FOE IN THE HOUSEHOLD. Boston, 1871.

CHILD, LYDIA MARIA (FRANCIS)
1802–1880

NO AMERICAN woman in her day and generation exerted a greater influence than Mrs. Child. Though not the equal of Miss Sedgwick as a novelist and craftsman, she shared with her the honor of being the most successful feminine writer of the early nineteenth century. Her influence as a molder of nation-wide feminine opinion transcended the boundaries of her literary achievement.

Mrs. Child was born in Medford and lived until middle life in Massachusetts. She wrote voluminously on many subjects and produced several works which entitle her to mention here. Her influence as a national character dates from her removal with her husband to New York, in 1841, to take editorial direction of the *Anti-Slavery Standard.*

Her first book, "Hobomok," is an idealized picture of Indian life, then the popular literary theme; her best novel "Philothea," a gentle, if unscholarly work, which Poe applauded, and which was the first American story of classic Greece. It is impossible to grant her the distinction of great literary merit—yet she wrote almost unfailingly with sympathy and charm.

HOBOMOK. A Tale of Early Times. By an American. Boston, 1824.

THE REBELS; OR, BOSTON BEFORE THE REVOLUTION. Boston, 1825.

PHILOTHEA, A ROMANCE. Boston, 1836.

FLOWERS FOR CHILDREN. 3 volumes. New York,

1844–5–6. No. I For Children Eight and Nine Years Old; No. II For Children Four to Six Years Old; No. III For Young Persons of Various Ages.

A small volume having the same title and published in New York in 1817 has been attributed to Mrs. Child. Her authorship of this book at the age of only fifteen is questionable.

CHIVERS, THOMAS HOLLEY
1809–1858

Chivers, one of the most extraordinary figures of American letters, was born near Washington, Ga. He was educated in medicine at Transylvania College, Ky., but, although an honor student, later practiced his profession only in a perfunctory way. He was married twice, but in the first instance was separated almost immediately from his girl wife. Later, while on a Northern trip, he met and married a Miss Harriet Hunt of Springfield, Mass. He early formed a friendship with Poe—to whom he once offered a home—and in spite of their occasional differences the bond of sympathy between them seems to have been genuine.

It appears hardly just to characterize Chivers as a mere imitator of the author of "The Raven." Poe accused him of plagiarism after the publication of "Eonchs of Ruby," but it is probable that their like conception of poetry as a thing of beauty was individually spontaneous.

Chivers' weird and haunting melody is displayed in both "Eonchs of Ruby" and "Virginalia." The latter, however, perhaps best evidences the absurdity of his dogmas and his total lack of coherence.

THE LOST PLEIAD; AND OTHER POEMS. New York, 1845.

EONCHS OF RUBY. A Gift of Love. New York, 1851.

MEMORALIA; OR, PHIALS OF AMBER FULL OF THE TEARS OF LOVE. A Gift for the Beautiful. Philadelphia, 1853.

VIRGINALIA; OR, SONGS OF MY SUMMER NIGHTS. A Gift of Love for the Beautiful. Philadelphia, 1853.

CHOPIN, KATE
1851–1904

FEW American writers present so many problems to the student of American Letters, determined to account for their career and genius, as Mrs. Chopin. All of her literary work, which of itself was all too little, was done in middle life after her return to her native St. Louis in 1889 or 1890, following her husband's death. All of her material, on the other hand, save that attributable to her native genius, was gathered during several years of residence in a remote Louisiana parish.

Mrs. Chopin's first book, a relatively unimportant novel, "At Fault," appeared in 1890. Four years later, she published "Bayou Folk," a collection of short stories of extraordinary character. This was followed in 1897, by another collection of real, if lesser merit, "A Night in Acadie." In 1899, chagrined at the adverse criticism which greeted her novel, "The Awakening," she ceased all writing as mysteriously as she began.

Mrs. Chopin's career was so brief, her manner so unusual and her work is generally so little known that a consensus of critical opinion regarding it is lacking. Yet many who know it rate her as one of the few great masters of short story art. To quote from Edward J. O'Brien's "The Advance of the American Short Story"—"Her pastels are narrow enough in their range, but faultless in the attainment of their end. Moreover, she could gather a whole drama into one quiet little final sentence, as practically none of the so-called masters of the surprise ending can pretend to do."

BAYOU FOLK. Boston, 1894.
A NIGHT IN ACADIE. Chicago, 1897.

CHURCHILL, WINSTON
1871–

CHURCHILL was born in St. Louis, Mo. He was educated at Annapolis, and while a student at the Naval Academy made an exhaustive study of the life of John Paul Jones. Following his graduation, he resigned from the service to take up literature, first in association with *The Army and Navy Journal* and later with *The Cosmopolitan*. Since 1903 he has been an active and important influence in New Hampshire politics.

Without reflection upon his works published since 1900, which have struck a responsive chord in the democratic outlook of a host of his countrymen, Churchill reached his height in his second novel, "Richard Carvel," a story of Revolutionary Maryland and John Paul Jones and a work of real historical value. Its portrayal of the life and character of Jones is excellent; it is a thrilling story, and it has the advantage of being written by a man who knows the sea.

RICHARD CARVEL. New York, 1899.
There must be no notices of republication on the copyright page.

CLARK, CHARLES HEBER
(Max Adeler)
1841–1915

CLARK's serious pursuit was journalism, his avocation humor. He was born in Berlin, Md., early secured a job as a reporter on the *Philadelphia Inquirer,* in due course became its editor, was later associated with the *Evening Bulletin,* in 1882 purchased the *Textile Record* and from 1887 to 1897 edited the *Manufacturer.*

Clark's humor was extravagantly burlesque, but a trace of narrative gives it occasional life. He was even more highly regarded in England than in America.

OUT OF THE HURLY-BURLY; OR LIFE IN AN ODD CORNER. Philadelphia, Today Publishing Co., 1874.

CLARK, LEWIS GAYLORD
1810–1873

CLARK was born at Otisco, N. Y., and educated at home by his father, a man of far more than average culture. Eventually he came to New York, and in 1834 succeeded Timothy Flint as editor of the *Knickerbocker Magazine* which under his management became one of the leading periodicals of its day.

Clark preserved his editorial reminiscences in a series of light and racy sketches which still retain a measure of their humor.

KNICK-KNACKS FROM AN EDITOR'S TABLE. New York, 1852.

CLARK, WILLIS GAYLORD
1810–1841

CLARK, a twin of Lewis Gaylord (supra) and like him an editor, gained a contemporary national reputation as a humorist and poet. The flavor of his timely humor is now diminished, yet his "Ollapodiana Papers," originally published in the *Knickerbocker Magazine,* are still worth reading.

LITERARY REMAINS OF THE LATE WILLIS GAYLORD CLARK: INCLUDING THE OLLAPODIANA PAPERS, THE SPIRIT OF LIFE, AND A SELECTION FROM HIS VARIOUS PROSE AND POETICAL WRITINGS. New York, 1844.

CLARKE, REBECCA SOPHIA
(Sophie May)
1833–1906

REBECCA CLARKE, better known by her pen name of Sophie May, was one of the disproportionately large group of writers of juveniles living in Maine during the latter half of the nineteenth century.

Born in Norridgewock, and forced to give up her profession of teaching because of deafness, Miss Clarke seriously took up writing at the age of twenty-eight. She first essayed poetry but, thanks to her mother's dissuasion, shortly abandoned it for the "series" juvenile.

Her books were extremely popular, and were clearly an advance upon their too precise forerunners; but one can hardly agree with Thomas Wentworth Higginson that "genius came in with Little Prudy." There was still too much tendency to moralize and too little plot. The characters and settings, however, are natural. "Dottie Dimple" was probably the most esteemed of all her works.

LITTLE PRUDY. Boston, 1864.
DOTTY DIMPLE. Boston, 1865.

CLEMENS, SAMUEL LANGHORNE
(Mark Twain)
1835–1910

TWAIN, perhaps the most many-sided interpreter of America in all our literature, was born in the little village of Florida, Mo., close to the sleepy river town of Hannibal where he spent his boyhood and which he afterwards made famous. His father died when he was twelve and circumstances forced him to make a living. After six years' service as printer and assistant editor on the *Hannibal Journal,* he set out for New York, working his way during the next few years as a printer in various Eastern and Middle-Western cities.

In 1857, while on his way to New Orleans in pursuit of an impracticable South American scheme, he made the chance acquaintance of Horace Bixby, a Mississippi River pilot, who employed him as an apprentice. The experiences and materials which he gained during his next three years as a river pilot were confessedly the most valuable assets of his later career.

The lure of the New West then drew him to the mining camps of Nevada and later on to California, where he stayed for approximately four years, broken only by a trip to the Hawaiian Islands.

Then, after wending his way Eastward, with numerous stops for lecturing as he went, he made his first and memorable trip to Europe and the Near East. Returning to the United States, he was for a short time editor of a Buffalo, N. Y., newspaper. Later he resumed his lecturing, revisited

England, took up his permanent residence in Hartford, wrote and in general responded to all sorts of public calls.

In 1895 the publishing house with which Twain was associated failed. The fevered but valiant struggle which he made to pay its debts tempered the excellence of his later work. But nothing more was needed to demonstrate his greatness. America had already accepted him as one of her first literary figures.

Every personal experience was grist to Twain's literary mill. His first book, "The Celebrated Jumping Frog," which earned him immediate recognition, was written during his early California days. His still earlier years in the West and on the Mississippi were admirably portrayed in "Roughing It," his novel "Pudd'nhead Wilson," and "Life on the Mississippi."

Of his two books, "Innocents Abroad" and "A Tramp Abroad," descriptive of his European and Near-Eastern trip in 1868, the former is the better, and ranks well in the list of his leading works. The "Prince and the Pauper," ostensibly a charming children's story, is in reality even more interesting as a satire for adults. That, too, is true of "A Yankee at King Arthur's Court." His brief against the hypocrisies of the Reconstruction Period is filed in his satire "The Gilded Age."

Twain's two great masterpieces are "Tom Sawyer" and its sequel "Huckleberry Finn"—both in different degree autobiographical of his boyhood days, and both inimitable. "Tom Sawyer" was sufficient to confirm his greatness, but only an American could have written "Huckleberry Finn"—and no American but Twain.

In form and feeling "Joan of Arc" stands quite apart from all Twain's other work. Of all his books he liked this best.

THE CELEBRATED JUMPING FROG OF CALAVERAS COUNTY, AND OTHER SKETCHES. Edited by John Paul. New York, 1867.

A page of tinted advertisements should precede the title. The "i" in "this" in the last line on page 198 is perfect.

THE INNOCENTS ABROAD; OR, THE NEW PILGRIMS' PROGRESS . . . Hartford, 1869.

The words "American News Co.," only, appear at the bottom of the backstrip; the chapter numbers are missing on pages XVII and XVIII; the word "Conclusion" is missing at the bottom of page XVIII; there is no picture on page 129.

ROUGHING IT. Hartford, 1872.

The "M" in the first word under "Contents" is in perfect type; "My," the first word on page 19, is in perfect type; the words "American Publishing Co." are at the bottom of the spine.

THE GILDED AGE. A Tale of To-day. Hartford, 1873 or 1874.

Written in collaboration with Charles Dudley Warner.

The illustration "Philip leaves Laura" does not appear on page 403.

THE ADVENTURES OF TOM SAWYER. Hartford, 1876.

Measures 1 inch across the tops of covers. The versos of the frontispiece, preface and half-title are blank.

A TRAMP ABROAD. Hartford, 1880.

The frontispiece is entitled "Moses," not "Titian's Moses."

THE PRINCE AND THE PAUPER: A TALE FOR YOUNG PEOPLE OF ALL AGES. Boston, 1882.

Must have the imprint of the "Franklin Press" at foot of the copyright page. Also 15 copies on India paper.

LIFE ON THE MISSISSIPPI. Boston, 1883.

There is a picture of Twain being cremated on page 441.

THE ADVENTURES OF HUCKLEBERRY FINN, (Tom Sawyer's Comrade) . . . New York, 1885.

Page 283 is on a stub; in the "List of Illustrations" the picture which is actually on page 87 is called for as on page 88; page 57, line 23, reads "was" for "saw." The recent controversy over the number on page 155 seems so far to have established nothing definitive.

A CONNECTICUT YANKEE AT KING ARTHUR'S COURT. New York, 1889.

Has figured end papers. The lettering on the covers and backstrip is all in gilt.

THE TRAGEDY OF PUDD'NHEAD WILSON, AND THE COMEDY, THOSE EXTRAORDINARY TWINS. Hartford, 1894.

PERSONAL RECOLLECTIONS OF JOAN OF ARC. By the Sieur Louis de Conte. New York, 1896.

CLIFFTON, WILLIAM

1772–1799

JUDGED by his literary output, Cliffton seems to have been little affected by the sobering influences of an early Quaker training. He was born in Philadelphia and during his few short years as a rising publisher, he wrote voluminously in light verse and in satire on many pressing topics of the day.

His "Rhapsody on the Times" is for its day a pleasing mock-epic. It is not so well known, however, as "The Group," a vigorous satire in favor of Jay's Treaty, serving up to ridicule the self-styled patriots who lay low during the Revolution. As a lyric poet, too, in such lines as "To a Robin" he wrote with comparative sincerity and grace.

THE GROUP, OR AN ELEGANT REPRESENTATION. Philadelphia, 1796. Engraved plate.

POEMS, CHIEFLY OCCASIONAL, BY THE LATE MR. CLIFTON . . . Engraved portrait. New York, 1800.

COBB, SYLVANUS, JR.
1823–1887

FEW writers of adventure stories attained such popularity as Cobb. He was born in Waterville, Me., amid surroundings strangely at variance with the backgrounds of his amazing tales. His success as a writer began, after two editorial ventures in New England, with his association with the *New York Ledger,* from the columns of which more than a score of his novelettes were later taken for republication.

He was one of the most voluminous writers of the blood and thunder stories of the forties and fifties—the logical successors of earlier popular adventure stories,—the Dime Novel, in short, in all but name. If sheer sensationalism is a criterion of excellence in such lurid melodramas, none of these writers attained a greater mastery than Cobb.

THE GUNMAKER OF MOSCOW; OR, VLADIMIR THE MONK. New York, 1888.

This story was written expressly for and published in the *New York Ledger* in 1856, and was at intervals three times republished in its columns in response to popular demand. Cobb's daughter in her "Memoir" of her father states that the "Cassell" (1888) edition was the first appearance in book form, but the above appears to have more logical claim to priority.

COFFIN, CHARLES CARLETON
1823–1896

COFFIN was born on a farm in Boscawen, N. H., to which, after a brief try at engineering, he returned. In 1835 he took up newspaper work, became an expert telegrapher and eventually gained a wide and enviable reputation as field correspondent of the *Boston Journal* during the Civil and Austro-Prussian Wars. Upon his return to the United States, he became a popular lecturer and author, serving meanwhile for a time as a member of the Massachusetts Legislature.

Coffin was a facile writer, with a vein of native New England humor which served him well. His juveniles for boys, covering the entire range of our history from the Colonial period to the Civil War, combine history and fiction in an instructive and pleasing blend. No American writer has yet arisen to dispute Coffin's supremacy in the field of juvenile short histories.

THE BOYS OF '76. A History of the Battles of the Revolution. New York, 1877.

COOKE, JOHN ESTEN
1830–1886

JOHN ESTEN COOKE, unquestionably the best of pre-Civil War Virginia novelists, was born in Williamsburg, in the historic Shenandoah Valley. Later he moved to Richmond, where he attended school. He first intended to be a lawyer, and was, in fact, admitted to the bar. But literature proved to be more attractive, and in 1854 he crossed his Rubicon by publishing three novels.

Cooke was an ardent Southerner and served throughout the Civil War with Lee. When hostilities ceased, he retired to his boyhood home in the Shenandoah, where he lived, engaged in writing and agriculture, until stricken with a fatal attack of typhoid fever.

As a writer Cooke belonged to the old school. Even his post-war novels evidence the leisurely manner of an earlier generation. His third book, "The Youth of Jefferson," and its sequel, "Henry St. John, Gentleman," are charming, and "The Virginia Comedians," published in the same year as the former, and undoubtedly his strongest work, is a dramatic and sympathetic picture of the elegance, the vice and the poverty of the Old Dominion. "Surry of Eagle's Nest" is an admirable story based upon his own Civil War experiences, and "My Lady Pokahontas," though less well known, is justly accounted one of his best tales. He left the younger generation, also, a legacy in a series of excellent historical sketches, "Stories of the Old Dominion."

LEATHER STOCKING AND SILK; OR, HUNTER JOHN MYERS AND HIS TIMES. A Story of the Valley of Virginia. New York, 1854.

THE VIRGINIA COMEDIANS: OR OLD DAYS IN THE OLD DOMINION. Edited from the MSS. of C. Effingham, Esq. 2 volumes. New York, 1854.

In Volume 2, page 249, line 3, the word "erased" is misspelled "earsed."

(Anonymous) THE YOUTH OF JEFFERSON; OR A CHRONICLE OF COLLEGE SCRAPES AT WILLIAMSBURG, IN VIRGINIA, A. D. 1764. New York, 1854.

THE LAST OF THE FORESTERS: OR, HUMORS ON THE BORDER; A STORY OF THE OLD VIRGINIA FRONTIER. New York, 1856.

HENRY ST. JOHN GENTLEMAN, OF "FLOWER OF HUNDREDS," IN THE COUNTY OF PRINCE GEORGE, VIRGINIA. A Tale of 1774–'75. New York, 1859.

SURRY OF EAGLE'S NEST; OR, THE MEMOIRS OF A STAFF OFFICER SERVING IN VIRGINIA. Edited from the MSS. of Col. Surry. New York, Bunce and Huntington, 1866.

Later editions published the same year have the imprint of F. J. Huntington, and so far as observed state the edition number on the title page.

HILT TO HILT, OR DAYS AND NIGHTS IN THE SHENANDOAH IN THE AUTUMN OF 1864. New York, 1869.

MOHUN; OR, THE LAST DAYS OF LEE AND HIS PALADINS . . . New York, 1869.

STORIES OF THE OLD DOMINION, FROM THE SETTLEMENT TO THE END OF THE REVOLUTION. New York, 1879.

MY LADY POKAHONTAS: A TRUE RELATION OF VIRGINIA. Writ by Anas Todkill, Puritan and

Pilgrim. With notes by John Esten Cooke. Boston, 1885.

COOKE, PHILIP PENDLETON
1816–1850

Philip Pendleton Cooke, an elder brother of John Esten, the novelist, was a Virginia aristocrat and sportsman. After graduation from Princeton he studied law, which he seems, however, to have practiced in a rather casual way. He was a friend of Poe, and though he viewed his own literary work chiefly as a diversion, was a considerable contributor of both prose and verse to the *Southern Literary Magazine* and other periodicals.

Cooke's prose is quite forgotten. A few of his poems, including the graceful but perhaps too sentimental "Florence Vane," may still be found in the anthologies.

Froissart Ballads, and other Poems. Philadelphia, 1847.

COOKE, ROSE TERRY
1827–1892

Mrs. Cooke was the real pioneer in the field of the local color short story, and as such deserves much of the credit generally accorded to Bret Harte. Her work is a fine blend of humor, sympathy and understanding. She was born near Hartford, Conn. Years of teaching in the remoter districts of her native Connecticut gave her a rare opportunity to see and sense the quaintness, amusing traits and sterling character of rural New England—in short, to look into its very soul.

Much of Mrs. Cooke's best work was done at least a decade

before the timely appearance of Harte's "Luck of Roaring Camp" prepared the country for its reception. Yet it was still more than another decade before the publication of the first collected group of her stories, "Somebody's Neighbors," brought her due recognition as a real force in American letters.

POEMS. By Rose Terry. Boston, 1861.

SOMEBODY'S NEIGHBORS. Boston, 1881.

HUCKLEBERRIES GATHERED FROM NEW ENGLAND HILLS. Boston, 1891.

COOLBRITH, INA DONNA
1842–1928

MISS COOLBRITH, one of the minor Pacific Coast poets, was born near Springfield, Ill., but spent most of her life in California. After a long residence in Los Angeles, she moved to San Francisco where she became Librarian of the Oakland Public Library. Her best work, "A Perfect Day and Other Poems," deserves passing mention.

A PERFECT DAY AND OTHER POEMS. San Francisco, 1881.
"Author's Subscription Edition."

COOPER, JAMES FENIMORE
1789–1851

COOPER, the first novelist to establish the complete independence of American letters, was born in Burlington, N. J. He spent his youth, from boyhood, among pioneer conditions in Cooperstown, N. Y., a frontier settlement founded by his father. Later he was sent to Yale, but was dismissed and entered the Navy, rising to the rank of lieutenant. In 1811 he married.

His first novel, "Precaution" (1820), written, it is said, to make good a boast to his wife, justly failed to win applause. Public recognition came the next year with the publication of "The Spy," an original and powerful tale which established American literature on its own feet. This was followed by "The Pioneers," beginning, although not chronologically, the famous "Leather-Stocking Tales"—"The Last of the Mohicans"—perhaps his greatest novel—, "The Prairie," "The Pathfinder" and "The Deerslayer." "The Pilot," inspired by the inaccuracies of the nautical incidents in Scott's "Pirate," appeared in 1823. This proved more popular even than "The Spy," and takes its place as the first of America's great novels of the sea.

In 1827 Cooper went to Europe. While there he became involved in a controversy over European conceptions of America, at the same time taking his countrymen to task for their subservience to the demagoguery of the times. He also wrote "The Red Rover"—the second of his sea tales—, "The Prairie," "The Wept of Wish-Ton-Wish," "The Water Witch," "The Bravo" and the two political novels, "The Heidenmauer" and "The Headsman."

On his return home in 1833 he explained his views in "A Letter to His Countrymen" and baited his fellow citizens with the remarkably prophetic essays published under the title of "The American Democrat" and "The Monikins," "Homeward Bound" and "Home as Found."

Cooper was now very unpopular. For a time he confined himself to historical and travel writing. But in 1840 he brought out "The Pathfinder" and followed it in rapid succession with "Mercedes of Castile," "The Deerslayer," "The Two Admirals," "The Wing-and-Wing," "Wyandotte," "Ned Myers" and "Afloat and Ashore."

Three political novels came next, the "Littlepage Tales," —"Satanstoe," "The Chainbearer," and "The Redskins"— followed by another sea tale "The Crater," "Jack Tier,"

"The Oak Openings," "The Sea Lions," and the last of his novels "The Ways of the Hour."

Cooper's greatest work is undoubtedly found in "The Leather-Stocking Tales" and in the best of his sea stories—"The Pilot," "The Red Rover," "The Two Admirals," "Wing-and-Wing," and the entertaining but often overlooked "Afloat and Ashore."

His position as the first great American novelist is secure. In this respect he looms so large, that, despite the great unevenness of his work little of it can be overlooked. At his best he was large-minded, original in character and setting, wholesome, spirited and of a fine inspiration; at his worst he was slipshod, inconsistent, stilted, heavy and dogmatic. But the worst serves only to accentuate his greatness. American Letters owe him an incalculable debt.

(Anonymous) PRECAUTION; A Novel. 2 volumes. New York, 1820. In some copies Volume I contains an errata leaf.

THE SPY; A TALE OF THE NEUTRAL GROUND. 2 volumes. New York, 1821.

THE PIONEERS; OR THE SOURCES OF THE SUSQUEHANNA; A DESCRIPTIVE TALE. 2 volumes. New York, 1823.

THE PILOT; A TALE OF THE SEA. 2 volumes. New York, 1823.

LIONEL LINCOLN; OR THE LEAGUER OF BOSTON. 2 volumes. New York, 1825–4.

THE LAST OF THE MOHICANS; A NARRATIVE OF 1757. 2 volumes. Philadelphia, 1826.

THE PRAIRIE; A TALE. 2 volumes. Philadelphia, 1827.

THE RED ROVER; A TALE. 2 volumes. Philadelphia, 1828–7.

NOTIONS OF THE AMERICANS: PICKED UP BY A TRAVELLING BACHELOR. 2 volumes. Philadelphia, 1828.

THE WEPT OF WISH-TON-WISH; A TALE. 2 volumes. Philadelphia, 1829.

THE WATER-WITCH; OR, THE SKIMMER OF THE SEAS. A Tale. 2 volumes. Philadelphia, 1831.

THE BRAVO: A TALE. 2 volumes. Philadelphia, 1831.

THE HEIDENMAUER; OR THE BENEDICTINES: A LEGEND OF THE RHINE. 2 volumes. Philadelphia, 1832.

THE HEADSMAN; OR, THE ABBAYE DES VIGNERONS. A Tale. 2 volumes. Philadelphia, 1833.

A LETTER TO HIS COUNTRYMEN. New York, 1834.

THE MONIKINS. 2 volumes. Philadelphia, 1835.

HOMEWARD BOUND; OR THE CHASE. A Tale of the Sea. 2 volumes. Philadelphia, 1838.

HOME AS FOUND (A SEQUEL TO HOMEWARD BOUND). 2 volumes. Philadelphia, 1838.

Some copies have "Notice to the Public" preceding the title in Volume I.

THE PATHFINDER; OR THE INLAND SEA. 2 volumes. Philadelphia, 1840.

Copyright notice is omitted from Volume I.

MERCEDES OF CASTILE; OR THE VOYAGE TO CATHAY. 2 volumes. Philadelphia, 1840.

THE DEERSLAYER: OR, THE FIRST WAR-PATH. A Tale. 2 volumes. Philadelphia, 1841.

THE TWO ADMIRALS; A TALE. 2 volumes. Philadelphia, 1842.

THE WING-AND-WING, OR LE FEU FOLLETT. A Tale. 2 volumes. Philadelphia, 1842.

WYANDOTTE; OR THE HUTTED KNOLL. A Tale. 2 volumes. Philadelphia, 1843.

AFLOAT AND ASHORE; OR THE ADVENTURES OF MILES WALLINGFORD. 2 volumes. Philadelphia, 1844.

The Same. Volumes 3 and 4. New York, 1844.

SATANSTOE; OR THE LITTLEPAGE MANUSCRIPTS. A Tale of the Colony. 2 volumes. New York, 1845.

Also 2 volumes in one.

THE CHAINBEARER, OR THE LITTLEPAGE MANUSCRIPTS. 2 volumes. New York, 1845.

THE REDSKINS; OR INDIAN AND INJIN: BEING THE CONCLUSION OF THE LITTLEPAGE MANUSCRIPTS. 2 volumes. New York, 1846.

THE CRATER; OR VULCAN'S PEAK. A Tale of the Pacific. 2 volumes. New York, 1847.

JACK TIER; OR THE FLORIDA REEFS. 2 volumes. New York, 1848.

THE OAK OPENINGS; OR THE BEE-HUNTER. 2 volumes. New York, 1848.

THE SEA LIONS; OR THE LOST SEALERS. 2 volumes. New York, 1849.

COX, PALMER
1840–1924

Cox's reputation as a children's author rests more upon his artistic creations than upon his literary achievement. As a young man he left his home in Canada for San Francisco, where he found employment as a ship's carpenter. While still at the Coast he contributed sketches and cartoons to the newspapers, which presently gained him a reputation and resulted in the offer of a position on one of the New York comic papers. In 1880 he began illustrating children's stories for *St. Nicholas* and quickly acquired an enthusiastic juvenile following.

Shortly thereafter he evolved the "Brownies," inspired by recollections of the folklore stories of his boyhood home. These appealing little people at once became immensely popular and still remain among the gentlest and most whimsical figures of American juvenile literature.

THE BROWNIES, THEIR BOOK. New York, The Century Co., (1887).

The Printer's emblem must appear ¼ inch below the copyright notice. It was later placed at the foot of the page.

COX, WILLIAM
?–1851

Cox, by birth an Englishman, by trade a printer, and as such for a time in the employ of the *New York Mirror,* became in due course a worthy member of the so-called "Knickerbocker" group which followed in the wake of Irving.

He was a frequent contributor to the journals of the day, a satirist of the literary frailties of the times, and a discriminating, if frank critic of the stage and its celebrities. He had the grace to include himself among the objects of his derision. The tales of himself and of the City Constable are, in fact, the best of the "Crayon Sketches" he reprinted from the columns of the *Mirror*.

CRAYON SKETCHES. By an Amateur. Edited by Theodore S. Fay. 2 volumes. New York, 1833.

COZZENS, FREDERICK SWARTWOUT
1818–1869

COZZENS, well known in his day as a humorist, was born in New York City. At the age of twenty-one he entered the wine and grocery business and until his failure in 1868 was reckoned one of the leading merchants of the city.

Cozzens was a frequent contributor to the *Knickerbocker Magazine* and published a trade journal known as the *Wine Press*. In the "Sparrowgrass Papers" he depicts with a certain degree of pleasing whimsicality the disillusionment of an urbanite who became a suburbanite.

THE SPARROWGRASS PAPERS: OR, LIVING IN THE COUNTRY. New York, 1856.

CRANCH, CHRISTOPHER PEARSE
1813–1892

CRANCH, a native of the District of Columbia, a member of the Transcendental Club and an occasional contributor to the short lived *Dial,* was a man of unusual versatility, esteemed by his contemporaries as above all else a poet, but with a pleasing talent for music, painting and ventriloquism.

His first book, "Poems," was published in 1844; his two

important juveniles, "The Last of the Huggermuggers" and "Kobboltozo," in 1856 and 1857. Judged from the standpoint of literary excellence neither of these books can be called distinguished, yet the combination of text and author's illustrations gives them a pleasant piquancy.

THE LAST OF THE HUGGERMUGGERS, A GIANT STORY. Boston, 1856.

KOBBOLTOZO: A SEQUEL TO THE LAST OF THE HUGGERMUGGERS. Boston, 1857.

CRANE, STEPHEN
1871–1900

PHYSICALLY delicate, intense, and endowed with a compelling energy which drove him relentlessly, Crane was one of the tragic figures of our literature. He was born in Newark, N. J., and save for periods of absence during his last years as war correspondent, resided there throughout his brief but brilliant career.

Though naturally romantic and creative, his experience as a newspaper reporter made him a stark realist. In no other way may one account for his first book, "Maggie," a brutally frank picture of degenerate New York. "Maggie," however, was a public failure, and success first came to him with the publication of "The Red Badge of Courage," a remarkable study of the psychology of fear in war—doubly remarkable in that it was a creation of the author's imagination.

"The Red Badge" is generally accepted as Crane's masterpiece, yet one may not overlook the fine quality of his free verse, so well exemplified in "The Black Riders," nor the excellence of the short stories collected in "The Open Boat."

MAGGIE, A GIRL OF THE STREETS: A TALE OF NEW YORK. By Johnston Smith. Privately printed. New York, (1893).

It was republished in cloth. New York, 1896.

THE RED BADGE OF COURAGE. An Episode of the American Civil War. New York, 1895.

The first page of advertisements is devoted to "Gilbert Parker's Best Books."

THE BLACK RIDERS AND OTHER LINES. Boston, 1895.

Also 50 copies on Japan paper.

THE OPEN BOAT AND OTHER TALES OF ADVENTURE. New York, 1898.

Only 1500 copies in all were issued, in three editions. The first is undetermined.

CRAWFORD, FRANCIS MARION
1854–1909

CRAWFORD, the most cosmopolitan of American novelists, was born in Bagni-di-Lucca, Italy, and was educated there and in America, England and Germany. His first book, "Mr. Isaacs," written while continuing his Sanskrit studies at Harvard, was published in 1882, and its instant success determined his choice of literature as a profession. After completing his studies he traveled for a while and then established a permanent residence in Italy.

Crawford's own definition of the novelist bears repetition: "We are not . . . teachers or professors, . . . We are nothing more than public amusers. Let us, then, accept our position cheerfully . . . without attempting to dignify it with titles too imposing for it to bear. . . ." Within the arbitrary limits he himself imposed he is brilliant,—one of the most, perhaps the most brilliant of our writers. The group of novels that make up the Saracinesca Series, "Saracinesca," "Sant' Ilario," "Don Orsino" and "Corleone," are probably his best known works.

MR. ISAACS: A TALE OF MODERN INDIA. London and New York, 1882.

The New York edition was assembled from sheets printed in Edinburgh.

SARACINESCA. New York, 1887.

SANT' ILARIO. A Sequel to Saracinesca. New York, 1889.

A CIGARETTE-MAKER'S ROMANCE. New York, 1890.

DON ORSINO. A Novel. New York, 1892.

CORLEONE. A Tale of Sicily. 2 volumes. New York, 1896.

CREVECOEUR, J. HECTOR, (MICHEL GUILLAUME), ST. JOHN de
1735–1813

FEW foreigners have contributed at once so delightfully and impressively to the literature of their adopted country as Crevecoeur. He was the son of a noble house in Normandy. After receiving his education in England and short sojourns in both Canada and Pennsylvania, he became a citizen of New York in 1764. Five years later he settled as a farmer in Ulster County, from which headquarters he traveled extensively throughout the Colonies. Upon attempting to return to France in 1779 he was imprisoned as a spy, but was quickly released and returned by way of England to Normandy, where, following the Revolution, save for a brief service as French Consul in New York, he remained until his death.

Crevecoeur was a man of fine intelligence and feeling, a keen and sympathetic student of nature, of which he became enamored as an Ulster County farmer, and a prophetic observer of the expanding American scene. His "Letters from an American Farmer," charmingly written, and for the most part highly modern in spirit, are perhaps the greatest contribution to literature made from America during the Revolution.

(Anonymous) LETTERS FROM AN AMERICAN FARMER. . . . London, 1782.

Has two folding maps.

The first American edition was published in Philadelphia in 1793.

CROCKETT, DAVID
1786–1836

COLONEL CROCKETT was born in Hawkins, Tenn. When he was thirteen he ran away from home, but returned three years later, began farming and married. In 1813–14 he served in the Creek War, and in 1815 moved to the western part of the state. He was elected to the State Legislature in 1821 and to Congress in 1827 and again in 1833. His opposition to Jackson caused his defeat in 1835, whereupon he went to Texas and was killed in the defense of the Alamo.

Crockett's autobiography, being in part political and in part, at least, factual, is usually omitted from a discussion of American literature. It is doubtful whether he really was the author, but whoever wrote it succeeded admirably in catching the spirit of the early backwoods. The exaggeration, the broad farce, the use of homely English are all typical of the development of the frontier. The book is an important document in the beginnings of Western realism.

A NARRATIVE OF THE LIFE OF DAVID CROCKETT, OF THE STATE OF TENNESSEE. Philadelphia, 1834.

CUMMINS, MARIA SUSANNA

1827–1866

MARIA CUMMINS, Augusta Jane Evans, Mary J. Holmes and Mrs. Southworth, with a following of less notable women writers, were the logical result of the sentimentalist wave which, swelled by the impulse of a flood of annuals and ladies' publications, reached its crest during the years immediately preceding the Civil War.

Miss Cummins was the daughter of a Salem, Mass., jurist. She was educated at Mrs. Sedgwick's fashionable school at Lenox, and almost immediately began her literary career with the publication of short stories in the *Atlantic Monthly* and similar periodicals.

Properly to understand her work and that of her feminine contemporaries necessitates a clear conception of the intellectual atmosphere and social standards of their day. For they were in reality as representative of their period as is the so-called modernist of the present time.

Of all the sentimental novels of this earlier period "The Lamplighter" is, perhaps, the best. If forty thousand copies issued during the eight weeks immediately following its publication measure the high tide of its popularity, there are still thousands living who would find in it a genuine appeal today.

(Anonymous) THE LAMPLIGHTER. Boston, 1854.
Other editions than the first give the number of thousands on the title page.

CURTIS, GEORGE WILLIAM

1824–1892

CURTIS, one of the most cultured and refining influences in our literature, was born in Providence, R. I., and received his first impressive intellectual experience as a pupil at the Brook Farm School. Later he traveled extensively in Europe and the Orient, where he found the inspiration for his delightful fancies and travel sketches which began their appearance in book form with the publication of his "Nile Notes of a Howadji."

Upon his return to the United States he lived for a time in Concord and there fell mildly under the spell of Emerson and others of the Transcendentalist Group. Returning to New York, he became editor of *The Easy Chair in Harper's* and later editor-in-chief of the magazine. From that point of departure began a long, useful and honorable career not only as an essayist and writer on social subjects, but also as an orator and a potent force in civic and national affairs.

Curtis lacked the spark of genius; yet his gentle philosophy, his culture and his moral integrity make him a welcome figure in the literature of the nation.

(Anonymous) THE POTIPHAR PAPERS. New York, 1853.

PRUE AND I. New York, 1856.

The first edition contains 214 pages only. There were a few copies issued in gilt and blind stamped morocco. Some of the cloth copies read "Prue and I" on the backstrip—some read also "Curtis's Works."

DANA, RICHARD HENRY, SR.
1787–1879

THOUGH a permanent resident of Massachusetts, the senior R. H. Dana was more closely affiliated with the New York group than with his New England literary contemporaries.

He was born in Cambridge a lineal descendant of Anne

Bradstreet, was a lawyer by profession, a brother-in-law of Washington Allston and a founder and one-time editor of the *Atlantic Monthly*. Though holding friendly relations with the Transcendentalists, his active and stimulating efforts to mold a broader literary taste were among the potent influences in preparing the way for the passing of the Transcendentalist epoch.

His name as a writer is popularly associated with his labored sea epic, "The Buccaneer," but his shorter poem, "The Little Beach Bird," in "Poems" (1827), is a more permanent contribution. "The Idle Man," though not the equal of the "Sketch Book" which inspired it, is its worthiest competitor.

(Anonymous) THE IDLE MAN. Six parts or two volumes. New York, 1821–22.

Bryant contributed six poems to this publication.

POEMS. Boston, 1827.

DANA, RICHARD HENRY, Jr.
1815–1882

AS WAS the case with several other American authors a physical disability was the immediate cause of R. H. Dana, Jr.'s distinguished literary achievement. He was born and educated in Cambridge, Mass. Weakened eyesight early in his college career, however, led to a protracted sea voyage as a common sailor, and that in turn to his admirable epic and masterpiece, "Two Years Before the Mast."

In this greatest of American sea sagas Dana pictures with vividness and an unrivaled fidelity to truth the charms and the brutalities of a seaman's life. He knew the sea in all its moods, its terrors and its gentleness; he reported them with a touch akin to genius.

(Anonymous) Two Years Before the Mast. A Personal Narrative of Life at Sea. New York, 1840.

Copies bound in tan cloth, with the list of "Harper's Family Publications" which is printed on the back cover ending with No. 105, are preferred. This book is No. CVI. Also in black cloth.

DAVIS, JOHN
1767–1816

Davis may fairly be styled a literary tramp. His nationality was English, but he called himself a citizen of the world. America may properly lay claim to him in part, as being the material source and inspiration of much of his most important literary work.

After having traveled in the East and many parts of Europe he came to the United States in 1798 and remained here for upwards of three years, working at odd times and tramping about the country, indulging his keen powers of observation and a naturally prying disposition. His place in American fiction is pre-eminently due to "The First Settlers of Virginia," a story of the "noble redman,"—the first treatment in novel form of the Pocahontas legend.

(Anonymous) The First Settlers of Virginia, an Historical Novel, Exhibiting a View of the Rise and Progress of the Colony at James Town, a Picture of Indian Manners, The Countenance of the Country, and Its Natural Productions. The Second Edition considerably enlarged. New York, 1805.

The above is the title by which this book is known and the earliest available edition. There is one known copy of the shorter first edition, "Captain Smith and Princess Pocahontas, An Indian Tale. Philadelphia, 1805."

DAVIS, RICHARD HARDING
1864–1916

RICHARD HARDING DAVIS, a native of Philadelphia, was a newspaper reporter at the age of twenty-four and later became a war correspondent of international fame. Quite apart from his journalistic work, Davis wrote voluminously, turning out short stories, novels, war tales and plays in a manner aptly described by Henry James as "journalese."

Like Crawford, though in lesser degree, he believed that the great end of fiction is entertainment. He was above all else a craftsman who valued effect and form far more than substance. His greatest literary success was "Gallegher." Probably his best novel, despite its extravagances, was "Soldiers of Fortune." Neither possesses in any true literary sense enduring quality, but his style unquestionably affected the literary development of a later generation.

GALLEGHER AND OTHER STORIES. New York, 1891.

This book as first published was printed on wove paper.

SOLDIERS OF FORTUNE. New York, 1897.

Must have the "Charles Scribner" imprint.

DAWES, RUFUS

1803–1859

DAWES was born in Boston and educated at Harvard, but subsequently moved to Baltimore, where he served for several years as editor of the *Emerald,* a weekly. Much of his literary work appeared in the columns of this paper and the *Literary Gazette.*

Dawes' chosen literary field was poetry, yet, save for a few of his shorter poems of minor merit, his verse is now forgotten. He wrote, however, a single work of fiction, which, despite a florid beginning and an occasional labored philosophical digression, deserves some recognition,—"Nix's Mate," a story of the revolt of Massachusetts Bay Colony against the oppressions of James II, with a glimpse of contemporary Harvard and a mild tirade against college pedantry. It presents a sympathetic and delightful portrayal of Governor Winthrop and an interesting conception of Indian character during the early Colonial days.

NIX'S MATE: AN HISTORICAL ROMANCE OF AMERICA. By the Author of "Athenia of Damascus, etc." 2 volumes. New York, 1839.

In Volume I in the seventh line from the bottom of page 64 "he" is repeated, and in the seventh line of page 67 "is" is repeated. In Volume II in the seventh line from the bottom of page 187 the text reads "fora" instead of "for a."

DE FOREST, JOHN W(ILLIAM)

1826–1906

"IT SEEMS reasonable that he should be lastingly recognized as one of the masters of American fiction, and I for one shall never be willing to own him less"—William Dean Howells.

De Forest, a man of real and varied intellectual attainments, was born in Seymour, Conn., educated in Europe, and thereafter spent several years in the Levant. Upon his return to America he compiled his first book,—the one with which his name is now commonly associated,—a scholarly "History of the Indians of Connecticut" (1851). He served with distinction during the Civil War and was discharged with the brevet rank of Major. He devoted the remainder of his life to historical research and literary work.

In the search for the beginnings of realism it has been the custom to start with Eggleston, but, without underestimating the importance of the Hoosier's position, it appears that he has been unduly honored. Before the War De Forest had made a good beginning in his first novel, "Seacliff," and after its close he wrote a number of stories in still more vigorous and natural vein. "Miss Ravenel's Conversion from Secession to Loyalty" was "of an advanced realism before realism was known," and Carl Van Doren, to whom we are indebted for its recovery, says of it, in his admirable "The American Novel," that "no other novel of the decade has been less dimmed by a century of realism. Coldly truthful in its descriptions of battles and camps, crisp and pointed in its dialogue, penetrating, if not over-subtle, in its character analysis, sensible in its plot, and in its general temper alert and sophisticated, it is almost as convincing as it once was precocious."

Much the same may be said of other of De Forest's novels. "Kate Beaumont" is an exceptional portrayal of certain phases of Southern life, and in some respects his most finished work, and "Honest John Vane" and "Playing the Mischief," in spite of some exaggeration and the author's obvious dislike for "statesmen," are perhaps the first believable pictures of everyday American politics in our literature.

SEACLIFF OR THE MYSTERY OF THE WESTERVELTS. Boston, 1859.

MISS RAVENEL'S CONVERSION FROM SECESSION TO LOYALTY. New York, 1867.

This book appears in two dissimilar bindings. Since internal errors are identical in both either would appear acceptable.

OVERLAND. A Novel. New York, Sheldon, (1871).

KATE BEAUMONT. Boston, 1872.

"Osgood's Library of Novels, No. 5."

HONEST JOHN VANE. A Story. New Haven, 1875.

PLAYING THE MISCHIEF. A Novel. New York, 1875.

DELAND, MARGARET (MARGARETTA WADE CAMPBELL)

1857–

MRS. DELAND, a native of Manchester, Pa., since her marriage to Lorin F. Deland has resided in Boston. She began her literary work at the close of the "local color period" and naturally fell to a degree under its influence. Yet in her broader sympathies she stands above it. She is at all times a careful student of human relations, and an intelligent observer and faithful delineator of their conflicts. Her best novel prior to 1900 is probably her second book, "John Ward, Preacher," a strong portrayal of the effect of religious differences on married life. Even more artistic and quite as penetrating are the delightful stories of her girlhood environment, grouped in her "Old Chester Tales."

JOHN WARD, PREACHER. A Novel. Boston, 1888.

Other than first printings have the edition number on the title page.

SIDNEY. Boston, 1890.

PHILIP AND HIS WIFE. A Novel. Boston, 1894.

THE WISDOM OF FOOLS. Boston, 1897.

OLD CHESTER TALES. New York, 1899.

In the sixth line from the bottom on page 5 the text reads "Chelsea" for "Chester." The advertisements of Mary E. Wilkins' books at the back are in smaller type than the advertisements which follow.

DEMING, P(HILANDER)

1829–1915

DEMING was born in Oneida County, N. Y., and after a brief experience in school teaching and operating a sawmill, entered the University of Vermont, from which he graduated with Phi Beta Kappa honors in 1861. He received his degree at the Albany Law School in 1872, and after a comparatively short experience as legislative reporter for the *Albany Journal* and *New York Times* and as editor of the *Burlington Free Press* became official court reporter at Albany.

In the early 'seventies Deming began contributing to the *Atlantic Monthly* a series of "Adirondack Stories," which he declared where honest tales of actual happenings, and which for stark realism can be compared only to Mary E. Wilkins' New England stories published more than a decade later. Though little read today, it would be difficult to overrate Deming as a pioneer force in the realistic movement of the eighteen-seventies and -eighties.

ADIRONDACK STORIES. Boston, 1880.

TOMPKINS AND OTHER FOLKS. Stories of the Hudson and the Adirondacks. Boston, 1885.

DENNIE, JOSEPH
1768–1812

DENNIE, contemporarily referred to as the "American Addison" and by far the most popular American essayist of his day, was born in Boston, and educated at Harvard. After graduating he moved to Walpole, N. H., to practice law, but abandoned his profession to devote his entire time to literature. Dennie published *The Tatler,* a weekly, in Boston, and simultaneously, in Walpole, *The Farmer's Museum,* to which he contributed his most famous essays "The Lay Preacher." Offered a clerkship in the State Department by Secretary Pinckney, he moved in 1801 to Philadelphia, where he established *The Port-Folio,* the most influential journal of its period, which he conducted until his death.

Dennie's style, judged by present canons, was stilted and regrettably subservient to British models; yet he was one of the first and most important essayists of the New Republic, and by his wit and intellect gave invaluable stimulus to a country still groping for literary light.

(Anonymous) THE LAY PREACHER; OR, SHORT SERMONS, FOR IDLE READERS. Walpole, N. H., 1796.

DERBY, GEORGE HORATIO
(John Phoenix)
1823–1861

DERBY, a native of Dedham, Mass., and an army officer who served in the Mexican War and as a Government Engineer, was the first to introduce the Pacific Coast as subject matter of typical American humor. He was a forerunner of the "Pike County" school and his talents were genuine. His influence on those who followed him,—even on Mark Twain, himself,—is appreciable.

PHOENIXIANA; OR, SKETCHES AND BURLESQUES. New York, 1856.

DICKINSON, EMILY
1830–1886

MISS DICKINSON was born in Amherst, Mass., and lived her entire life within her native town. Although she had a few intimate friends, to the world she was a recluse, but whether from preference or because of an unfortunate love affair is a matter of dispute among her recent biographers.

Miss Dickinson's verse was written for her own delectation, and with the exception of one poem none of it appeared until Thomas Wentworth Higginson, her literary sponsor, arranged for its publication after her death. Her poetry displays an amazing caprice and personality, and its vivid insight, playful irony and curious sense of detachment go far toward justifying the claims of her admirers. Some rank her as the best of American poetesses. The "Single Hound" (1914) contains some of her finest work.

POEMS. Boston, 1890.

POEMS. Second Series. Boston, 1891.

LETTERS OF EMILY DICKINSON, EDITED BY MARY LOOMIS TODD. 2 volumes. Boston, 1894.

POEMS. Third Series. Boston, 1896.

DODGE, MARY ELIZABETH MAPES
1836–1905

TO THE children of the middle eighteen-seventies and -eighties Mrs. Dodge needed no introduction. She was born and educated in New York, and began writing as an avocation. Following the death of her husband she took up literature as a profession, and in 1873 assumed the editorship of the *St. Nicholas Magazine,* which under her guidance prospered amazingly.

Meanwhile, she had written her masterpiece, "Hans Brinker," one of the most famous of American juveniles, which was quickly translated into five languages and crowned by the French Academy. Later, in 1883, she published a second important book for children, "Donald and Dorothy,"—less well known, but little inferior in simplicity and charm. She published also three volumes of poems.

HANS BRINKER; OR, THE SILVER SKATES: A STORY OF LIFE IN HOLLAND. New York, 1866.

DONALD AND DOROTHY. Boston, 1883.

DRAKE, BENJAMIN
1794–1841

AMONG the prose writers of the early West, Drake, a lawyer by profession, is a figure in importance second only to Flint and Hall. He was born in Mason County, Kentucky, but later moved to Cincinnati, where he conducted with ability and taste a literary and family weekly of far reaching influence. He was the author of important biographies of Black Hawk and Tecumseh and of a valuable sketch of "Cincinnati in 1826."

Drake was not by any stretch of the imagination a great literary figure, yet his tales are a valuable part of the record of an important though vanished day.

TALES AND SKETCHES FROM THE QUEEN CITY. Cincinnati, 1838.
The copyright notice is omitted.

DRAKE, JOSEPH RODMAN
1795–1820

DRAKE was born in New York City, and, though educated as a physician, was clearly marked by natural talent for literary work. He early contributed poems to various publications, but first attracted attention when he and Halleck collaborated in the "Croaker Papers," a series of lively satires on leading local politicians which became at once the talk of the town.

Drake's masterpiece is unquestionably "The Culprit Fay," completed in two days and one of the few fine fairy tales in American verse. By his untimely death American poetry lost a writer of real attainment and of even greater promise.

POEMS BY CROAKER, CROAKER & CO., AND CROAKER, JUN., AS PUBLISHED IN THE EVENING POST. New York, 1819.

THE CULPRIT FAY AND OTHER POEMS. New York. 1835.

Has an engraved portrait and title page.

This book was published posthumously at the instigation of his family. There is said to be a separate 1819 edition of the title poem, but copies of it seem curiously elusive. Among the other poems in this collection is his famous poem "The American Flag."

DU CHAILLU, PAUL BELLONI
1831–1903

DU CHAILLU's father was the agent of a Paris firm located on the west coast of Africa. It is doubtful whether the son was born in New Orleans or in France, but he grew up in Africa and was educated at a Jesuit Mission there.

In 1852 he secured the backing of the Philadelphia Academy of Natural Sciences, and after burying himself for four years in the jungle returned with some startling material and the first group of gorillas ever exhibited in this country. His first book, which appeared in 1861, was widely ridiculed, though most of its statements were later corroborated by other scientists. He visited Africa again in 1863, returning two years later with new evidence substantiating his earlier contentions. Later still he went to Norway and Sweden, and eventually to St. Petersburg, where he died.

Du Chaillu was a careful observer and entertaining writer, and his descriptive work is excellent. "Stories of the Gorilla Country" stands well among the thrilling narratives of fact for children.

STORIES OF THE GORILLA COUNTRY. Narrated for Young People. New York, 1868.

THE LAND OF THE MIDNIGHT SUN; SUMMER AND WINTER JOURNEYS THROUGH SWEDEN, NORWAY, LAPLAND AND NORTHERN FINLAND. 2 volumes. New York, 1882.
Also 2 volumes, London, 1881.

DUNBAR, PAUL LAWRENCE
1872–1906

DUNBAR, since Phillis Wheatley the first American Negro to achieve literary notability, was born in Dayton, Ohio, and was educated in the public schools. He began his active life in connection with a New York City paper, but abandoned journalism as a profession to join the staff of the Congressional Library in Washington. Meanwhile the first volume of his poems, "Oak Leaves and Ivy" (1893), was attracting increasing attention. He was later much in demand as a public reader of his own verse.

Although Dunbar's work includes a volume of short stories, a novel or two and some verse in standard English, his chief claim to distinction rests upon his dialect poems. Howells considered him the first of his race "to feel the negro life aesthetically and to express it lyrically."

MAJORS AND MINORS. (Toledo, 1895).
Reprinted, for the most part, as "Lyrics of Lowly Life." New York, 1896. It appears in two bindings with smooth and beveled edges. No priority has been demonstrated.

FOLKS FROM DIXIE. New York, 1898.

DUNNE, FINLEY PETER
1867–

FINLEY PETER DUNNE was born in Chicago, and well into the period of his most important work was associated editorially with one or another of the leading Chicago daily papers.

Dunne reached his greatest popularity in the early days of the Spanish-American War, in bringing his overwrought countrymen-at-large to earth through the satiric Irish wit of his "Mr. Dooley." He bids fair to live as one of our genuine humorists.

MR. DOOLEY IN PEACE AND IN WAR. Boston, 1898.

MR. DOOLEY IN THE HEARTS OF HIS COUNTRYMEN. Boston, 1899.
It is said that all copies seem to have on the

copyright page a record of several printings "before publication."

DWIGHT, TIMOTHY

1752–1817

DWIGHT, a grandson of Jonathan Edwards, was born in Northampton, Mass., and was educated at Yale. At the close of the Revolution, during which he served as an army chaplain, he became both pastor and principal of the famous boys' school at Greenfield, Conn., and thereafter, from 1795 until his death, was president of Yale.

As a preacher and theologian Dwight had no contemporary equal. He was unquestionably a man of great ability, of which, unfortunately, he seems to have been too much aware. His literary memory rests solely upon his contributions to the work of the so-called "Hartford Wits," who, despite their long and tedious poems, almost alone, save for Freneau, kept American poetry alive during the troubled years that followed the Revolution.

Dwight's major personal contributions were "The Conquest of Canaan," sometimes called the first American epic, and "Greenfield Hill," a discursive poem typical of the period, written, as he averred, for the amusement and enlightenment of his countrymen. Though dull and labored and lamentably subservient to English models, on which they certainly made no improvement, they have here and there a stanza, phrase or sentence prophetic of a national literature to come.

THE CONQUEST OF CANAAN; A POEM, IN ELEVEN BOOKS. Hartford, 1785.

GREENFIELD HILL: A POEM, IN SEVEN PARTS. . . . New York, 1794.

EDWARDS, HARRY STILWELL

1854–1927

EDWARDS was born in Macon, Ga., and attended private school until he was fifteen. A short service as a clerk in the Auditor's office in Washington and several years of book-keeping, again in Macon, were followed by his graduation in law from Mercur University. He then became an associate editor and owner of the *Macon Telegraph* and later of other local papers.

His tales are full of quaint conceits, and at least one of them, "Eneas Africanus" (1919), is a Southern classic.

TWO RUNAWAYS AND OTHER STORIES. New York, The Century Co., (1889).

EGGLESTON, EDWARD

1837–1902

FEW figures stand out more boldly than Eggleston's as marking a turning point in the history of American fiction. He was born in Vevay, Ind., was essentially self-educated, began life as a circuit rider, and later entered a larger field as agent of the Minnesota Bible Society,—two experiences which proved rich in the materials utilized in his later literary work.

In 1866 he moved to Evanston to become the editor of *Hearth and Home,* in which he first published his famous story "The Hoosier Schoolmaster." Shortly afterwards he went to Chicago to engage in Sunday School work, and while there began contributing to the *New York Independent,* of which he presently became literary editor. In 1879 he retired to Lake George to devote himself to writing.

While the literature of the Atlantic Seaboard was still struggling in the last throes of sentimentalism, Harte in California and Eggleston in the Middle West were successfully developing a new type of fiction. The essential note in all of Eggleston's work was its fidelity to fact. He portrayed life exactly as he saw it. His influence on the subsequent trend of the American novel was profound. *

THE HOOSIER SCHOOLMASTER. A Novel. New York, Orange, Judd, (1871).
Page 71, line 1 reads "was" not "is."

THE CIRCUIT RIDER: A Tale of the Heroic Age. New York, 1874.
The word "Illustrated" must not appear on the title page.

ROXY. New York, 1878.

THE HOOSIER SCHOOLBOY. New York, 1883.
The question of priority between the Scribner and Orange Judd imprints is undetermined. The copy in the Library of Congress, filed for copyright, bears the Scribner imprint but other factors make this evidence inconclusive.

THE GRAYSONS: A STORY OF ILLINOIS. New York, The Century Co., (1887).

ELLIOTT, SARAH BARNWELL
1848–1928

MRS. ELLIOTT was the daughter of Bishop Stephen Barnwell of Beaufort, Ga. During her early girlhood her father

* Eggleston is generally regarded as the first American realistic novelist. This is not literally true. De Forest had started his realistic writing before the Civil War and of the two was unquestionably the greater artist, but he came before his time. De Forest's influence was unfortunately negligible, while Eggleston's, being timely, was profound.

moved to the Tennessee plateau, where, save for an interval of seven years in New York City, she spent the rest of her days. Throughout her life she took a deep interest in the equal suffrage movement, and made important contributions to its cause. She was likewise a playwright of no mean distinction.

As a novelist Mrs. Elliott is in some ways the complement of Mary Noailles Murfree. Miss Murfree's characters are sometimes hazy, Mrs. Elliott's generally men and women of life and fire. A certain timidity, undoubtedly a concession to an audience not yet ready for stark realism, prevented her greater success. Nevertheless, in a way, she was the Southern representative of the new school of which Crane, Norris, Kirkland, Howe, Fuller and Garland were the Northern and Western exponents. "Jerry," her best known story, caused a sensation when it first appeared in *Scribner's Magazine.*

JERRY. A Novel. New York, 1891.

THE DURKET SPERRET; A NOVEL. New York, 1898.

ELLIS, EDWARD S(YLVESTER)
1840–1916

CROWDING the heels of Ned Buntline (Judson) and Sylvanus Cobb, Jr., at the end of the eighteen-fifties, appeared a new element in the development of sensationalism, the "Dime Novel." Crude, swashbuckling stories at best, they had little save a startling rapidity of action to recommend them, yet for many years they were eagerly read by a considerable portion of the public.

The Dime Novel was an innovation of the enterprising firm of Beadle & Adams. Among the earliest authors employed by this firm was Edward S. Ellis, a native of Geneva, Ohio, who had come to New York for an education, had remained as a teacher, and some years later was to do excellent historical research work as well as to continue the writing of juveniles.

Ellis was the author of "Seth Jones," the most popular of the early ten cent thrillers, and justifiably selected here as an example of the type. Within six months of its release more than four hundred and fifty thousand copies of it were sold, not to mention certain foreign printings. Its keynote is action; every page is sensational.

SETH JONES, OR THE CAPTIVES OF THE FRONTIER. New York, (1860).
"Beadle's Dime Novel. No. 8."

EMBURY, EMMA CATHARINE (MANLEY)
1806–1863

WRITING over the signature of "Lanthe" Mrs. Embury became a popular magazine contributor years before her identity was known. One trusts that no undue significance attaches to the fact that, whereas nearly all of her literary work prior to her marriage to a Brooklyn gentleman in 1828 was poetry, virtually all of her subsequent output was prose. Her tales were for the most part of the romantic type current in the contemporary magazines. Whatever recognition they receive must be credited to her mild powers of observation and invention.

PICTURES OF EARLY LIFE; OR, SKETCHES OF YOUTH. Boston, 1839.

EMERSON, RALPH WALDO
1803–1882

EMERSON was born in Boston and completed his education at Harvard. He then took up teaching, and, while so engaged, prepared himself for the ministry. After a short pastorate, he resigned by reason of personal religious scruples. Following the death of his first wife, and broken in health, he traveled extensively in Europe, where, in personal contact, he cemented his friendship with Carlyle, Coleridge, Wordsworth and other men of note. Upon his return to the United States he settled permanently in Concord, and began what may be called his life work.

No man has so profoundly influenced the thought of America as Emerson, few have attained to his stature as a figure in her literature. Nothing that he wrote is unimportant, yet the essence of his greatness is embodied in his "Nature," his "Essays" and his "Poems."

As an ethical stimulator appealing to those willing to listen to inner promptings Emerson stands supreme among our philosophers and men of letters. If he was, indeed, the leader of the Transcendentalists, he transcended them all in his singular aloofness from their controversies.

(Anonymous) NATURE. Boston, 1836.

Bound in varied colored cloths. In earlier copies page 94 is in error numbered 92.

AN ORATION DELIVERED BEFORE THE PHI BETA KAPPA SOCIETY, AT CAMBRIDGE, AUGUST 31, 1837. Boston, 1837.

ESSAYS. Boston, 1841.

The words "First series" must not appear on the spine.

ESSAYS. Second Series. Boston, 1844.

POEMS. Boston, 1847.

Has four pages of advertisements.

NATURE, ADDRESSES AND LECTURES. Boston, 1849.

This appeared in part four years earlier in England, under the title "Nature; an Essay."

REPRESENTATIVE MEN: SEVEN LECTURES. Boston, 1850.

Must measure ¾ of an inch across the top of the covers and have an hour glass design on both the front and back cover.

ENGLISH TRAITS. Boston, 1856.

THE CONDUCT OF LIFE. Boston, 1860.

Must contain no leaf of advertisements in front in any form, and the verso of the half title must be blank. The advertisement at the back should not be dated January, 1861.

MAY DAY AND OTHER PIECES. Boston, 1867.

SOCIETY AND SOLITUDE. Boston, 1870.

LETTERS AND SOCIAL AIMS. Boston, 1876.

ENGLISH, THOMAS DUNNE
1819–1902

DR. ENGLISH, editor, politician and playwright, was born in Philadelphia and graduated from the University of Pennsylvania Medical School. He subsequently studied law and was admitted to the bar. He began his literary activities in 1839, with a contribution to *Burton's Gentleman's Magazine,* and continued them with the establishment of two papers, the *Aurora* and the *Aristidon,* both of which failed.

English distinguished himself by a quarrel with Poe, resumed his practice of law in 1852, settled in Bergen County, N. J., served in the New Jersey legislature from 1863 to 1864, started another magazine, became a member of the literary staff of the *Newark Sunday Call* and again served in the New Jersey legislature from 1891 to 1895.

Although English was never more than a second rate

poet, he had the honor of being the author of one lyric, "Ben Bolt," which, whatever its literary merit, is still one of the most popular ballads ever written in America.

American Ballads. Harper's Half-Hour Series. New York, 1880.

"Ben Bolt" was first printed in the *New York Mirror,* September 2, 1842.

FAWCETT, EDGAR
1847–1904

Fawcett, a native of New York City and a graduate of Columbia, was in a sense a man of leisure. Writing, at least, was not to him a necessary means of livelihood. Nevertheless his range was almost as wide as his truly remarkable quality of fancy, embracing poetry, drama, essays and the novel. He was something of an iconoclast, and his biting though often accurate satires of New York society made him most unpopular,—were the cause in fact of Henry Stoddard's well remembered *bon mot,* "Won't somebody turn this Fawcett off?"

Partly on account of his local unpopularity, Fawcett moved to England at the age of fifty and remained there until his death.

An Ambitious Woman. A Novel. Boston, 1884.

The House at High Bridge. A Novel. Boston, 1887.

FAY, THEODORE SEDGWICK
1807–1898

Though educated as a lawyer, Fay, a native of New York, never seriously practiced his profession. Apart from his lifelong interest in writing, his more active years were marked by two distinctive experiences, editorial association for several years with the *New York Mirror* in his native city, and, after 1837, distinguished foreign diplomatic service, first as Secretary of Legation at Berlin and later as Minister to Switzerland.

His literary activities were varied,—a little poetry of ordinary merit, certain travel sketches, a half dozen popular but mediocre novels, a group of fugitive papers on Shakespeare, and a considerable number of timely essays, for the most part published in the *Mirror*. The best selection from these was first published in book form in "Dreams and Reveries of a Quiet Man," most of which is interesting today chiefly for its lively historical pictures of contemporary New York life. The "Little Genius" essays, however, remain delightful satires, and the travesty, "Extracts from Mrs. Trollope's Travels" is still a gem.

Dreams and Reveries of a Quiet Man, Consisting of The Little Genius, and Other Essays. By one of the Editors of the *New York Mirror*. 2 volumes. New York, 1832.

FESSENDEN, THOMAS GREEN
(Christopher Caustic)
1771–1838

Fessenden, journalist and traveling salesman, and perhaps the most notable and bitter satirist between Trumbull and Lowell, was born in Walpole, N. H. After working his way through Dartmouth and making a try at law, he went to England in 1801, to sell American goods. On his return to the United States in 1804, he edited the *New York Weekly Inspector* until 1808, when he removed to Brattleboro, Vt., to practice law. He subsequently became editor of the

Brattleboro Reporter and the *Bellows Falls Advertiser* and in 1822 established the *New England Farmer* in Boston.

His political poems, particularly "Democracy Unveiled," in which he attacks Jefferson and others with incredible coarseness, are probably the most virulent American diatribes of their kind.

DEMOCRACY UNVEILED; OR, TYRANNY STRIPPED OF THE GARB OF PATRIOTISM. By Christopher Caustic, LL. D. Boston, 1805.
There is an errata note on page 220.

FIELD, EUGENE
1850–1895

EUGENE FIELD was born in St. Louis, lived as a boy in Amherst, Mass., and went to college at Williams and the University of Missouri. After several years of newspaper experience in St. Louis and Kansas City he became managing editor of the *Denver Tribune*. In 1881 he reprinted some of his sketches in a little book called the "Tribune Primer," and the enthusiasm which this volume aroused quickly translated itself into a position on *The Chicago News*.

Despite the amusing cleverness of the "Tribune Primer" Field's true worth as a paragrapher and poet is better evidenced in "Culture's Garland" and a "Little Book of Western Verse." From these one gains an estimate of him as a clever critic, a singularly happy interpreter of childhood, and, above all else, a master of humorous verse. Field's sentimental touch amounted almost to genius. A wide understanding of humanity and a deftness of rhythm characterize all of his best work.

CULTURE'S GARLAND; BEING MEMORANDA OF THE GRADUAL RISE OF LITERATURE, ART, MUSIC AND SOCIETY IN CHICAGO AND OTHER

WESTERN GANGLIA. With an Introduction by Julian Hawthorne. Boston, 1887.

A LITTLE BOOK OF WESTERN VERSE. Chicago, 1889.

Two hundred and fifty copies on large paper.

LOVE SONGS OF CHILDHOOD. New York, 1894.

Fifteen copies on Japan paper; one hundred and six copies on Van Gelder paper.

THE LOVE AFFAIRS OF A BIBLIOMANIAC. New York, 1896.

One hundred and fifty copies, large paper.

FIELDS, JAMES T(HOMAS)
1816–1881

AT FOURTEEN Fields left his home at Portsmouth, N. H., to enter the employ of a Boston publishing house; at twenty he was the junior member of Ticknor, Reed & Fields. His later progress as a publisher is sketchily indicated by the successive changes of the firm's name to Ticknor & Fields, and later to Fields, Osgood & Co. In 1862 he founded the *Atlantic Monthly*. He retired in 1870 to take up public lecturing.

It is questionable whether any other publisher personally enjoyed the intimate acquaintance of so many authors. He was a man of exceptional charm and grace which, coupled with his commanding position as a publisher, gave him an unusual opportunity for association with the foremost writers of the world. Fortunately, he has left a pleasing record of these contacts in a book notable for its keen insight and its excellent perspective.

YESTERDAYS WITH AUTHORS. Boston, 1872.

FINLEY, MARTHA (MARTHA FARQUHARSON)
1828–1909

MISS FINLEY, a voluminous writer of girls' serials, was born in Chillicothe, Ohio. Most of her life, however, was spent in the East, where she finally settled in Elkton, Md. Having an aversion to seeing her name in print, she adopted a nom-de-plume, Martha Farquharson, at the insistence of her publishers. After the appearance of "Elsie Dinsmore" there was a continuous popular demand for her work, and she became enormously successful.

The Elsie books were the climax of the pious didacticism which, save for Goulding's "Young Marooners," and a few other stories, had previously dominated the American juvenile. Though there is a certain tenderness in Miss Finley's glorification of the "angel child," the reader cannot cavil at Professor Tassin's comment that the "Elsie Series," "made all previous prigs appear reticent and recreant." *

ELSIE DINSMORE. New York, 1867.

FLINT, TIMOTHY
1780–1840

FLINT enjoys the unique distinction of being the first American author with a genuinely Western point of view, and shares honors with James Hall as a pioneer of Western literature.

He was born in Reading, Mass., where he was for several years a Congregational pastor before his appointment in 1815 as missionary to the Valley of the Mississippi. There, during ten years of itinerant teaching and preaching, he gained the broad and accurate knowledge of the country and people which made his "Recollections of Ten Years

* Cambridge History of American Literature, Book II, Chapt. VII.

in the Mississippi Valley" (1826) an authoritative work, and furnished, as well, the background and material for much of his important fiction. He was for three years editor of the *Western Monthly Magazine.*

Flint's first novel, "Francis Berrian," remained for some time our only intimate picture of Southwestern frontier life. Miss Mitford, the well known contemporary English critic, characterized his "George Mason" as almost equal to Defoe. Neither of these novels, nor "The Shoshonee Valley" warrants great praise, but all three are among the fountain heads of Western literature.

(Anonymous) FRANCIS BERRIAN, OR THE MEXICAN PATRIOT. 2 volumes. Boston, 1826.

THE LIFE AND ADVENTURES OF ARTHUR CLENNING. . . . 2 volumes. Philadelphia, 1828.

GEORGE MASON, THE YOUNG BACKWOODSMAN; OR "DON'T GIVE UP THE SHIP." A Story of the Mississippi. Boston, 1829.

THE SHOSHONEE VALLEY; A ROMANCE. 2 volumes. Cincinnati, 1830.

FOOTE, MARY HALLOCK
1847–

MRS. FOOTE, known as an illustrator in black and white as well as an author, was born in New York and educated in the East. After her marriage she visited Idaho, Colorado and California with her husband, a civil engineer. Mrs. Foote's chief distinction came to her as a pioneer romancer of the Western mining camps. For a time she had a tremendous vogue. But though she tells a story well, her work is quite conventional. Its priority is its chief claim to recognition.

THE LED HORSE CLAIM: A ROMANCE OF A MINING CAMP. Boston, 1883.

FORD, PAUL LEICESTER
1865–1902

FORD was above all else a distinguished historian and bibliographer, and his fiction, by which he is best known to the general public, was written almost solely by way of relaxation. He was born in Brooklyn, N. Y., and was educated privately. Later, after extended travel both in the United States and abroad, he plunged wholeheartedly into most painstaking research, and his studies of the sources of American history have proved extremely valuable.

It is natural, therefore, that his "Janice Meredith," perhaps our best literary picture of social conditions during the Revolution, and "The Honorable Peter Stirling," a truthful story of ward politics in a later day, should be characterized by a singular exactitude and fidelity of detail. It is far more unexpected to find him writing a fine detective story like "The Great K. & A. Train Robbery."

THE HONORABLE PETER STIRLING AND WHAT PEOPLE THOUGHT OF HIM. New York, 1894.
"Stirling" is so spelled on the title page and misspelled "Sterling" on the covers and the backstrip.

THE GREAT K. & A. TRAIN ROBBERY. New York, 1897.
Should be at least 7¼ inches tall.

JANICE MEREDITH. A Revolutionary Romance. New York, 1899.
The 2 volume edition is later.

FOSTER, HANNAH WEBSTER
1759–1840

Mrs. Foster was the daughter of a Boston merchant and the wife of the Rev. John Foster of Brighton, Mass. After her husband's death she resided with a daughter in Montreal, Canada. She was a frequent contributor of political articles to various magazines, and the author of one of the most popular novels ever published in America.

"The Coquette" is a tale of seduction, with the inevitable moral. Unlike its near contemporaries and its only rivals in early popularity, "Charlotte" and "Alonzo and Melissa," its characters, though priggish and wooden, possess some resemblance to human beings and the story has a consecutive plot. It was enormously popular, at least one edition appearing yearly until 1833, to say nothing of later printings. Altogether it remains the most readable of the earliest American novels written by a feminine author.

The Coquette; or, the History of Eliza Wharton; A Novel; Founded on Fact. By a Lady of Massachusetts. Boston, 1797.

FOX, JOHN (WILLIAM) JR.
1863–1919

Fox was born at Stony Point, Ky., and was educated at Transylvania College and Harvard. After graduation he worked on the *New York Sun* and the *Times* until failing health compelled him to return to Kentucky, where he engaged in a mining venture in the Cumberland Mountains. For a time he wrote and taught school. When the Spanish-American War broke out he joined the Rough Riders and later served as a war correspondent during the Russo-Japanese conflict.

Fox was thoroughly conversant with the manners and customs of the Tennessee-Kentucky mountain folk. He was, moreover, a good story teller, and handled his subjects in a realistic manner. His best known books are probably "The Trail of the Lonesome Pine" and "The Little Shepherd of Kingdom Come," both published after 1900.

A CUMBERLAND VENDETTA AND OTHER STORIES. New York, 1896.

FREDERIC, HAROLD
1856–1898

FREDERIC, one of the more important figures in the renaissance of realism, was born in Utica, N. Y., and, following an apprenticeship as news photographer and proofreader, received his early training as a writer on the editorial staff of the *Albany Journal*. Subsequently he moved to New York and later went to Europe, where he won fame as a foreign correspondent of the *New York Times*.

At his best, Frederic was a brilliant writer. Unfortunately a certain carelessness militated against a full realization of his true abilities. But for this, "The Damnation of Theron Ware,"—a story of real power,—would rank as one of the great American novels.

Frederic's first book was a boldly realistic story of scenes and characters in rural New York, his boyhood home. "In the Valley," an excellent novel of the French and Indian War, and "The Market Place" also deserve a word of genuine praise.

SETH'S BROTHER'S WIFE: A STUDY OF LIFE IN THE GREATER NEW YORK. New York, 1887.

IN THE VALLEY. New York, 1890.

THE DAMNATION OF THERON WARE. Chicago, 1896.

THE MARKET PLACE. New York, Stokes, (1899).

(FREEMAN), MARY ELEANOR WILKINS
1862–1930

MRS. FREEMAN was born in Randolph, Mass., was educated at Mt. Holyoke Seminary, and was well fitted by both training and environment to become a standard bearer of the later "New England School."

Her earlier tales are rugged, grimly convincing studies of the vanishing tradition of Puritanism, which owe little to any previous literary models. Both "A Humble Romance" and "A New England Nun" are entitled to rating as among the best groupings of American short stories. As a novelist Mrs. Freeman is of lesser rank, but "Pembroke" and perhaps "Jane Field" are among the better realistic studies of the transition period of the late eighteen hundreds.

A HUMBLE ROMANCE AND OTHER STORIES. New York, 1887.
Later editions are undated.

A NEW ENGLAND NUN AND OTHER STORIES. New York, 1891.

JANE FIELD. A Novel. New York, 1893.

PEMBROKE. A Novel. New York, 1894.
The first page of advertisements in the back must not contain reviews of this book.

FRENCH, ALICE
(Octave Thanet)
1850–

MISS FRENCH was born in Andover, Mass., but for the greater part of her life has been a resident of Iowa and a frequent visitor in Arkansas. She belongs to the later local color school, though responsible for no innovations. Her work is often dramatic, but lacks in intensity. She is an observer rather than a participator in life. Nevertheless, there is some value in the sociological aspects of her studies of labor. Her short stories are undoubtedly better handled than her novels.

KNITTERS IN THE SUN. Boston, 1887.
THE HEART OF TOIL. New York, 1898.

FRENEAU, PHILIP
1752–1832

FRENEAU, most important American poet of the eighteenth century, was born in New York of Huguenot ancestry, and was graduated from Princeton at the age of nineteen. He taught school for a time, but presently moved to Philadelphia to conduct a newspaper. While on a trading venture to the West Indies during the Revolution he was captured and imprisoned by the English on one of the famous prison hulks in New York Harbor, an experience which inspired his best known poem, "The British Prison-Ship." After the war he wrote voluminously, again went to sea for a time, and later served as editor of several New York papers. His last years were spent on a New Jersey farm, where he died as a result of exposure during a snowstorm.

Freneau's range was wider and his talents were more pronounced than those of any American poet prior to the nineteenth century. His popular reputation as the "Poet of the Revolution" has to a degree deprived him of the broader recognition due him. Many of his ballads, lyrics, satires and descriptive poems display real beauty and imaginative power.

THE AMERICAN VILLAGE, A POEM. To which are added. Several Other Original Pieces in Verse. New York, 1772.

(Anonymous) A Poem, on the Rising Glory of America; being an Exercise Delivered at the Public Commencement at Nassau-Hall, September 25, 1771. Philadelphia, 1772.

Written in collaboration with H. H. Brackenridge.

(Anonymous) The British Prison-Ship: A Poem; in Four Cantos. . . . To which is added, a Poem on the Death of Capt. N. Biddle, who was blown up, in an engagement with the Yarmouth, near Barbadoes. Philadelphia, 1781.

The Poems of Philip Freneau. Written chiefly during the late war. Philadelphia, 1786.

In some copies the page number 257 is missing.

Poems written between the years 1768 & 1794, By Philip Freneau. . . . A New Edition, Revised and Corrected by the Author; Including a Considerable Number of Pieces never before published. Monmouth, (N. J.), 1795.

This book was set up and printed by Freneau himself. Some copies omit the last line of text.

FULLER, HENRY BLAKE
1857–1929

Fuller was a native and lifelong resident of Chicago, which furnished him the background for much of his best work.

His first two books were romances, the better of which, "The Chevalier of Pensieri-Vani," won the approbation of both Norton and Lowell. Later he turned to realism and produced as his initial novel of this type "The Cliff-Dwellers," a relentless story of Chicago life. Fuller's reputation and possibly his final ranking may to a degree suffer by reason of his limited output, yet it is clear that he rendered valiant service in the vanguard of the realistic movement.

THE CHEVALIER OF PENSIERI-VANI, TOGETHER WITH FREQUENT REFERENCES TO THE PROREGE OF ACOPIA. By Stanton Page. Wrappers. Boston, J. A. Cupples, (1890).
Later issues were bound in boards.

THE CLIFF-DWELLERS: A NOVEL. New York, 1893.

WITH THE PROCESSION: A NOVEL. New York, 1895.

GALLAGHER, WILLIAM DAVIS
1808–1894

GALLAGHER, the most important of the early Western poets, was born in Philadelphia, but went with his parents to Cincinnati at the age of eight. At seventeen he entered a printing office and shortly began contributing anonymously to various periodicals. He then became progressively associated with several journals, notably the *Cincinnati Mirror,* the *Western Literary Journal* and the *Western Monthly Magazine.* From 1849 to 1853 he served as confidential clerk to Mr. Corwin, Secretary of the Treasury, resigning to join the editorial staff of the *Louisville Courier.* At the close of the Civil War he became U. S. Pension Agent for the district of Kentucky.

Gallagher's influence upon the development of the earlier

literature of the West was great, both by reason of his own writings and through the helpful encouragement which he gave to others. His style is to a degree imitative and he is at times careless in his work; yet he is the sole representative of the early West,—still essentially a frontier,—whose verse evidences some genuine poetic feeling.

Erato. Number I. Cincinnati, 1835. 36 pp.
Number II. Cincinnati, 1835. 60 pp.
Number III. Cincinnati, 1837. 60 pp.

GARLAND, HAMLIN

1860—

Garland was born amid the drear surroundings of a modest farm near West Salem, Wisc. After bitter early struggles for an education, he graduated from Cedar Valley Seminary, in Iowa. He taught school until 1883, when he moved to Boston to devote himself exclusively to literature. A strenuous course of reading in the Boston Public Library imbued him with the spirit of the French "Veritists," and profoundly influenced his subsequent career.

Garland's "Main-Traveled Roads" and its companion pieces, "Prairie Folk" and "More Main-Traveled Roads" (1910), are tales of the bleak, inhospitable Mid-Western plains. Their art is manifest; yet the new force, authenticity and broadened Americanism which they display are of far greater importance. Garland's literary significance is truly national. He is a fervent protagonist of Americanism in literature, art and culture. His creed is summed up in a book of striking essays, "Crumbling Idols." "A Son of the Middle Border" is perhaps his best work subsequent to 1900.

Main-Traveled Roads: Six Mississippi Valley Stories. Wrappers. Boston, 1891.

The words "first thousand" appear at the bottom of the front wrapper. A few copies were issued in cloth for presentation purposes.

PRAIRIE FOLK. Chicago, 1893.

CRUMBLING IDOLS: TWELVE ESSAYS ON ART DEALING CHIEFLY WITH LITERATURE, PAINTING AND THE DRAMA. Chicago, 1894.

GILDER, RICHARD WATSON
1844–1909

GILDER, a native of Flushing, N. Y., published a paper at the age of twelve, and while yet in his 'teens saw service in the Civil War. At the close of the war he joined the staff of the *Newark Advertiser,* and within a year, in his leisure moments, was again editing his own paper, *Hours at Home.* In 1870 he joined the staff of *Scribner's Magazine,* now *The Century,* and after Dr. Holland's death became its editor-in-chief.

Gilder was the author of several volumes of verse which though characterized by Stedman as "each a collection of flawless poems," have unfortunately little other than this flawlessness to recommend them. His true importance lay rather in his far reaching influence as an editor, in which field he was one of the last classicists of our later nineteenth century literature.

THE NEW DAY: A POEM IN SONGS AND SONNETS. New York, 1876.

GLASGOW, ELLEN ANDERSON GHOLSON
1874–

PRACTICALLY all of Mrs. Glasgow's work has been published in the twentieth century. Yet the genuine promise (later fulfilled) of her first book, "The Descendant," entitled her to mention here.

(Anonymous) THE DESCENDANT. A Novel. New York, 1897.

The advertisements at the back must not mention Twain's "American Claimant."

GOODRICH, SAMUEL GRISWOLD
(Peter Parley)
1793–1860

GOODRICH was born in Ridgefield, Conn., and eventually became a publisher both in Hartford and in Boston, Mass. His literary activities were vast and varied, but they are of slight interest now save for the one hundred and seventy juveniles which bear his name. Most of these were written under the pseudonym of Peter Parley, and most of them (for example, Hawthorne's "Peter Parley's Universal History"), were in reality the work of other authors. Yet, though only nine can be definitely attributed to Goodrich's own pen, he deserves the credit for the initiative and enterprise behind them.

It is difficult to imagine a modern child enjoying Peter Parley's tales,—even such a one as the "Story of the Umbrella and the Tiger." But to a youngster of the earlier eighteen hundreds, fed upon a daily diet of contemporary Sunday School Tracts, they must have been a source of endless delight. In 1856 Goodrich published his "Recollections of a Lifetime." Though not a work of great distinction, it throws many fascinating sidelights on the progress of American culture.

THE TALES OF PETER PARLEY ABOUT AMERICA. Boston, 1827.

RECOLLECTIONS OF A LIFETIME; OR MEN AND THINGS I HAVE SEEN. 2 volumes. Boston, 1856.

GOULDING, FRANCIS ROBERT
1810–1881

DIDACTICISM remained the dominant motif of the American juvenile until the middle of the nineteenth century. It was not until 1852 that a boy's story appeared, written for no other purpose than to amuse the young reader. The author was a Georgia minister.

Goulding was educated at Franklin College, Ga., and prepared for the ministry at the Theological Seminary at Columbia, S. C., an institution founded by his father. After several years in the ministry he resigned his pastorate in 1853 to open a boys' school. Following the Civil War, which left him utterly impoverished, he supported himself and his family by contributing to various literary journals.

Goulding left behind him two notable achievements in widely separated fields, the invention of one of the first practical sewing machines, and "The Young Marooners," a simple little tale of the adventures of five children who came to grief on an island off the Florida coast. Despite the lapse of nearly eighty years, "The Young Marooners" retains its charm. But its deeper significance lies in the fact that, though the "instructive" child's story continued to be produced in diminishing quantity for at least two decades, "The Young Marooners" marks the passing of an epoch in the history of the American juvenile.

ROBERT AND HAROLD OR THE YOUNG MAROONERS ON THE FLORIDA COAST. Map. Philadelphia, 1852.

MAROONER'S ISLAND. OR DR. GORDON IN SEARCH OF HIS CHILDREN. Philadelphia, 1869.

GRANT, ANNE (McVICAR)
1755–1838

THOUGH by strict interpretation an English writer, Mrs. Grant's "Memoirs of an American Lady" should include her in any comprehensive grouping of American authors. She was born in Glasgow, Scotland, but came to America when a mere infant, with her father, a Captain in the British army. After a short stay in New York City, she settled with her parents near Albany, where her father was stationed for several years. It had been his intention to stay in America, for which purpose he had taken up land on the eastern New York frontier, but the encroachments of the Vermonters during the boundary dispute sent him home in disgust in 1768. Miss McVicar was later married to the Rev. Mr. Grant in Scotland, but following his death took up writing for a livelihood.

"Memoirs of an American Lady" is in part an extremely flattering eulogy of Mrs. Philip Schuyler, one of the leading *grandes dames* of pre-Revolutionary Albany society, in whose home Mrs. Grant spent a large part of her girlhood days. Though well and vivaciously written and a manifestly honest and instructive document, it is at times a bit tedious. Yet it retains a genuine charm for the modern reader, and its pictures of life and manners in and about colonial Albany are, in their way, unique.

(Anonymous) MEMOIRS OF AN AMERICAN LADY: WITH SKETCHES OF MANNERS AND

SCENERY IN AMERICA, AS THEY EXISTED PREVIOUS TO THE REVOLUTION. 2 volumes in one. Boston, 1809.

The English edition appeared in 1808.

GRANT, ROBERT

1852–

JUDGE GRANT, a well known lawyer in his native Boston, early had something of a local reputation as a satirical poet, but is better known as a novelist. He is generally considered to have done his best work after 1900, but he scored at least one minor success before that time with "Confessions of a Frivolous Girl," a satire on New York society, and one of the sensations of the year 1880.

THE CONFESSIONS OF A FRIVOLOUS GIRL. A Story of Fashionable Life. Boston, Williams, New York, Brentano's, 1880.

Later copies as far as observed omit the Brentano imprint, and state the edition number.

GREENE, ALBERT GORTON

1802–1868

GREENE was born in Providence, R. I. He studied law, became City Clerk and later a magistrate, and in the course of a lifetime made one of the finest collections of American poetry then in existence. He was an occasional poet for his own amusement, without pretensions of any sort, but with a natural gift for humorous rhyme. "Old Grimes" was written in 1818, when he was sixteen. Its gentle benevolence and structural oddity have made it survive the intervening years.

OLD GRIMES. Providence, 1867.

This poem first appeared anonymously in the *Providence Gazette* in 1822. It was also printed in "Miscellanies Selected from The Public Journals," Boston, 1822.

GREENE, ASA
1788–1837

GREENE was born in Ashburnham, Mass., graduated from Williams in 1813, took a medical course and finally settled as a book seller in New York, where for a time he edited the *Evening Transcript*..

His contemporaries regarded him as a man of ready wit. His half-quack, half-serious character, "Dr. Dodimus Duckworth," still remains amusing and there seems to be no reason to quash their verdict. It is interesting to note that the Doctor's "Life and Adventures" appeared in the same year as Seba Smith's "Jack Downing."

THE LIFE AND ADVENTURES OF DR. DODIMUS DUCKWORTH. A. N. Q. To which is added the History of a Steam Doctor. 2 volumes. New York, 1833.

GREENE, SARAH PRATT McLEAN
1856–

MRS. GREENE was born in Simsbury, Conn., educated at Mt. Holyoke Seminary, and married in 1887. She gained wide notoriety through her book, "Cape Cod Folks," in which she treated in a rather cavalier manner certain local characters. The book became the cause of numerous law suits and locally aroused much adverse criticism.

(Anonymous) CAPE COD FOLKS. Boston, 1881.

GRISWOLD, RUFUS WILMOT
1815–1857

DR. GRISWOLD was born in Benson, Vt., and as a young man engaged for a time in the printing business. He traveled extensively, was ordained to the ministry and subsequently, in addition to his clerical duties, engaged in literary work in association with the *New Yorker, The New World, Graham's* and the *International Magazine*. Discarding as unimportant Griswold's single novel, his historical writings and his own verse, his energy and enthusiasm made him an extremely valuable propagandist in the dissemination of a larger knowledge of American letters. He was the author of three carefully compiled anthologies, "Poets and Poetry of America,"—which ran into seventeen editions by 1856,—the "Prose Writers of America" and the "Female Poets of America." His critical judgment is frequently at fault, but his works still remain among the books most valuable to the student of American literature. He is best known today through his much criticized relations with Poe.

THE POETS AND POETRY OF AMERICA, WITH AN HISTORICAL INTRODUCTION. Philadelphia, 1842.

THE PROSE AND PROSE WRITERS OF AMERICA WITH A SURVEY OF THE HISTORY CONDITIONS AND PROSPECTS OF AMERICAN LITERATURE. Philadelphia, 1847.

THE FEMALE POETS OF AMERICA. Philadelphia, 1848.

GUINEY, LOUISE IMOGEN
1861–1920

MISS GUINEY was born in Boston, was educated for the most part by private tutors and in 1901 went to England where she resided until her death. Her poetry is vigorous and facile and her ideals were praiseworthy. But her work in general is not of great consequence.

GOOSE-QUILL PAPERS. Boston, 1885.

A ROADSIDE HARP. Boston, 1893.

PATRINS. Boston, 1897.

GUNTER, ARCHIBALD CLAVERING
1847–1907

GUNTER, an Englishman, born in Liverpool, came to the United States as a mining engineer, settled in California, became a stockbroker and at the age of forty took up writing. As an author, Gunter broke all accepted precepts. He had, however, a remarkable gift for narrative, to which he added an axiom of his own,—that something should happen every five hundred words. By the same token he was a literary failure, yet the sheer swiftness with which one incident follows another and the lure of the story itself make such novels as "Mr. Barnes of New York" and "Mr. Potter of Texas" fascinating reading.

MR. BARNES OF NEW YORK. A Novel. New York, 1887.

Must have the imprint of "Deshler Welch & Company."

Mr. Potter of Texas. A Novel. New York, 1888.

HABBERTON, JOHN

1842–1921

Habberton was born in Brooklyn, and learned the printing trade in New York City. He served in the Civil War, and afterwards was associated in editorial work with the *Christian Union* and also with the *New York Herald.*

In 1876 he published "Helen's Babies," which immediately struck the popular fancy and sold heavily both here and abroad. Aside from its frankly stated purpose to amuse, the book has no significance as a literary achievement. Nevertheless, it succeeded so admirably in its intention that it bids fair to hold its place as a bright spot in our humor.

Helen's Babies. With Some Account of their Ways Innocent, Crafty, Angelic, Impish, Witching and Repulsive. . . . By Their Latest Victim. Boston, (1876).

There are several variations; priority undetermined.

HALE, EDWARD EVERETT

1822–1909

Hale, noted clergyman, author and philanthropist, and a grand-nephew of the Revolutionary patriot Nathan Hale, was born in Boston and educated at Harvard. After spending two years as a tutor, he became pastor of a Unitarian Church in Worcester, and later preached in Boston, where he continued to reside until his death. In 1903 he was appointed Chaplain of the U. S. Senate.

"The Man Without a Country," "Ten Times One is Ten" and "Philip Nolan's Friends" are fairly representative of his voluminous writings. The first, which appeared during the closing days of the Civil War, and is generally accepted as Hale's masterpiece, was, though as a story little if any better than "My Double and How He Undid Me," one of the most timely pieces of fiction ever published. The second, though less well known, gave a world-wide impulse to far reaching movements of a religious and charitable nature, such as the "In His Name" societies, etc. The third is an entertaining novel of the conquest of the West, with an excellent historical background.

THE MAN WITHOUT A COUNTRY. Boston, 1865.

A very few copies contain a publisher's "Announcement" slip tipped in between the title page and the front wrapper.

IF, YES AND PERHAPS. Four Possibilities and Six Exaggerations with some Bits of Fact. Boston, 1868.

This is the first collected edition of Hale's stories. "The Man Without a Country" first appeared in pamphlet form in 1865 (supra); "My Double and How He Undid Me" in "Atlantic Tales," 1866.

TEN TIMES ONE IS TEN: THE POSSIBLE REFORMATION. Boston, 1871.

PHILIP NOLAN'S FRIENDS. A Story of the Change of Western Empire. New York, 1877.

HALE, LUCRETIA PEABODY
1820–1900

MRS. HALE, a native of Boston and a frequent contributor to various magazines, was the author of "The Peterkin Papers," in which she describes the doings of a family of harmless morons in a spirit of hilarious farce, and adds for good measure an occasional bit of pungent satire. Her method is so unusual and effective that she seems entitled to a permanent and possibly unique place among American humorists.

THE PETERKIN PAPERS. Boston, 1880.

HALE, SARAH J(OSEPHA) (BUELL)
1788–1879

MRS. HALE labored prodigiously for the intellectual development of women, particularly through her close personal association with annuals and lady's books. She was born in Newport, N. H., but moved to Boston, and, after her husband's death in 1822, took up literature as a profession. She became editor of the *Boston Lady's Magazine* in 1828, and remained in charge until it consolidated with *Godey's Lady's Book* in 1837, when she moved to Philadelphia as editor of the joint publication. Incidentally, she published several annuals,—for example, "The Opal,"—was largely instrumental in the establishment of Thanksgiving as a national holiday and was a prominent factor in the public financing of Bunker Hill Monument.

Her writings were considerable and varied,—numerous poems, several anthologies, at least two novels, two dramas, a few stories and some sketches and essays standing to her credit. Among her poems is the immortal "Mary's Little Lamb."

SKETCHES OF AMERICAN CHARACTER. Boston, 1829.

POEMS FOR OUR CHILDREN. Designed for Families, Sabbath Schools, and Infant Schools. Part first. Boston, 1830.

Contains the first printing of "Mary's (Little) Lamb" found in any edition of Mrs. Hale's work. Whether its appearance in "The Juvenile Miscellany for 1830" is prior is still in dispute.

HALL, JAMES
1793–1868

WITH the possible exception of Timothy Flint, no writer accomplished as much as Hall in making the Western Frontier a matter of our national literary consciousness. He was born in Philadelphia, entered the army in 1812, and in 1815 served with Decatur in Algiers. Meanwhile, as occasion permitted, he studied law. He began to practice in Illinois, in 1820, but later removed to Cincinnati, where he prospered as a lawyer and a banker, served as editor of the *Western Souvenir* and later of the *Western Monthly Magazine,* and speedily became one of the foremost figures in his adopted state.

Hall's tales and novels, especially his "Legends of the West," "Tales of the Border" and "The Wilderness and the Warpath" are valuable assets of our literature. He frequently glosses over the crudities of frontier conditions with a fine abandon, his sense of structure is defective and his style is florid, but his work is fresh and preserves an invaluable record of thitherto unheeded material which but for him would doubtless have been lost. Though not a master workman, he deserves consideration as a moving force in the intellectual development of the West.

THE WESTERN SOUVENIR . . . for 1829. Cincinnati, 1829.
Edited by Hall.

LEGENDS OF THE WEST. Philadelphia, 1832.

TALES OF THE BORDER. Philadelphia, 1845.

THE WILDERNESS AND THE WARPATH. New York, 1846.

HALLECK, FITZ-GREENE
1795–1867

HALLECK, the only American whose work can be compared at all favorably with that of the contemporary popular English romanticists, came to New York in 1811, and in 1813 entered the employ of John Jacob Astor, who later appointed him Trustee of the Astor Library. He was a bachelor, residing with his sister, and was actively engaged in mercantile pursuits until his retirement in 1849, when he returned to Guilford, Conn., his boyhood home.

Halleck was a man of striking personality, who entered zestfully into the stimulating whirl of New York life. In 1819 he found a congenial spirit in Joseph Rodman Drake, with whom he collaborated in the production of the famous "Croaker Papers," and whose death he mourned in his exquisitely beautiful lines beginning,

"Green be the turf above thee,
Friend of my better days!"

His first book, the long popular but ponderous "Fanny," was published in 1819; his "Alnwick Castle," containing his memorial to Drake, "Marco Bozzaris" and "Burns," in 1827. Contemporary critics decried his imitative tendency.

Though a few of his poems are still remembered, their judgment would appear to have been correct.

(Anonymous) FANNY. New York, 1819.

(Anonymous) ALNWICK CASTLE, WITH OTHER POEMS. New York, 1827.

HALPINE, CHARLES GRAHAM
1829–1868

HALPINE, one of the most popular humorists of the Civil War period, was born in Ireland, but came to the United States from London in early manhood and for a time assisted Shillaber on the *Boston Carpet Bag*. Later, he continued his writing in New York. He served with distinction during the Civil War, meanwhile continuing his O'Reilly verse and sketches in the *Herald*, and was retired with the rank of Brigadier General. He devoted his few remaining years to politics. Halpine's humor was not brilliant, but it was clever, timely and useful, and it is still mildly amusing.

(Anonymous) THE LIFE AND ADVENTURES, SONGS, SERVICES, AND SPEECHES OF PRIVATE MILES O'REILLY. . . . New York, 1864.

HARDY, ARTHUR SHERBURNE
1847–1930

HARDY was born in Andover, Mass., from which district he entered the United States Military Academy at West Point. Later he became professor of civil engineering at Iowa College, and later still he taught mathematics at Dartmouth College. In 1893 he entered the diplomatic service, becoming progressively U. S. Minister to Greece, Rumania,

Switzerland and Spain. He was the author of several important works on higher mathematics as well as of some novels of merit.

Hardy's first work of fiction, "But Yet a Woman," is a penetrating tale of contemporary France. But it hardly measures up to the standard of "Passe Rose," which, with Mrs. Catherwood's "Romance of Dollard," ushered in the era of the modern historical novel. "Passe Rose" is an idealization of Europe during the time of Charlemagne, and, although one of the first, is also one of the best novels of its type.

BUT YET A WOMAN; A NOVEL. Boston, 1883.

PASSE ROSE. Boston, 1889.

HARRIS, GEORGE WASHINGTON
1814–1869

HARRIS, the best among the imitators of Baldwin's Southwestern "Flush Times" stories, was born in Allegheny City, Pa., and later served as a jeweler's apprentice and as a steamboat captain on the Tennessee River. Eventually he became a political writer, furnishing racy yarns meanwhile to his newspaper under the name of Sut Lovengood. A number of these yarns were subsequently published in a collected edition in 1867.

SUT LOVENGOOD. Yarns Spun by a Nat'ral Born Durn'd Fool. Warped and Wove for Public Wear. New York, Dick and Fitzgerald, (1867).

HARRIS, JOEL CHANDLER
1848–1908

FEW writers have succeeded more notably than Harris in giving a unique touch to American literature. When no more than twelve years old he secured a position on *The Countryman,* a local journal published on a typical Southern plantation nine miles from Hillsborough, Ga., and owned by Mr. J. A. Turner, who, to encourage Harris' literary taste, put the plantation library at his disposal. After remaining four years with Mr. Turner, Harris spent the next twelve in association with newspapers in different Southern cities. In 1876 he joined the staff of the *Atlanta Constitution,* with which he remained associated until his death.

Harris' first "Uncle Remus" story appeared in 1879. It was written hurriedly when Sam Small, the *Constitution's* regular dialect writer, failed to put in an appearance. Its success was so complete and immediate that Harris was given a permanent assignment.

As told by Uncle Remus the adventures of Br'er Rabbit are important contributions to American folklore. They are likewise masterpieces. In "Mingo and Other Sketches" Harris has sketched the Georgia "cracker" with almost equal understanding.

UNCLE REMUS: HIS SONGS AND HIS SAYINGS; THE FOLK-LORE OF THE OLD PLANTATION. New York, 1881.
The first page of advertisements contains no reviews of this book.

MINGO AND OTHER SKETCHES IN BLACK AND WHITE. Boston, 1884.

UNCLE REMUS AND HIS FRIENDS; OLD PLANTATION STORIES, SONGS, AND BALLADS, WITH

SKETCHES OF NEGRO CHARACTER. Boston, 1892.

HART, CATHERINE JULIA
Dates Unknown

MISS HART was not, in the customary usage of the term, an American author, but rather the first Canadian novelist. Yet she wrote of the United States in her "Tonnewonte," which is sufficiently American in its scene and spirit to warrant its inclusion here. Its pictures of pioneer conditions in Western New York are both interesting and instructive. Its plot is subservient to the literary conventions of the period, but it admirably serves the author's major purpose of contrasting the privileges and advantages of American democratic social institutions with the artificial restraints and injustices of a European aristocratic régime.

TONNEWONTE, OR THE ADOPTED SON OF AMERICA. A Tale, containing Scenes from Real Life, by an American. 2 volumes in one. Volume I, Watertown, N. Y. 1825, Volume II, Watertown, N. Y., 1824.

Copies are also known bearing the imprints —Volume I, Albany, 1825, Volume II, Watertown, 1824; also Volume I, Watertown, 1825, Volume II, Albany, 1824.

HART, J(OSEPH) C.
?–1865

SAVE that he resided for a time in Nantucket, was in the Consular service and wrote at least two novels, there seems to be no procurable biographical information about Hart. His "Miriam Coffin" is the first novel of whaling written in the United States. It was inspired in part by a desire to obtain Congressional support for the industry, but it is of greater importance today as a picture of whaling days in Nantucket and New Bedford. In spite of its occasional melodrama, it remains a readable book.

(Anonymous) MIRIAM COFFIN, OR THE WHALE FISHERMEN. 2 volumes. New York, 1834.

HARTE, FRANCIS BRET
1839–1902

THOUGH other authors have done greater work, few have had a more profound influence on American letters than Bret Harte. He was the son of a school teacher in Albany. His father died when he was six, leaving as a heritage little more than a fine library,—fortunately the very thing to direct the lad's attention to fields in which he later attained marked success.

Harte spent the next nine years of his boyhood with his sister in New York, but ran away at fifteen to cross the plains and join his mother, then living in California with her elder son. For the sake of a living, he turned his hand to whatever was nearest,—typesetting, teaching, express riding,—until he found a position with the *Golden Era.* Secure in this employment, he married in 1862. Shortly thereafter he was appointed Secretary of the California Mint.

Harte later became editor of the *Overland Monthly,* in the second number of which he published "The Luck of Roaring Camp," and found himself almost over-night internationally famous. Shortly thereafter the *Atlantic Monthly* offered him a retainer of ten thousand dollars to write for it exclusively, and in 1871 he left the Coast, never to return. After a temporary sojourn in the East he went to Europe, where he remained, for the most part in England, until his death.

In a literary sense Harte's writings are historically among the most important of the local color school. In the larger sense he failed to report the forces which were developing the frontier. Yet despite his posturing and tendency to caricature, there was vitality in his method, and he was the first to create a type and form which, with timely modifications, have until recently dominated American short story literature.

That at the end he could write of life truthfully is evidenced by certain of his later stories, for example, the "Passing of Enriquez." That his inventiveness extended to his poetry is clearly demonstrated by the original note he sounded in numerous poems, of which "Plain Language from Truthful James" is probably the most important example.

THE LUCK OF ROARING CAMP AND OTHER SKETCHES. Boston, 1870.

Contains two hundred and thirty-nine pages only; without the story of "Brown of Calaveras."

PLAIN LANGUAGE FROM TRUTHFUL JAMES (THE HEATHEN CHINEE).

Nine lithographed cards in an envelope, with flap. (Chicago, 1870).

The first issue is as yet undetermined. The drawings vary considerably—evidently having been revised several times.

POEMS. Boston, 1871.

The second line at the top of page 136 reads "S.T.K."; the imprint is "Fields Osgood & Co."

GABRIEL CONROY. Hartford, 1876.

The first binding has a picture of a bear on the backstrip.

STORIES IN LIGHT AND SHADOW. Boston, 1898.

HAWTHORNE, NATHANIEL
1804–1864

HAWTHORNE was born in Salem, Mass. Undoubtedly one of the important formative influences of his career was the seclusion of the Maine farm to which his mother retired after his father's death. Following his graduation in 1825 from Bowdoin in the same class with Longfellow and Franklin Pierce, he spent the next twelve years as a recluse at his birthplace in Salem, studying, writing, destroying and rewriting, in a fixed determination to perfect his art.

His first separately published work, "Fanshawe," which he later tried to suppress, was an immature production. "Twice-Told Tales," his first great work, appeared in 1837, but was a failure. Later, while an employee in the Salem Customs House, he published three charming juveniles, "Grandfather's Chair," "Famous Old People" and "Liberty Tree," which met a kindlier reception. Presently dismissed from the Customs House for political reasons, after a brief residence at Brook Farm, he married and removed to Concord in 1842, and in the same year brought out a second volume of "Twice-Told Tales." "Mosses from an Old Manse" followed four years later, almost coincident with his appointment as Surveyor of Customs at Salem by President Pierce. Following a second dismissal in 1849, he moved to Lenox, then to West Newton and finally again to Concord.

His return to Concord seems to have been a veritable home-coming, for the next two years found him at the height of his powers,—the years of "The Scarlet Letter" and "The House of the Seven Gables," two of the nation's greatest works of fiction. Three excellent juveniles and a volume of short stories quickly followed,—"True Stories," "A Wonder Book," "Tanglewood Tales" and "The Snow-Image,"—and one fine novel, "The Blithedale Romance." After his appointment as Consul at Liverpool, however, the compelling urge was gone. "The Marble Faun," often called a "guidebook to Rome," though good, was below his standard, and the work which followed had the form but not the inspiration. His end came suddenly, when on a trip to the White Mountains, with his old friend, Franklin Pierce.

It is as an analyst that Hawthorne ranks supreme. An early critic described his characters as "psychological problems, wandering in search of a solution." To his powers of observation he added a penetrating intelligence, a power of graphic description and a command of and insistence upon artistic perfection which place him almost in a class apart.

(Anonymous) FANSHAWE, A TALE. Boston, 1828.

TWICE-TOLD TALES. Boston, 1837.
In the "Table of Contents" "The May-Pole of Merry Mount" must be noted incorrectly as on page 78.

GRANDFATHER'S CHAIR: A HISTORY FOR YOUTH. Boston, 1841.

FAMOUS OLD PEOPLE: BEING THE SECOND EPOCH OF GRANDFATHER'S CHAIR. Boston, 1841.

LIBERTY TREE: WITH THE LAST WORDS OF GRANDFATHER'S CHAIR. Boston, 1841.
Page 24, line two, reads "in a con;" page 30, line thirteen, "half burned out."

MOSSES FROM AN OLD MANSE. 2 volumes, wrappers, or 2 volumes in one, cloth. New York, 1846.

The names of the printer and stereotyper must appear in opposite lower corners on the verso of the title page. In wrapper copies, those in the earliest state list only fifteen titles on the back wrappers.

THE SCARLET LETTER; A ROMANCE. Boston, 1850.

Page 21, line twenty, reads "reduplicate." Page 61, line five, reads "Madam." Page 199, line four, reads "Known of it." Page 26 was entirely reset in later editions. There are four pages of advertisements in front.

THE HOUSE OF THE SEVEN GABLES, A ROMANCE. Boston, 1851.

The advertisements are variously dated. The earliest are March, but May are probably also acceptable.

TRUE STORIES FROM HISTORY AND BIOGRAPHY. Boston, 1851.

Must have the imprint "Cambridge, Printed by Bolles and Houghton" at the foot of the copyright page.

THE SNOW-IMAGE AND OTHER TWICE-TOLD TALES. Boston, 1852.

Has four pages of advertisements. The earliest dating is January, 1852. An edition appeared with a London, 1851, imprint, but probably without priority.

THE BLITHEDALE ROMANCE. Boston, 1852.

Has four pages of advertisements. The earliest dating is April, 1852.

A WONDER-BOOK FOR GIRLS AND BOYS. Boston, 1852.

The decorations on the backstrip must be at the top only.

TANGLEWOOD TALES FOR GIRLS AND BOYS: BEING A SECOND WONDER-BOOK. Boston, 1853.

The imprint on the verso of the title page must read "Stereotyped at the Boston Stereotype Foundry." The price of the book (88c) must be omitted from the advertisements, and the book announced as "Just out."

THE MARBLE FAUN; OR THE ROMANCE OF MONTE BENI. 2 volumes. Boston, 1860.

Volume 2 must end at page 284 (omitting the "Conclusion"). The earliest dating of the advertisements is February, 1860.

OUR OLD HOME: A SERIES OF ENGLISH SKETCHES. Boston, 1863.

A single leaf of advertisements must be present in the back.

HAY, JOHN

1838–1905

HAY, one of the most distinguished public men of his generation, was a native of Salem, Ind., a graduate of Brown University and, though considerably younger, an intimate friend of Lincoln, whom he served as assistant secretary during most of the latter's administration. He was later Attaché of Legation at Paris, Vienna and Madrid, and later still, save for a brief service as Assistant Secretary of State under Hayes, was a member of the editorial staff of the *New York Tribune.* He was appointed Ambassador to Great Britain in 1897. His service as Secretary of State was one of the most distinguished in our history.

Mark Twain claimed, probably with a measure of justice, that Hay, not Harte, was the originator of the "Pike County Balladry." Whether or not "Pike County Ballads" and "Jim Bludsoe" have claims of priority, they contributed enormously to the popularity of that type of verse. Hay's novel of labor, "The Breadwinners," although it created a sensation, is handicapped by the author's prejudices and can be accorded only a minor place. His greatest work, the "Life of Abraham Lincoln" (in collaboration with John G. Nicolay), falls outside the scope of this volume.

Pike County Ballads, and other Pieces. Boston, 1871.

Jim Bludsoe of the Prairie Belle, and Little Breeches. Boston, 1871.

(Anonymous) The Breadwinners, a Social Study. New York, 1884.

HAYNE, PAUL HAMILTON
1830–1886

Hayne, perhaps the most beloved of all Southern poets, was born in Charleston, S. C., and was educated at Charleston College. He was graduated in law, but shortly thereafter renounced his profession for literary pursuits, and quickly became the leading spirit of a coterie of writers who made Charleston the pre-War literary center of the South. He edited *Russell's Magazine* for a time, but when the Civil War broke out joined the staff of General Pickens. In the Southern debacle which followed the conclusion of peace, he lost most of his fortune. He retired to Georgia and spent his last years in partial seclusion.

Hayne's potential rank as a poet was affected by his lack of a compelling message. Yet he was a sweet and pleasing singer in many keys, and as such deserves high place among the relatively small band of Southern writers who struck a true note prior to the Civil War.

POEMS. Boston, 1855.

HEARN, LAFCADIO
1850–1904

HEARN'S whole intellectual life was spent in a baffled search for beauty,—now satisfied for a brief interval, now, again, adrift. He was born on an Ionian island, of a Greek mother and an Irish father. At nineteen he came to the United States. After spending a short time in New York City, he moved on to Cincinnati and then to New Orleans, where, amid Creole surroundings he seems for a time to have found the romance which he was seeking. A commission from *Harper's* then took him to Japan. The strangeness of the Orient delighted him. He married a Japanese and became a Japanese citizen. Later when the glamour palled, he died, exhausted by his own intensity.

Hearn's literary genius is beyond dispute. He is fragmentary rather than coherent, yet his work possesses a barbaric splendor which belongs to him alone. His impressionistic pictures of the American tropics are extraordinary, and his interpretation of the Orient is, perhaps, unrivaled.

STRAY LEAVES FROM STRANGE LITERATURE. . . . Boston, 1884.

SOME CHINESE GHOSTS. Boston, 1887.

CHITA. A Memory of Last Island. Boston, 1889.

YOUMA, THE STORY OF A WEST-INDIAN SLAVE. New York, 1890.

GLIMPSES OF UNFAMILIAR JAPAN. 2 volumes. Boston, 1894.

In black or green cloth. No priority has been established.

HENTZ, NICHOLAS MARCELLUS

1797–1856

HENTZ, the best of Cooper's early contemporaries who essayed the historical Indian tale, was born in France, but came to the United States and became a teacher, first in association with George Bancroft, the historian, at the Round Hill School, and later with his wife, Caroline Whiting, a popular novelist and poet, at various places in the South.

Hentz's literary output was limited, but his novel, "Tadeuskund," a somewhat involved story of the struggles of an Indian chieftain to be loyal to his friendship with the whites, played a useful part in the development of frontier fiction. Though its descriptions of natural scenes are at times labored, its action is spirited and its workmanship painstaking.

(Anonymous) TADEUSKUND, THE LAST KING OF THE LENAPE. An Historical Tale. Boston, 1825.

HIGGINSON, THOMAS WENTWORTH

1823–1911

HIGGINSON, a man of great culture and varied intellectual interests, was born in Cambridge, Mass., and graduated from Harvard at the early age of seventeen. A short period of teaching was followed by a pastorate in Newburyport, from which he resigned because of his parishioners' resentment of his pronounced anti-slavery views.

During the Civil War he served as a captain and later as colonel of a negro regiment. When peace was declared, he returned to Boston and spent the balance of his life as a patron of the arts and literature. To him particularly we owe our appreciation of Thoreau and Emily Dickinson, as well as of other authors of lesser note. His own best writings were for the most part in essay form—among them his "Out-Door Papers," a graceful argument touching the joys and virtues of exercise and outdoor living, which anticipated the studies of Burroughs and others by several years. His one pretentious work of fiction, "Malbone," though amusing, is more notable for its display of culture than for its power.

Out-Door Papers. Boston, 1863.

Malbone: An Oldport Romance. Boston, 1869.

Atlantic Essays. Boston, 1871.

Old Cambridge. New York, 1899.

HILDRETH, RICHARD
1807–1865

Hildreth, perhaps best known as an historian, was born in Deerfield, Mass. He graduated from Harvard in 1826, and for a short time practiced law. In 1832 he became editor of the *Boston Atlas*. Several years later, following a year in Florida for recuperation, he went to Demarara, British Guiana, where he engaged in editorial work in support of the British Government's efforts to abolish slavery. He became U. S. Consul at Trieste in 1861.

Aside from his valuable historical work, Hildreth's literary consequence rests entirely on his "Memoirs of Archy Moore," an indifferent story, but the first anti-slavery novel published in the United States.

THE SLAVE; OR, MEMOIRS OF ARCHY MOORE. 2 volumes. Boston, 1836.

HILL, GEORGE
1796–1871

HILL was born in Guilford, Conn., graduated from Yale at the age of twenty and in 1827 became an instructor of mathematics in the Navy. In 1831 he was made Librarian of the State Department, and in 1839 was appointed Consul to Asia Minor. He returned to the United States in 1859 and worked in the Department of State until his death. Hill is not at his best in "The Ruins of Athens," his principal effusion, but he wrote an occasional shorter poem with a graceful and assured touch.

THE RUINS OF ATHENS; TITANIA'S BANQUET, A MASK; AND OTHER POEMS. Boston, 1839.

This is a more representative work than "The Ruins of Athens, with other Poems. By a Voyager," Washington 1831.

HIRST, HENRY BECK
1813–1874

HIRST, a Philadelphia merchant and lawyer, owes a certain notoriety to his quarrel with Poe. Yet his imaginative qualities entitle him to a more substantial recognition. "The Funeral of Time" and "The Coming of the Mammoth," the latter the epic of a herd survivor who crossed the continent to elude his pursuers, are handled with a genuine, if sometimes hesitant dramatic touch.

THE COMING OF THE MAMMOTH, THE FUNERAL OF TIME AND OTHER POEMS. Boston, 1845.

HITCHCOCK, ENOS
1744–1803

THE second American novelist, Dr. Hitchcock, was a native of Springfield, Mass., and a graduate of Harvard. He was ordained to the ministry in 1771, became a chaplain in the Revolutionary Army, and in 1783 settled in Providence, R. I.

As might be expected of the beginnings of American fiction, Hitchcock's two novels are sermons in fictional form—fine examples, in other words, of the didactic essay. Even more than W. H. Brown's "Power of Sympathy" they represent the cultural outlook of contemporary America.

MEMOIRS OF THE BLOOMSGROVE FAMILY. In a Series of Letters to a Respectable Citizen of Philadelphia. . . . 2 volumes. Boston, 1790.

THE FARMER'S FRIEND, OR THE HISTORY OF MR. CHARLES WORTHY. . . . Boston, 1793.

HOFFMAN, CHARLES FENNO
1806–1884

HOFFMAN was a native New Yorker of marked versatility, who, among other important literary activities, established the *Knickerbocker Magazine*. He wrote an occasional good poem, and his Indian and Revolutionary romance, "Greyslaer," though at times tedious, merits a word of commendation. It is by no means devoid of action, and its pictures of contemporary men and manners and its historical background are at once instructive and reliable.

GREYSLAER: A ROMANCE OF THE MOHAWK. 2 volumes. New York, 1840.

A leaf of errata follows the title page in Volume I.

THE VIGIL OF FAITH, AND OTHER POEMS. New York, 1842.

HOLLAND, JOSIAH GILBERT
1819–1881

DR. HOLLAND, who played a major part in the democratization of American letters during the latter half of the nineteenth century, was the son of a mechanic. He was born in Belchertown, Mass., and early decided on a literary career. As a young man he had to struggle as a photographer, teacher and doctor before realizing his first ambition as assistant editor of the *Springfield Republican.*

He attracted general attention through his "Timothy Titcomb Letters," published in 1858. His true influence, however, first found full expression in 1870, when he established *Scribner's Monthly,* later *The Century,* where he gathered about him many of the writers destined to mold our literature.

Dr. Holland's own writings are nicely calculated to please the popular taste, and perhaps for that reason lack a measure of distinction. Nevertheless, as early as 1857 he hinted at realism with his tale of early Massachusetts, "The Bay-Path," one of the best historical romances so far written in America. "Arthur Bonnicastle," his story of college life, though more typical of his aims, is less impressive. His poetry, though well written and immensely popular, is of less significance than his novels.

THE BAY-PATH; A TALE OF NEW ENGLAND COLONIAL LIFE. New York, 1857.

TITCOMB'S LETTERS TO YOUNG PEOPLE, SINGLE AND MARRIED. New York, 1858.
Timothy Titcomb, pseudonym.

BITTER SWEET. A POEM. New York, 1859.
Later editions are so marked on the title page.

LETTERS TO THE JONESES. By Timothy Titcomb. New York, 1863.

KATHRINA: HER LIFE AND MINE, IN A POEM. New York, 1867.
Later editions are so marked.

ARTHUR BONNICASTLE: AN AMERICAN NOVEL. New York, 1873.

HOLLEY, MARIETTA
(Josiah Allen's Wife)
1844–1926

MISS HOLLEY, a native of Jefferson County, Mo., and a resident of upper New York State, began her literary labors as a contributor to the *Christian Union,* and found a productive vein in a crude and blundering type of humor. Her work was extremely popular, but quite without distinction.

SAMANTHA AT SARATOGA; OR "FLIRTIN' WITH FASHION." By Josiah Allen's Wife. Philadelphia, 1887.

There are at least three editions bearing the 1887 date. Priority is as yet undetermined.

HOLMES, MARY JANE (HOWE)
1839–1907

LIKE many of her sister authors of the middle nineteenth century, Miss Holmes is more deserving than many critics of the sentimentalists will admit. She was born in Brookfield, Mass., and while still a young girl taught district school. Immediately following her marriage she removed to Kentucky, with which, if one may judge from the scene of her "'Lena Rivers," she was already measurably familiar.

She published her first book, "Tempest and Sunshine," when only fifteen years of age, and her best work, "'Lena Rivers," but three years later. Both books are morally unobjectionable; yet the latter shows a subtle understanding of feminine character little short of uncanny for so young an author, and a human interest which makes her immense appeal to the contemporary younger generation quite understandable. A reliable estimate places the total sales of her works during her lifetime at two million copies.

'LENA RIVERS. New York, 1857.

An 1856 publication date (the date of copyright) is frequently assigned to this book. No copy so dated, however, has so far been located, and it seems reasonable to accept 1857 as the year of publication. The imprint should be Miller, Orton and Mulligan.

HOLMES, OLIVER WENDELL
1809–1894

HOLMES' spontaneous humor stood all but alone during the middle eighteen hundreds. He was the son of the Rev. Abiel Holmes, a Calvinist minister in Cambridge, Mass., but fortunately for posterity inherited none of the rigid orthodoxy of his ancestors. As was natural, Holmes went to Harvard, intending to study law, but after a year at law books he turned to medicine as more congenial. During his college days he evidenced his talent for humorous and social verse. He was an undergraduate when he wrote "The Last Leaf," which, with his famous "Old Ironsides," appeared in his collected "Poems" (1836). But even after the pronounced success of this book he considered the poetic side of his nature secondary, and continued to devote himself assiduously to his profession, in which he later attained eminent success as Professor of Anatomy at Dartmouth and at Harvard.

It was not until 1857 that Holmes leaped from local into national literary fame. Entreated by Lowell to make a contribution to the new *Atlantic,* he obligingly dug up two random papers written in 1831 and extended them in series into the now famous "Autocrat of the Breakfast-Table." Their success put *The Atlantic* on its feet. Thereafter, Holmes devoted himself exclusively to literary work, producing shortly "The Professor" and later "The Poet" and "Over the Teacups," all in the same vein. These four constitute the brilliant, witty series on which his larger reputation rests.

Holmes also wrote three novels, all of lesser merit, only one of which, "Elsie Venner," calls for mention here. He also continued to add to his store of popular verse such poems as "The Wonderful One Hoss Shay." He lingered until 1894,—the last leaf of the old "New England Group" to fall.

POEMS. Boston, 1836.

There is a preference for the Boston imprint,

though it has no demonstrable priority over the Boston and New York imprint.

(Anonymous) THE AUTOCRAT OF THE BREAKFAST-TABLE. Every man his own Boswell. Boston, 1858.

Correct copies have an engraved half title. The third end paper is entitled "Poetry and the Drama," and the fourth "School Books." The type on page 95 is perfect. A very few known copies have five circles on the backstrip.

There is also a large paper edition dated 1859.

THE PROFESSOR AT THE BREAKFAST-TABLE; WITH THE STORY OF IRIS. Boston, 1860.

The Boston imprint is preferred, though it has no demonstrable priority over the Boston and Philadelphia imprint.

There is also a large paper edition.

ELSIE VENNER: A ROMANCE OF DESTINY. 2 volumes. Boston, 1861.

The necessity for the presence of the "r" in "richer" in the second line of the second paragraph of page 13, Volume I, is contested. The advertisement facing the title page announcing "Currents and Counter-Currents" is headed "Nearly Ready."

SONGS IN MANY KEYS. Boston, 1862.

THE POET AT THE BREAKFAST-TABLE. HIS TALKS WITH HIS FELLOW-BOARDERS. . . . Boston, 1872.

Reads "Talle" for "Table" in the headline of page 9.

There is also a large paper edition.

Songs of Many Seasons. 1862–1874. Boston, 1875.

Over the Teacups. Boston, 1891.

The edges and end papers are yellow. The advertising leaf facing the title does not mention any price for this book.

HOOPER, JOHNSON J.

1815–1863

Hooper probably was born in North Carolina, but early moved to Alabama, where he became influential both as a lawyer and newspaper editor. He attained considerable political eminence, and was for a time Secretary of the Provisional Confederate Congress.

Hooper, like Joseph Glover Baldwin, was well acquainted with the "Flush Times" bar, which he sketched in his own fashion in "Simon Suggs." Fortunately, he preferred to depict life rather than to rely solely on the mechanics of humor,— a fact which insured his work a certain permanence. "Simon Suggs" is not, however, the equal of Judge Baldwin's later classic.

Some Adventures of Captain Simon Suggs, Late of the Tallapoosa Volunteers; together with "Taking the Census," and other Alabama Sketches. By a Country Doctor. Philadelphia, 1845.

HOPKINSON, FRANCIS
1737–1791

HOPKINSON, author of the first bit of original fiction written and published in America, was born and educated in Philadelphia, where, before removing to New Jersey, he practiced law. He was later appointed a member of the Continental Congress from his adopted state, assisted in the drafting of the Articles of Confederation and was a signer of the Declaration of Independence. Toward the close of his life he held several offices in the Federal Government.

His prose work, "A Pretty Story," was a satirical allegory calling for separation from Great Britain. He is better known, however, for the "Battle of the Kegs," a rollicking skit inspired by the abortive attempt of the Americans to drive away the British fleet stationed in the Delaware River. This poem, which first appeared in book form in his "Poems" (1792), was first published as a broadside in 1778, and brought endless cheer to the American soldiery stationed in near-by camps.

A PRETTY STORY WRITTEN IN THE YEAR OF OUR LORD 2774, BY PETER GRIEVOUS, ESQ. Philadelphia, 1774.

The second edition is so marked on the title page. There are also other 1774 editions with other than Philadelphia imprints. This is the first fiction to be written and published in America.

POEMS ON VARIOUS SUBJECTS. . . . Philadelphia, 1792.

This is Volume 3 of (Hopkinson's) "Miscellaneous Essays". . . .

HOPKINSON, JOSEPH
1770–1842

Hopkinson, a Philadelphian, and a son of Francis Hopkinson, one of the signers of the Declaration of Independence and a poet of distinction, was himself a public man of note. After completing his legal education at the University of Pennsylvania, he began to practice law. Later, from 1815 to 1819, he served as a member of the House of Representatives, and in 1828 was appointed Judge of the U. S. District Court, which position he filled with distinction until his death.

He was the author of "Hail Columbia," a martial poem of great historical importance, but save for this single effort, time has obliterated all memory of his literary work.

Song (Hail Columbia) Adapted to the President's March, Sung at The Theatre by Mr. Fox, at His Benefit. Composed by Joseph Hopkinson, Esq. Printed by J. Ormrod, 41, Chestnut-Street. (Philadelphia, 1798). 6 pages.

HOVEY, RICHARD
1864–1900

Hovey was born in Normal, Ill., educated at Dartmouth, studied theology and thereafter spent a few short, busy years as poet, journalist, actor and dramatist and as instructor in English at Columbia University.

He belonged to a select group that struck a new note in American poetry,—a sound and healthy, gay and boisterous note, aptly suggested by the name of "Vagabondia," which he and Carman gave to the series of three books on which they collaborated. Of the entire group none was more virile than

Hovey. "For it's always fair weather," the chorus of his joyous "Stein Song," is the perennial delight of every college generation.

LAUNCELOT AND GUENEVERE; A POEM IN DRAMAS. New York, United States Book Co. (1891).

MORE SONGS FROM VAGABONDIA. Boston, 1896.
Contains the "Stein Song," later incorporated in the ode "Spring" first appearing in "Along the Trail." Written in collaboration with Bliss Carman. Also 60 copies on large paper.

ALONG THE TRAIL. A BOOK OF LYRICS. Boston, 1898.

HOWE, EDGAR WATSON
1853–

SINCE the age of twelve, Howe has been associated with the printing business in some capacity. He was born in Treaty, Ind. At nineteen he was publisher of the *Golden Globe* at Golden, Colo., and from 1877 to 1911 was proprietor of the *Atchison (Kansas) Daily Globe.* Since 1911 he has been both editor and publisher of *E. W. Howe's Monthly.*

Howe's work makes up in quality for what it lacks in quantity. He is the author of only three novels, but the first of them, "The Story of a Country Town," is one of the most genuinely American stories ever published. Undoubtedly it owes some of its inspiration to the local color school, but it moves, untrammeled, beyond the limits of its local prairie setting. It is the first American novel fully to measure up to the ideal expressed in Garland's great plea for a national literature.

THE STORY OF A COUNTRY TOWN. Atchison, Kansas, 1883.

The book varies considerably in make-up, but there was only one printing.

HOWE, JULIA WARD
1819–1910

MRS. HOWE, a native of New York, was one of the most energetic and influential figures in the history of American feminism. The list of her activities is formidable. Before the Civil War she assisted her husband, Samuel G. Howe of Boston, in his philanthropic work, edited with him the anti-slavery *Boston Commonwealth,* wrote for the *New York Tribune* and the *Anti-Slavery Standard* and edited the *Woman's Journal.* At the close of the struggle, she engaged in further social and philanthropic work, was a founder of the New England Women's Clubs, President of the "Association for the Advancement of Women," preached in Boston pulpits, and came to be looked upon as almost a national institution.

Mrs. Howe's poetry was deeply religious. Yet it is this quality which makes "The Battle Hymn of the Republic" probably the best known and perhaps the soundest and most enduring of all Civil War lyrics.

LATER LYRICS. Boston, 1866.

The "Battle Hymn" appeared first in the February, 1862, number of the *Atlantic.* Ditson immediately published it as a song. Its first appearance in a collected edition is in "Later Lyrics."

HOWELLS, WILLIAM DEAN
1837–1920

CRITICALLY, personally and by example Howells was one of the foremost figures in American letters during the latter quarter of the nineteenth century. He was born in Martin's Ferry, Ohio, and spent his years to maturity in his native state in labored and conscientious preparation for the career which he had definitely planned. As a young man he made a "literary pilgrimage" to Boston and wrote a "Campaign Life" of Lincoln, the latter activity leading to his appointment as Consul at Venice. After four delightful years in Europe he returned to Boston as assistant editor of the *Atlantic Monthly,* of which he later became the editor-in-chief. He retired in 1881 to devote himself to literature. His last years were spent as the incumbent of *Harper's Editor's Easy Chair.*

Howell's first literary efforts were in verse of mediocre merit. It was not until 1871 that he produced a work of promise, "Suburban Sketches." With certain reservations in sporadic cases, the modern realistic movement dates from the publication in 1882 of "A Modern Instance." This, in the opinion of many critics, is also his best work. A still larger number prefer "Silas Lapham," while he himself selected "Indian Summer." These three, with "A Hazard of New Fortunes," which has been called the best novel of New York, and "The Kentons" (1902), complete the group of his most outstanding works.

Howells was a true champion of realism—in his own case a realism tempered by classicism and a deference for the critical opinion of his readers. In diction, dialogue and expression he is faultless, but his perfection is the product of deep study of his art and not of genius. His influence upon the development of literary form and trend was probably greater than that of any other American author of his generation.

SUBURBAN SKETCHES. New York, 1871.

A CHANCE ACQUAINTANCE. Boston, 1873.

A Modern Instance. A Novel. Boston, 1882.
Measures 1¼ inches across the top of covers; thinner copies were published later.

The Rise of Silas Lapham. Boston, 1885.
The page of advertisements facing the title must be headed, "Mr. Howells' Latest Works."

Indian Summer. Boston, 1886.

A Hazard of New Fortunes. New York, 1890.
The two volume edition is later.

A Boy's Town. Described for "Harper's Young People." New York, 1890.
Has a woodcut on the verso of the "Contents" page.

Christmas Every Day, and Other Stories Told for Children. New York, 1893.

My Literary Passions. New York, 1895.

HUBBARD, ELBERT
1859–1905

In his younger days Hubbard was manager and half owner of a soap factory, to which estate he rose after leaving the Illinois farm where he was born. Later he sold out his interest, traveled for a period and eventually established the Roycroft Press, at East Aurora, N. Y., from which point of vantage he preached oracularly to an admiring audience.

During the stirring days of the Spanish War Hubbard wrote a story-essay, "A Message to Garcia," which took the country by storm. It is one of the most dramatic of American writings, and its prestige is such that its title has since been incorporated into our speech as connoting a difficult task well done.

A MESSAGE TO GARCIA. . . . East Aurora, Erie County, New York, U. S. A., . . . (1898).

Must read "homily" not "preachment" on the title page. The story first appeared in the *Philistine* for March, 1898.

HUMPHREYS, DAVID
1752–1818

HUMPHREYS, the son of a Derby, Connecticut, clergyman and a Yale graduate, was an aide-de-camp to Washington and remained his close friend after the Revolution. Upon returning to his native state, he became a fellow of the "Hartford Wits," and took part in the preparation of the "Anarchiad." His public services both at home and abroad were numerous and important.

As a poet Humphreys was not the equal of his collaborators, Dwight, Barlow and Trumbull, but his faith in the material and cultural future of America was a potent force when such a force was sorely needed.

A POEM ON THE HAPPINESS OF AMERICA; ADDRESSED TO THE CITIZENS OF THE UNITED STATES. London, Printed 1780. Hartford: Reprinted by Hudson and Goodwin, (1780).

There was also a New Haven, 1780, imprint.

POEMS. Philadelphia, 1789.

INGRAHAM, JOSEPH HOLT
1809–1860

INGRAHAM, a native of Portland, Me., began his literary work as an imitator of Cooper, whom, however, he soon outstripped in lurid quality. Later, after becoming a clergyman, he published "The Prince of the House of David," a sort of lesser "Ben Hur," which, though not the equal of Wallace's masterpiece, has to this day retained a measure of its earlier popularity.

(Anonymous) LAFITTE; OR, THE PIRATE OF THE GULF. 2 volumes. New York, 1836.

THE PRINCE OF THE HOUSE OF DAVID; OR, THREE YEARS IN THE HOLY CITY. New York, 1855.

IRVING, JOHN TREAT (JR.)
1812–1905

JOHN T. IRVING, a nephew of Washington Irving, was born in New York. He attended Columbia College, and after graduating was admitted to the New York Bar.

About 1833 Irving made a trip to the trans-Mississippi country and returned East to relate his experiences in "Indian Sketches" (1835). Later he made use of the same material in a novel, "The Hawk Chief," a tale of the early fur trade. Centered about a war between the Pawnees and the Konzas, enemies and friends respectively of the white man, it is a graphic and well-written story as well as an informative document touching the difficulties encountered by the early trappers and the customs and culture of the mid-continent Indians.

THE HAWK CHIEF. 2 volumes. Philadelphia, 1837.

IRVING, WASHINGTON
1783–1859

IRVING's father, scion of a cultured old Scotch family, settled in New York before the Revolution. Washington, his youngest son, was educated in New York City, and planned to enter Columbia to study law when ill health interfered. To recuperate, he made a trip to Europe, where he remained for two years. Returning to New York in 1806, he entered a law office, and in 1807–8 collaborated with his brother William and James K. Paulding in the publication of the famous "Salmagundi" Papers, a series of humorous but kindly essays touching contemporary New York. The following year, 1809, he published the "Knickerbocker History," which, though originally intended as a hoax, was at once hailed as a masterly piece of work.

In 1815 Irving went to England as representative of the firm of P. Irving & Co. His duties seem not to have been arduous, and the next three years were spent largely in pleasant relaxations. Unfortunately for his own peace of mind, but fortunately for the world of letters, the firm failed in 1819, compelling him to turn to writing for a livelihood.

The first number of the "Sketch Book" appeared in New York in March, 1819, and with its appearance the adolescent period of American literature came to an end. When, a little later, it was published in England, through the good offices of Scott, Irving's international reputation was secure. In 1822 he published "Bracebridge Hall" and two years later "Tales of a Traveller," both worthy successors of the "Sketch Book."

He then turned his attention to Spain, and after three years of careful research, wrote his "Life and Voyages of Christopher Columbus," his most profitable book, "The Conquest of Granada" and "The Alhambra."

After a period of service as Secretary of Legation in Great Britain, he returned to the United States in 1831 and devoted nearly all of the next ten years to the New West. To this period belong "The Crayon Miscellany," "Astoria" and the "Rocky Mountains."

Thereafter, following four years of service as U. S. Minister in Spain, he retired to his estate at "Sunnyside" on the Hudson, and devoted the last years of his life exclusively to his elaborate "Life of Washington," the last volume of which appeared only three months before he died.

Irving is one of the few American authors who have been unqualifiedly accepted by the Old World. His work is uniformly of high quality; his artistry in tales with a folklore background like "Rip Van Winkle," "Sleepy Hollow" and "Wolfert Webber" is well-nigh perfect. He was the first man of his nationality to answer adequately Sidney Smith's sneering query, "Who reads an American book?"

SALMAGUNDI; OR THE WHIM-WHAMS AND OPINIONS OF LAUNCELOT LANGSTAFFE, ESQ., AND OTHERS. 2 volumes or 20 numbers. (January, 1807 to January, 1808). New York, 1807–8.

Later editions are so styled at the top of the first page of each number. To secure all parts in the first edition is practically impossible.

A HISTORY OF NEW YORK FROM THE BEGINNING OF THE WORLD TO THE END OF THE DUTCH DYNASTY. . . . By Diedrich Knickerbocker. 2 volumes. New York, 1809.

Volume I has a folding plate of New Amsterdam.

THE SKETCH BOOK OF GEOFFREY CRAYON, GENT. . . . 7 parts in wrappers. Parts I–V, New York, 1819; parts VI and VII, New York, 1820.

For a complete discussion of the bibliography of the Sketch Book the reader is referred to the monograph by W. R. Langfeld published in the *Bulletin of the New York Public Library* for July, 1932. Among the many changes between the first and second printings the following may be noted. In Part I, page 94, line 3, the first issue reads "Charles V"—later changed to "Emperor Frederick." The last word on page 104 must be "servile" in Part II and line 21 must read "compete" instead of "contend." Parts III, IV and V were paged consecutively in the first issue, but later were paged separately. In Part VI the last line on page 38 should begin with "species." Part VII, page 33, line 19 reads "some shrew" instead of "some pestilential shrew." There are many other variations in text, copyright notices, etc., which are too voluminous to list here.

BRACEBRIDGE HALL; OR THE HUMOURISTS. A MEDLEY, BY GEOFFREY CRAYON, GENT. 2 volumes. New York, 1822.

TALES OF A TRAVELLER. . . . BY GEOFFREY CRAYON, GENT. 4 parts. Philadelphia, 1824. Part II, p. 99, l. 13, reads "at housand."

A HISTORY OF THE LIFE AND VOYAGES OF CHRISTOPHER COLUMBUS. 3 volumes. Map. New York, 1828.

A CHRONICLE OF THE CONQUEST OF GRANADA. BY FRAY ANTONIO AGAPIDA. 2 volumes. Philadelphia, 1829.

This was also published in a large paper edition.

THE ALHAMBRA: A SERIES OF TALES AND SKETCHES OF THE MOORS AND SPANIARDS. 2 volumes. Philadelphia, 1832.

THE CRAYON MISCELLANY. 3 volumes. Philadelphia, 1835. 1, "A Tour of the Prairies;" 2, "Abbotsford and Newstead Abbey;" 3, "Legends of the Conquest of Spain."

ASTORIA; OR, INCIDENTS OF AN ENTERPRISE BEYOND THE ROCKY MOUNTAINS. 2 volumes. Maps. Philadelphia, 1836.

THE ROCKY MOUNTAINS; OR, SCENES, INCIDENTS, AND ADVENTURES IN THE FAR WEST. . . . 2 volumes. Maps. Philadelphia, 1837.

THE LIFE OF GEORGE WASHINGTON. 5 volumes. New York, 1855–59.

Volumes I and II, 1855; Volume III, 1856; Volume IV, 1857; Volume V, 1859. A publisher's announcement slip is tipped in in the back of Volume III, in some copies. Also large paper, 110 copies.

JACKSON, HELEN (HUNT)
(H. H.)
1831–1885

"H. H." WAS the daughter of Professor Fiske of Amherst College, and a neighbor and girlhood acquaintance of Emily Dickinson. Her early life was one of tragedy. She lost her husband, Capt. Hunt, in a marine accident, and later, following the death of her two sons, sought refuge in seclusion.

Her first book, a volume of verses, was published in 1870, and "Saxe Holm's Stories" (First Series), correctly attributed to her, in 1874. Later, following her marriage to Mr. Jackson of Colorado, she visited California, and while there became so impressed by the deplorable conditions among the Indians that she wrote her novel "Ramona" as a protest.

There is little doubt that all thought of literary accomplishment on Mrs. Jackson's part was submerged in the sincerity of her purpose. But the glamorous nature of its background, the truly American theme and her passionate interest in the subject have obscured the good which "Ramona" accomplished as a recital of Indian wrongs and have caused it, rather, to be accepted as one of America's notable national romances.

VERSES BY H. H. Boston, 1870.

(Anonymous) SAXE HOLM'S STORIES. New York, 1874.

The "L" must be present in "Longer" in the second line from the bottom on page 88.

RAMONA. A STORY. Boston, 1884.

JAMES, HENRY, JR.

1843–1916

AS A novelist and short story writer, many critics and students consider James the most finished product of American literature.

He was brought up in the atmosphere of a cultured and aristocratic New York home. His father, a man of wealth and personal attainment, a disciple of Swedenborg and a firm believer in individual intellectual development, insisted that his sons should be trained by private tutors. Henry was sent to Europe for further study at the age of twelve. When, on his return from Europe, he entered the Harvard Law School, his literary instincts were already strong. After achieving the publication of a few short stories, he abandoned law for a literary career. Shortly thereafter, in 1869, he returned to Europe, and save for infrequent visits home, remained there until his death. He became a British subject on the outbreak of the World War.

James was a finished artist even in his first book, "A Passionate Pilgrim and Other Tales." He carried a sustained brilliance through "Roderick Hudson,"—his first novel of consequence,—"An International Episode," "Washington Square," "The Princess Casamassima," "The Spoils of Poynton," "What Maisie Knew" and the fine trio which crowned his literary career—"The Wings of the Dove" (1902), "The Ambassador" (1903) and "The Golden Bowl" (two volumes, 1904). He came nearest to attaining popularity with "Daisy Miller." But by common consent his best novels are "The American" and "The Portrait of a Lady,"—the latter the choice of the majority; while many consider his almost perfect ghost story, "The Turn of the Screw" (in "The Two Magics"), the finest thing he ever wrote.

Even in his earlier, more natural days James had but a relatively small audience. When changed methods brought him even less popular recognition, he devoted himself to his art solely for its own sake. His failure to appeal to the average reader was due chiefly to the slow development of his plots and to the increasing involvement of his style.

A PASSIONATE PILGRIM AND OTHER TALES. Boston, 1875.

RODERICK HUDSON. Boston, 1876.

THE AMERICAN. BOSTON, 1877.

THE EUROPEANS. A Sketch. Boston, 1879.

The 2 volume London, 1878, edition has priority.

DAISY MILLER. A Study. New York, 1879.

The last number in the list of works on page 4 is 79.

An International Episode. New York, 1879.
The last number on page 4 is 87.

Washington Square. New York, 1881.

The Portrait of a Lady. Boston, 1882.
Measures 1 3/16 inches across the top of covers; later issues are on thicker paper. The 3 volume London, 1881, edition has priority.

The Princess Casamassima: A Novel. Three volumes. London, 1886.

The Bostonians. A Novel. Three volumes. London, 1886.
Also 1 volume.

The Lesson of the Master, The Marriages, The Pupil, Brooksmith, The Solution, Sir Edmund Orme. New York, 1892.

The Spoils of Poynton. Boston, 1897.

What Maisie Knew. Chicago, 1897.

The Two Magics. The Turn of the Screw. Covering End. New York, 1898.

JEWETT, SARAH ORNE
1849–1909

Summer boarders who infested the Maine coast even in her childhood days were anathema to Miss Jewett. She tells us that, as a young girl in South Berwick, she heard them lording it over the country folk, and how, even then, she determined to vindicate the people of her native state. Her own life appears to have been a peaceful one, its dominant note her attachment to her father whom she so charmingly and successfully portrays in "A Country Doctor."

Miss Jewett wrote entirely of New England, and like Mrs. Freeman treated her subject exquisitely. Unlike Mrs. Freeman, however, she is gently optimistic. Her sympathies are apparent but well controlled, and she never expresses them to the detriment of the quality of her work. She is probably at her best in "Deephaven" and "The Country of the Pointed Firs." In "Betty Leicester" she has left us an appealing juvenile.

DEEPHAVEN. Boston, 1877.

A COUNTRY DOCTOR. Boston, 1884.

Later editions are so noted on the title page.

A WHITE HERON AND OTHER STORIES. Boston, 1885.

BETTY LEICESTER; A STORY FOR GIRLS. Boston, 1890.

The advertisement facing the title must not mention "Tales of New England." There is also a large paper edition.

THE COUNTRY OF THE POINTED FIRS. Boston, 1896.

The first binding was a silken rather than a linen texture cloth.

JOHNSON, RICHARD MALCOLM
1822–1898

JOHNSON began writing at about the close of the Civil War, and must therefore be classed among the post-war Georgians, though in reality he belongs to the Old South. He was born in the early eighteen-twenties, and was brought up on his father's plantation in Hancock County, Ga. In 1841 he graduated from Mercer College and presently began to practice law. Following his marriage, he accepted a professorship of

Belles-Lettres, but after the Civil War opened a boys' school in Hancock County. His last years were devoted entirely to literary work.

Johnson harks back to Longstreet, and his rambling sketches owe much to "Georgia Scenes." His range was small, his control of large materials uncertain, but he performed a timely service in focusing literary attention on the South.

DUKESBOROUGH TALES. By Philemon Perch. Baltimore, 1871.

JOHNSON, ROSSITER
1840–1931

JOHNSON was born in Rochester, N. Y., and educated at the University there. For a time, following his graduation, he edited the *Rochester Democrat,* and later the *Concord, N. H. Statesman.* Thereafter, he devoted most of his time to the compilation of such publications as the "American Cyclopaedia" and the "World's Great Books."

Johnson's earlier writings consist of historical essays, novels and boys' juveniles. "Phaeton Rogers," one of the latter, is an amusing and veracious account of the haps and mishaps of a couple of lively youngsters, sufficiently sophisticated to satisfy the modern taste.

PHAETON ROGERS. A NOVEL OF BOY LIFE. New York, 1881.

JONES, JAMES ATHEARN
1791–1854

JONES was born in Tisbury, Mass. He received a common school education, and as a young man made several voyages to the West Indies. Later he taught school, resided in England for three years and at various times engaged in editorial work in Philadelphia, Baltimore and Buffalo. From the time of his boyhood Jones was an indefatigable collector of Indian legends. The fascinating "Tales of an Indian Camp" which he published in 1829 seems to be the first major effort to preserve the folklore of the American aborigines. He also wrote a novel "Haverhill," a story of Colonial Salem, Wolfe's campaign and the West Indies—at times startlingly good in its dialogue and particularly interesting in its descriptions of everyday life in the regions depicted.

TALES OF AN INDIAN CAMP. 3 volumes. London, 1829.
Later reprinted as "Traditions of the North American Indians."

HAVERHILL; OR, MEMOIRS OF AN OFFICER IN THE ARMY OF WOLFE. 2 volumes. New York, 1831.

JUDD, SYLVESTER
1813–1853

THOUGH born in Westhampton, Massachusetts, of an orthodox family and trained in its traditions, Judd was profoundly influenced by the prevailing religious unrest. After his graduation from Yale and from the Harvard Divinity School his doubts found their solution in the acceptance, in 1840, of a Unitarian pastorate in Maine, where he remained until his death.

In 1845 Judd produced his "Margaret," in certain respects a remarkable book. Though uneven in construction, sometimes to the point of incoherence, it had the then rare merit of being faithful to the neglected materials of everyday American life. Lowell called it "the most emphatically

American book ever written," undeniably too strong a statement, but one which holds a modicum of truth.

(Anonymous) MARGARET. A Tale of the Real and Ideal, Blight and Bloom; including Sketches of a Place not before described, called Mons Christi. Boston, 1845.

RICHARD EDNEY AND THE GOVERNOR'S FAMILY. A Rus-urban Tale . . . of Morals, Sentiment, and Life . . . containing, also, hints on being good and doing good. Boston, 1850.

JUDSON, EDWARD L. C.
(Ned Buntline)
1822–1886

IT WOULD be difficult to name an American author who led so crowded and turbulent a life as Judson. He was born in Philadelphia, ran away to sea at the age of eleven, and when thirteen was appointed ensign by President Van Buren for an act of bravery. He served in the Levant, qualified as the best shot in the Navy and became a New York gangster.

His first story, "The Captain's Pig," was published in the *Knickerbocker Magazine* for 1838. Later he started *Ned Buntline's Own,* a weekly paper. Shortly thereafter he was sentenced to a fine of two hundred and fifty dollars and a year in jail as one of the instigators of the Astor Place Riots. Following his release he wrote prolifically, meanwhile finding time to organize the Know-Nothing Party, an anti-Catholic movement, in 1853. During the Civil War he was the Government's chief scout among the Indians. Frequent temperance lectures and a literary output of something over four hundred books, published in magazine form, cap the climax of his amazing career.

THE BLACK AVENGER OF THE SPANISH MAIN, OR THE FIEND OF BLOOD, A STORY OF BUCCANEER TIMES. Boston, 1847.

JUDSON, EMILY CHUBBUCK
(Fanny Forester)
1817–1854

MRS. JUDSON was born in Eaton, N. Y. Her early interest in missions led to her marriage to Dr. Adoniram Judson, the founder of the Burmah Missions, with whom she went to the East. Following his death in 1850, she returned to the United States, an invalid, and after a lingering illness, died at her brother's home in Hamilton, N. Y., in 1854.

Mrs. Judson was the author of various novels, sketches and poems, all of a definitely moral tone. A series of these, republished from the columns of the *New York Mirror,* appeared in a collected edition in 1847.

ALDERBROOK. A Collection of Fanny Forester's Village Sketches, Poems, etc. 2 volumes. Boston, 1847.

(KALER), JAMES OTIS
1848–1912

JAMES OTIS KALER, better known by his Christian names, was a native of Winterport, Me., who, though handicapped by the limitations of an education which ended with the common schools, achieved measurable success as a journalist and as a writer of boys' stories.

"Toby Tyler," his best performance, is the story of a boy who ran away from home to join a circus, only to find that life under the "big top" was not all that it was painted. Toby's adventures were just the kind to satisfy the young critic and to make the story one of the most popular juveniles of its day.

TOBY TYLER OR TEN WEEKS WITH A CIRCUS. New York, 1881.

KELLOGG, ELIJAH

1813–1901

KELLOGG, the author of the most famous declamatory piece in American literature, was born in Portland, Me. He graduated from Bowdoin in 1840, and thereafter took a course in the Andover Theological Seminary, during which he wrote "Spartacus to the Gladiators," an oratorical exercise that has thrilled a host of youngsters. After ordination he became an acting pastor in his native state. Later he was for a time Chaplain of the Boston Seaman's Friend Society.

Kellogg's last years were devoted to writing juveniles, a field in which he was extremely successful. His stories are wholesome tales of adventure, without sentiment or moralizing, admirably adapted to the juvenile taste, and are, on the whole, the equal of any "series" boys' stories yet published in America. Perhaps the most popular of them was the first book of the "Elm Island" series,—"Lion Ben."

STANDARD SPEAKER; Containing Exercises in Prose and Poetry for Declamation. By Epes Sargent. Philadelphia, 1852.

Contains the first book form printing of "Spartacus to the Gladiators" which has been traced by the compiler.

LION BEN OF ELM ISLAND. Boston, 1869.

KENNEDY, JOHN PENDLETON
1795–1870

KENNEDY, who combined politics and literature with eminent success, was born, educated and resided in Baltimore. He served in the War of 1812, and was subsequently three times elected to the National House of Representatives. He was appointed Provost of the University of Maryland in 1849, and Secretary of the Navy by President Fillmore in 1852. At the outbreak of the Civil War he espoused the Union cause.

Kennedy was a close friend of Poe, Thackeray and Irving, and, with the exception of the last, was the most cultured of the early nineteenth century American authors. He began his writing with the "Red Book," in obvious imitation of "Salmagundi," and continued in the Irvingesque manner in "Swallow Barn," a skillful and graceful sketch of life in the Old Dominion. "Horse-Shoe Robinson" which followed, based upon actual incidents of the Revolution, and one of the best novels of its day, met with an enthusiastic reception. Few, if any books of the period remain more readable than this and "Rob of the Bowl," a whimsical tale which, despite its swashbuckling theme, admirably catches the spirit of Maryland under Charles the second.

THE RED BOOK. 2 volumes. Baltimore, 1818–19.
Written in collaboration with Peter Hoffman.

(Anonymous) SWALLOW BARN, OR A SOJOURN IN THE OLD DOMINION. 2 volumes. Philadelphia, 1832.
An errata note for Volume 1 appears at the end of "Contents" in Volume 2.

HORSE-SHOE ROBINSON: A TALE OF THE TORY ASCENDENCY. 2 volumes. Philadelphia, 1835.

(Anonymous) ROB OF THE BOWL: A LEGEND OF ST. INIGOES. 2 volumes. Philadelphia, 1838.

KETTELL, SAMUEL
1800–1855

KETTELL, an accomplished linguist, sometime editor of the *Boston Courier* and in later life a member of the Massachusetts House of Representatives, was a native of Newburyport, Mass. He was also closely associated with S. G. Goodrich, at whose suggestion he compiled a monumental anthology of American poetry. That few authors of note appear in the three volumes of his anthology is more the fault of the times than of Kettell. Even so, the painstaking if uncritical nature of the work makes it an extremely valuable reference book.

SPECIMENS OF AMERICAN POETRY, WITH CRITICAL AND BIOGRAPHICAL NOTICES. 3 volumes. Boston, 1829.

KEY, FRANCIS SCOTT
1780–1843

THE author of our National Anthem was a native of Frederick County, Maryland, and a graduate of St. John's College, Annapolis. He was a lawyer by profession, and for a short time practiced in Fredericktown. Subsequently he removed to Washington, where he became District Attorney for the City. During the War of 1812 he was held as a hostage while the British were bombarding Fort McHenry, near Baltimore, in 1814.

The inspiration for "The Star-Spangled Banner" came to him after an anxious night, when, looking out over the water just before sunrise, he saw the American flag still waving over the walls of the fort. The first book form printing of this poem in a work issued under his name was in his "Poems" (1857), though it appeared originally as a broadside entitled "The Bombardment of Fort McHenry," was reprinted in the *Baltimore American* and took final form in the *Analectic Magazine* for November 1814 under the title, "The Defense of Fort McHenry."

POEMS. With an Introductory Letter by Chief Justice Taney. New York, 1857.

The poem also appeared in the "National Songster," 1814.

KING, GENERAL CHARLES
1844–

GENERAL KING was born in Albany, but after retiring from the Army settled in Milwaukee, where he now resides. He is the author of more than fifty half-sensational, half-sentimental novels, dealing for the most part with Army life and frontier scenes and incidents. Apart from any question of outstanding literary excellence, their value as accurate pictures of the opening of the West is guaranteed by the author's intimate association with the settlement of the country, during a long period of active Army service following the Civil War.

THE STORY OF FORT FRAYNE. Chicago, Neely, (1895).

Measures one inch across the top of covers.

TROOPER ROSS AND SIGNAL BUTTE. Philadelphia, 1896.

KING, GRACE (ELIZABETH)

1852–1932

Miss King was born and educated in New Orleans, La., where she continued to reside. She first gained recognition through her story, "Monsieur Motte" (1888), inspired by what she considered Cable's too romantic treatment of the Creole character. Though she lacked Cable's exotic mastery, it is probable that, of the two, she is the more faithful delineator of the life and character of the Louisiana native.

Monsieur Motte. New York, 1888.

Balcony Stories. New York, 1893.

KIRK, ELLEN WARNER (OLNEY)

(Henry Hayes)

1842–

Mrs. Kirk, a native of Southington, Conn., and the wife of the historian J. F. Kirk, may be credited with a minor contribution to the advancement of feminine letters through her clever and, for the time, daring handling of the characters of a divorced wife and an adventuress in her novel of New York, "The Story of Lawrence Garthe."

The Story of Lawrence Garthe. Boston, 1894.

KIRKLAND, CAROLINE MATILDA (STANSBURY)

1801–1864

The best realistic literary pictures of the early Western settlements were the work of a woman, Mrs. Kirkland, a native of New York and the wife of a professor at Hamilton College, who emigrated to Michigan in 1839 as a pioneer in that newly settled region. In 1842 she returned East, to New York, and established a boarding school.

Mrs. Kirkland was almost the only early feminine writer untouched by the repressive influence of the "Lady's Books." Her work is sometimes weak in structure, but her sketches are convincing, rugged and of an almost masculine vigor. She depicts the early Western settlements with accuracy and humor. Poe called her "one of our best writers," and commented enthusiastically on her wit, verisimilitude and freshness of style. Time has confirmed his verdict.

A NEW HOME, WHO'LL FOLLOW? OR GLIMPSES OF WESTERN LIFE. By Mrs. Mary Clavers. New York, 1839.

WESTERN CLEARINGS. New York, 1845.

KIRKLAND, JOSEPH
1830–1894

LIKE his mother, Caroline Matilda Kirkland (supra), Joseph Kirkland turned to the frontier as the scene of his more important literary work. He was born in Geneva, N. Y., but moved to Chicago in 1856, enlisted during the early days of the Civil War, and rose to the rank of major. Again in Chicago, he was admitted to the bar, and built up a successful legal practice.

Kirkland was fifty-seven when his first book appeared, and he had but seven years in which to make his literary mark; yet he succeeded admirably. In "Zury" and in "The McVeys" he tells the story of the middle Western frontier with a cold truthfulness and rugged vigor almost unique among the writings of his generation. There have been greater books than "Zury," but it is fine, honest work, and as one of our first sincere novels of the soil it must be accorded a place of honor.

ZURY; THE MEANEST MAN IN SPRING COUNTY. A Novel of Western Life. Boston, 1887.

THE McVEYS. (AN EPISODE.) Boston, 1888.

LAMAR, MIRABEAU BUONAPARTE
1798–1859

LAMAR was born in Louisville, Ga., and after relatively brief experiences as an agriculturist, business man and editor in his native state, moved to Texas in 1835, where he immediately became identified with the revolutionary movement looking to Texan independence. Upon the proclamation of the Republic he was chosen its first President, and, following annexation, became commander of the Rangers. He was appointed U. S. Minister to Nicaragua in 1857.

In the same year Lamar published a collection of his verse, without, however, "The Daughter of Mendoza," his best known poem, which, though often printed, does not seem to have appeared in any collected edition of his poetry. His work is light and graceful, if not notable.

VERSE MEMORIALS. New York, 1857.

LANIER, SIDNEY
1842–1881

LANIER, the first important figure in the literature of the new South, and a scion of the old aristocratic régime, was born in Macon, Ga. He inherited a love of music from both of his parents, and during his boyhood taught himself to play expertly on the piano, banjo, violin and flute. At the age of fourteen he entered Oglethorpe College, from which he graduated with highest honors, afterwards accepting a position on the faculty.

At the outbreak of the Civil War he enlisted in the Confederate army. During the four years of campaigning ensuing he contracted consumption. Subsequently he went to Alabama to recuperate, published his first book, "Tiger-Lilies," in 1867, served as principal of a school at Prattville, and later married. But his health continued delicate, and he was advised by his physician to take up residence in Texas.

Unfortunately the change did him little good. Convinced at last that he had but a short time to live, he returned to Macon, but presently moved on to Baltimore, where he had secured a position in an orchestra. His next four years, though he was nominally resident in Baltimore, were spent for the most part in a vain search for health through various regions of the South. His hopeless struggles ended in Alabama, in 1881, following four years of brilliant service at Johns Hopkins in the chair of English Literature, to which he had been appointed in 1877.

Lanier's theories of poetry, expounded in his "Science of English Verse," had much in common with Poe's. He conceived music to be the basis of all poetic writing, and his own work contains some almost flawless examples of harmonious expression. "Corn" and "The Marshes of Glynn," are two of the fine poems in American Literature.

It is difficult to classify Lanier's one novel, "Tiger-Lilies." The first half of it is chaotic, but it ends in a note of true realism. In a way, it seems to bridge the gap between the old and the new in Southern literature.

TIGER-LILIES. A Novel. New York, 1867.

Lilies is spelled "Lillies" on the backstrip—"Lilies" on the title.

POEMS. Philadelphia, 1877.

THE SCIENCE OF ENGLISH VERSE. New York, 1880.

THE ENGLISH NOVEL AND THE PRINCIPLES OF ITS DEVELOPMENT. New York, 1883.

POEMS OF SIDNEY LANIER. Edited by his Wife. . . . New York, 1884.

LARCOM, LUCY
1824–1893

MISS LARCOM was a protégée and lifelong friend of Whittier, whose attention she first attracted through her poems printed in a paper published by the Lowell cotton mill in which she worked. She was born in Beverly, Mass. For a time she resided with her sister in Illinois. Later, she became a teacher at Wheaton Seminary, and later still, from 1866 to 1874, was editor of *Our Young Folks*. Her declining years were spent in Beverly, Mass.

If Miss Larcom's verse is marred by an excess of sentimentality, it at times gives evidence of genuine poetic gifts. Yet her relatively neglected prose possesses more enduring qualities,—particularly her reminiscences of girlhood.

POEMS. Boston, 1869.

A NEW ENGLAND GIRLHOOD; OUTLINED FROM MEMORY. Boston, 1889.

LAWSON, JAMES
1799–1880

LAWSON, a Scotchman, came to the United States in 1815 and entered business. Subsequently he became an assistant editor on several newspapers, eking out a livelihood as a salesman of marine insurance. He essayed a little drama and some poetry, but is important today chiefly as one of the first authors to bring American letters to the attention of English readers.

TALES AND SKETCHES, BY A COSMOPOLITE. New York, 1830.

LAZARUS, EMMA
1849–1887

MISS LAZARUS, perhaps the foremost nineteenth century American poetess of Hebrew extraction, was a native of New York. Her family came to the United States by way of Portugal. She grew up in a cultured atmosphere, and was educated by private tutors. Her intellectual attainments gained her the friendship of many of the best minds of her day.

Though Miss Lazarus published her first book before she was eighteen, she first won wide recognition in 1867, with "Admetus and Other Poems," which merited in large measure the praise bestowed upon it. Ten years later, deeply stirred by the persecutions of the Jews in Russia, she took their cause to heart and brought out her "Songs of a Semite," a remarkable example of the impassioned heights to which the Hebrew soul can rise. Thereafter she gave herself to the relief of Russian refugees.

ADMETUS AND OTHER POEMS. New York, 1871.
SONGS OF A SEMITE; THE DANCE OF DEATH, AND OTHER POEMS. New York, 1882.

LEGGETT, WILLIAM
1802–1839

WHILE still a lad, Leggett accompanied his father from New York City to the newly opened Illinois country, but returned East to Georgetown to complete his education, and in 1822 was appointed a midshipman in the Navy. Four years later he resigned to engage in literary work in New York as editor of *The Critic,* and afterwards of *The Mirror,* when the two were merged. Subsequently, he became associated with *The Evening Post,* and established the *Plaindealer.* He was a friend of Bryant and other leading contemporary literary lights, and was active in the current Abolition movement. In 1839 he was appointed diplomatic representative to Guatemala, but died before sailing to assume his post.

In 1829 Leggett published a book called "Tales and Sketches. By a Country Schoolmaster," which gained him the title of "Father of Western Literature." Despite this title, however, the book save historically is of minor importance, and is inferior to the work of Flint and Hall. On the other hand, some of his half forgotten "Naval Stories," such as "The Main Truck," though occasionally marred by a superfluous final paragraph, are among the best of early American sea yarns.

TALES AND SKETCHES. By a Country Schoolmaster. New York, 1829.

NAVAL STORIES. New York, 1834.

LELAND, CHARLES GODFREY
1824–1903

LELAND,—globe-trotter, poet, journalist, humorist and Germanic student,—was born in Philadelphia and educated at Princeton. During a life of restless movement through America and Europe he found time to write ably on travel, politics, history, and numerous other subjects.

His real contribution to American literature, however, is his humorous character, "Hans Breitman," despite an occasional boisterous crudeness, a successful portrayal of the emigrant German temperament when first brought into contact with American conditions.

HANS BREITMAN'S PARTY AND OTHER BALLADS. Philadelphia, T. B. Peterson & Bros. (1868).

"Ringwalt and Brown, Prs" must appear in small type at the bottom of the front wrapper.

LESLIE, ELIZA
1787–1858

MISS LESLIE was another of the relatively small, not vastly gifted but highly important group of early nineteenth century American authoresses who were responsible for a definite cultural advance among the women of America. She came of a fine Philadelphia family, and inherited from her father, a friend of Jefferson and Franklin, a quick perception and a ready mind, which she subsequently put to excellent use. Most of her active life was devoted to literature. She was at different times editor of *The Gift, The Violet* and other like annuals, a contributor to *Graham's* and *Godey's,* the author of a famous cook book and a writer of girls' juveniles.

Perhaps her most striking work is her "Pencil Sketches," published in three series,–fair in narrative, mildly good in characterization, but evidencing a knowledge of the fundamentals of good writing which cannot have failed to exert a steadying influence on the literature of the day.

PENCIL SKETCHES, OR, OUTLINES OF CHARACTER AND MANNERS.
(First series.) Philadelphia, 1833.
Second series. Philadelphia, 1835.
Third series. Philadelphia, 1837.

LEWIS, ALFRED HENRY
1858–1914

Fortunately for literature, when only twenty-one Lewis gave up a promising career as City Attorney of his native Cleveland for the more romantic occupation of "cow-puncher." Later he returned to practice in Kansas City, was for a time Washington correspondent of the *Chicago Times* and then of the Hearst papers. After 1898 he edited a political paper, *The Verdict,* published by Perry Belmont, in New York.

Lewis has had many imitators, but he seems to have been the first to see the fictional possibilities of life on the range, and like Harte, though less manifestly, to have started a new school of fiction. In "Wolfville" he presents the first authentic picture of the hard riding, hard living cowboy of the Southwest.*

Wolfville. New York, Stokes, (1897).
Later editions are noted on the title page.

LEWIS, CHARLES BERTRAND
(M. Quad)
1842–1927

Lewis was born in Liverpool, Ohio, was educated in Michigan, served in the Union army during the Civil War and later became associated with the *Detroit Free Press.* The contemporary popularity of his writings is attested by their translation into German, French and Japanese. The essence of his humor lay in his exaggeration of the foibles of the negro.

* See Charles Wilkins Webber.

Brother Gardner's Lime-Kiln Club: being the Regular Proceedings of the Regular Club for the last three years. . . . By M. Quad and Brother Gardner. Chicago, 1882.

LINN, JOHN BLAIR
1777–1804

Dr. Linn, a brother-in-law of Charles Brockden Brown, was born at Shippensburg, Pa., but upon entering the ministry took up his residence in Philadelphia. He was something of a dramatist and essayist, but more than either a poet. His "Powers of Genius" is one of the few American poems that can be compared at all favorably with contemporary British models.

The Powers of Genius, a Poem, in Three Parts. Philadelphia, 1801.

LOCKE, DAVID ROSS
(Petroleum V. Nasby)
1833–1888

Locke was a native of Vestal, N. Y., where he received only a common school education. He began his career as a printer's apprentice, but soon left home for Ohio where he finally became a newspaper editor. The "Nasby Papers," which made their first appearance in the *Finlay Jeffersonian* in 1860, gained him a national reputation, and brought him tenders, which he declined, of public office. He subsequently became editor of the *New York Mirror,* and eventually, returning West, took up his residence in Kentucky.

There was nothing subtle about the "Rev. Petroleum V. Nasby of Confederit X Roads Kentucky, Proponent of free

Whiskey and Opponent of Slavery." He evidenced no literary greatness; he was little more than a buffoon. But he was contagious, and though his work was little more than timely, it is impossible not to laugh at many of his sallies.

THE NASBY PAPERS. Letters and Sermons containing the Views on the Topics of the Day. . . . Indianapolis, 1864.

"SWINGIN' ROUND THE CIRKLE". . . . Ideas of Men, Politics, and Things. Boston, 1867.

LOCKWOOD, RALPH INGERSOLL
1798–1855

LOCKWOOD, a native of Greenwich, Conn., but later a New York lawyer, was the author of one of the most convincing of the earlier American novels.

The "Insurgents" is a story of Shay's Rebellion. It has many literary deficiencies, but, whether by accident or design, Lockwood hit upon one of the fundamental conflicts in American life, the long struggle between Republicanism and Federalism. Because the characters are genuine, the humor good and because the story as a whole reaches a credibility rare in contemporary fiction, it deserves to be lifted from the obscurity in which it has lain too long.

(Anonymous) THE INSURGENTS: AN HISTORICAL NOVEL. 2 volumes. Philadelphia, 1835.

LONGFELLOW, HENRY WADSWORTH
1807–1882

LONGFELLOW, the only American poet to be honored with a memorial in Westminster Abbey, was born in Portland, Me.

The influence of a cultured home stimulated his poetic ambitions, and at thirteen he had written his first verse. He graduated from Bowdoin in the class with Hawthorne, and for a time essayed law in his father's office. Later he went to Europe for a three year study period, from which he returned to Bowdoin to occupy the chair of Modern Languages. He was married in 1831. Four years later he again went abroad, on a trip which was saddened by the death of his wife. After his return he accepted a professorship at Harvard which he held for seventeen years. He resigned in 1854 to devote himself wholly to literary work. In 1861 his second wife was burned to death. He continued, however, to reside in Cambridge save for two years spent in Europe, during which he was the recipient of extraordinary honors.

It has been the fashion of late to class Longfellow as little more than a mediocre poet; and, if the familiar "Psalm of Life," "Village Blacksmith" and poems of that ilk are to be accepted as ultimate criteria, the criticism is warranted. But such a judgment ignores the strong American flavor of "Evangeline," "Hiawatha" and the "Courtship of Miles Standish," and the vitality of such ballads as "Paul Revere's Ride" and "The Skeleton in Armor." They mark him, not, perhaps, with greatness, but at least with permanence.

Probably no better estimate of Longfellow's final ranking has been made than that of Edmund Clarence Stedman—"His admirers may form no longer a critical majority, yet he surely helped to quicken the New World sense of beauty, and to lead a movement which precedes the rise of a national school."

(Anonymous) OUTRE-MER; A PILGRIMAGE BEYOND THE SEA. 2 parts, in wrappers. Boston, 1833–34.

Part 2 was also issued in boards. Some copies of part 1 do not have a 5 line quotation from Mandeville on the cover. Sometimes found 2 parts in 1, cloth.

VOICES OF THE NIGHT. Cambridge, 1839.

Copies of the first issue, which reads "His Hector's arm and his the might" on page 78, line ten, are excessively rare.

BALLADS AND OTHER POEMS. Cambridge, 1842.

Has a small "t" in "teacher" in the last line on page 88.

POEMS ON SLAVERY. Cambridge, 1842.

In later copies the words "Second Edition" appear on both the front wrapper and the title.

EVANGELINE, A TALE OF ACADIE. Boston, 1847.

The first issue has a tiny black diamond ornament under the author's name on the title page, and a minute break in the "g" of "Long" in the first line on page 61. The "ng" in "long" later dropped out.

THE SEASIDE AND THE FIRESIDE. Boston, 1850.

There is also a large paper edition.

THE GOLDEN LEGEND. Boston, 1851.

THE SONG OF HIAWATHA. Boston, 1855.

Reads "Dove" in the seventh line on page 96; "In the Moon when nights are brightest," in the eleventh line on page 32.

THE COURTSHIP OF MILES STANDISH, AND OTHER POEMS. Boston, 1858.

Reads "treacherous" instead of "ruddy" in the third line on page 124. The leaf of advertisements pasted between the front end papers is not a necessary indication of the first edition; it appears in later printings.

TALES OF A WAYSIDE INN. Boston, 1863.

In some copies this book is listed as "Nearly Ready" on page 11 of the advertisements. Whether this constitutes priority is debatable. The presence of the imprint of Welch, Bigelow at the bottom of page 225 appears to be a more reliable indication of first printing.

LONGSTREET, AUGUSTUS BALDWIN
1790–1870

LONGSTREET, historically the second of the many important authors whom Georgia has given to our literature, was the first local literary inspiration to her later sons. He was born in Augusta and graduated from Yale in 1813, immediately began to study law, and after his return to Georgia was made a judge in 1822. Later, after the death of his eldest son, he forsook the bench for the Methodist ministry. In 1840 he was called to the presidency of Emory College. He was afterwards President of Centenary College in Louisiana, of The University of Mississippi and of South Carolina College at Columbia.

Though Longstreet tried to suppress "Georgia Scenes" after his "conversion," it is now the one book on which his literary reputation rests. Broadly humorous, crude, rough, but with the true roughness of the "cracker," not literature precisely, but certainly life, it may fairly be regarded as one of the fountainheads of Southern realism.

GEORGIA SCENES, CHARACTERS, INCIDENTS, ETC., IN THE FIRST HALF CENTURY OF THE REPUBLIC. By a Native Georgian. Augusta, Ga., 1835.

LOTHROP, HARRIET MULFORD (STONE)
(Margaret Sidney)
1844–1924

Mrs. Lothrop was born in New Haven, Conn., was educated at private schools and during early womanhood traveled extensively throughout the United States. Later she married D. Lothrop of Boston, who became her publisher.

Mrs. Lothrop confined herself largely to writing juveniles and became so popular that, at one time, "Five Little Peppers" was an almost necessary part of a young girl's education. Her books are still entertaining, but a later generation finds them too sweetly unsophisticated.

Five Little Peppers and How They Grew.
Boston, D. Lothrop, (1880).
Later editions are copyrighted 1881.

LOWELL, JAMES RUSSELL
1819–1891

Though popularly acclaimed above all else as a poet, Lowell, the youngest of the so-called "New England Group," was perhaps even greater as an essayist and critic. He grew up in the literary atmosphere of his birthplace, Cambridge, and after graduation from Harvard and an early marriage was for a time engaged in journalistic work in Philadelphia. Returning shortly to Cambridge, he began his real life work in earnest.

A European trip in 1851 was unfortunately terminated by the death of Lowell's wife. In 1856 he was appointed Professor of Modern Languages at Harvard. The next year, following his remarriage, he became editor of the *Atlantic Monthly,* and in due course of the *North American Review,* which he served from 1863 to 1872. He revisited Europe in

1872, was Minister to Spain from 1877 to 1880, and ended his active public career as Ambassador to England.

Lowell's first recognized success was his "Poems" (1841), but the high tide of his achievement came in 1848, with "The Biglow Papers," a telling political satire in dialect verse, "A Fable for Critics," an amusing but withal penetrating satire on contemporary authors and his romantic poem "The Vision of Sir Launfal." Of his shorter poems the most notable are found in his "Poems" (1844), "Commemoration Ode" and "Under the Willows."

In the field of criticism and scholarship Lowell ranks undoubtedly as one of our leading men of letters. His critical works, like "Conversations on Some of the Old Poets," "Among My Books," first and second series, and "My Study Windows" contribute as much to his enduring fame as do his poems.

A YEAR'S LIFE. Boston, 1841.

First copies contained no errata slip; later copies had it tipped or pasted in. In the case of this book, since the errata slip is easily removed, the usual rule regarding priority is reversed, with the result that copies containing the slip are generally preferred.

POEMS. Cambridge, 1844.

A very few copies were issued on large paper. They are very rare but are not the first issue.

CONVERSATIONS ON SOME OF THE OLD POETS. Cambridge, 1845.

MELIBOEUS-HIPPONAX. The Biglow Papers, edited, with an Introduction, Notes, Glossary, and Copious Index, by Homer Wilbur, M. A. . . . Cambridge, 1848.

Preferred copies have only the Cambridge imprint, not Cambridge and New York, though there is no proof of their priority.

THE VISION OF SIR LAUNFAL. Cambridge, 1848.

A FABLE FOR CRITICS. . . . By a Wonderful Quiz. (New York), (18)48.

Of the large number of errors in this book, the determining one seems to be that page 64 should be misnumbered 63.

ODE RECITED AT THE COMMEMORATION OF THE LIVING AND DEAD SOLDIERS OF HARVARD UNIVERSITY, JULY 21, 1865. Cambridge, 1865.

Only fifty copies were issued—privately printed.

MELIBOEUS-HIPPONAX. The Biglow Papers. Second Series. Boston, 1867.

This is the first American edition. It must have Ticknor & Field's monogram on the backstrip, and perfect type in the word "writing" in the fourth line from the bottom of page V. The first edition was published in England in 1862—three parts in wrapper.

UNDER THE WILLOWS AND OTHER POEMS. Boston, 1869.

Has an erratum slip at the end. Line seven of page 224 reads "Thy thread-like windings" instead of "Its thread," etc.

AMONG MY BOOKS. Boston, 1870.

THE CATHEDRAL. Boston, 1870.

The first issue has nineteen lines which were deleted from later issues. In the second issue line three on page 19 begins "Eluding these."

My Study Windows. Boston, 1871.

The first issue has the Fields, Osgood monogram in gilt on the backstrip.

Among My Books. Second Series. Boston, 1876.

The first issue bears the copyright date of 1875, and reads "Belles-Letters" instead of "Belles-Lettres" on the title page.

LOWELL, ROBERT TRAILL SPENCE
1816–1891

Robert Lowell, the elder brother of James Russell Lowell, abandoned a medical career in 1839 to study theology. He was ordained in Bermuda in 1843, and shortly thereafter was transferred to Newfoundland. He returned to the United States in 1847 and after a short ministry in Newark became head master of St. Mark's School at Southboro, Mass., and later professor of Latin in Union College. During his long career he made a number of attempts at fiction.

Lowell's only novel meriting consideration is "The New Priest in Conception Bay." It is a true and sometimes powerful story of contemporary Newfoundland life but is interrupted by frequent theological discussions, which certainly add nothing to its interest.

(Anonymous) The New Priest in Conception Bay. 2 volumes. Boston, 1858.

McHENRY, JAMES
1785–1845

McHenry was born in northern Ireland and was educated at Dublin and Glasgow as a physician. He emigrated to the United States in 1817, and practiced his profession here until 1842, when he was appointed U. S. Consul at Londonderry, Ireland.

Though the scene of much of McHenry's literary output is American, his work would fail of mention save for one quite seriously intended but extraordinarily amusing tale. His literary ambition was to give the neglected Ulsterman, transplanted or otherwise, his due,—a theme which quite pervades his fiction. Yet time has defeated his obsession by remembering him for a very different reason, his authorship of a grotesque story of Washington's first romance during his service in the wilderness of western Pennsylvania.

(Anonymous) The Wilderness, or, Braddock's Times. A Tale of the West. 2 volumes. New York, 1823.

MABIE, HAMILTON WRIGHT
1846–1916

Mabie, well known in his day as an editor, essayist and critic, was a native of Cold Springs, N. Y., and a graduate of Williams College and of Columbia University Law School. In 1879 he joined the staff of the *Christian Herald,* later *The Outlook,* of which he eventually became assistant editor.

My Study Fire. New York, 1890.
Second Series, 1895.

MAJOR, CHARLES
(Edwin Caskoden)
1856–1913

MAJOR, an obscure Indiana lawyer, born in Indianapolis and educated in the public schools, became overnight a national figure with the appearance of his first novel, "When Knighthood Was in Flower," a story of sixteenth century England. It had an immediate and huge success, but there is little chance of its retaining a permanent place in American literature.

WHEN KNIGHTHOOD WAS IN FLOWER, OR THE LOVE STORY OF CHARLES BRANDON AND MARY TUDOR. . . . By Edwin Caskoden. Indianapolis, 1898.

In later copies Major's name appears in brackets under "Edwin Caskoden" on the title page. There should be no notice of reprintings on the copyright page.

MARKHAM, EDWIN
1852–

MARKHAM was born in Oregon City, Ore., spent his boyhood on a California ranch, attended the State Normal School and later studied law. Instead of practicing he became a teacher, and was from time to time head master of several California schools. His present residence is on Staten Island, N. Y. Markham is the author of the vigorous, impressive and much printed "Man with the Hoe"—widely acclaimed as one of the great poems of the generation.

THE MAN WITH THE HOE. San Francisco, 1899.

There is also a later New York, 1899 edition.

The first separate printing of this poem was in a special supplement to the *San Francisco Examiner* (1899).

MATHEWS, CORNELIUS
1817–1889

MATHEWS was born in Port Chester, N. Y., was educated at New York University and later became a member of the New York City bar. He was a well known and prolific writer of poems, novels and dramas, and a critic of contemporary repute. His "Career of Puffer Hopkins" is an amusing satire on politics in his adopted city.

THE CAREER OF PUFFER HOPKINS. New York, 1842.

MAYO, WILLIAM STARBUCK
1812–1895

MAYO was born in Ogdensburg, N. Y., and was graduated from the College of Physicians and Surgeons in 1833. Following a short period of practice, he made an extended foreign trip which took him, among other places, to Africa and Spain. Upon his return to the United States he gave up his profession to undertake a literary career, and using his African experiences as a basis, published as his second book an extraordinary novel, "Kaloolah." The story was well received, in good measure, no doubt, because of its bizarre and thrilling nature. It is enlivened by some rather pertinent satire and it still appeals to a small reading public.

KALOOLAH; OR, JOURNEYINGS TO THE DJÉBEL KUMRI. An Autobiography of Jonathan Romer. New York, 1849.

THE BERBER; OR, THE MOUNTAINEER OF THE ATLAS. A Tale of Morocco. New York, 1850.
Later editions are so marked.

MEEK, ALEXANDER BEAUFORT
1814–1865

MEEK was born in Columbia, S. C., was admitted to the bar in Alabama, served in the Seminole War, became a judge and a member of the State Legislature and for a time was associate editor of the *Mobile Register*. The desultory manner in which Meek composed his verse is evident in all his work, although it contains an occasional flash of inspiration.

SONGS AND POEMS OF THE SOUTH. New York, Mobile, 1857.
Both the first and second editions contain an errata slip, but the second edition is so marked, and omits the New York imprint.

MELVILLE, HERMAN
1819–1891

MELVILLE'S present accepted recognition as a great writer was a long time in the making. He was born in New York, and spent his boyhood on a farm, interrupted only by a brief runaway trip to sea. Later, after a period of teaching and more farming, the tedium of farm life drove him again to sea, this time on a whaler bound for the South Pacific. Upon reaching a port in the Marquesas, driven by the inhumanities of the captain, he deserted with a companion, was presently captured by a warlike band of natives and held in a sort of friendly bondage for four months, until rescued by an Australian whaler.

These experiences and his subsequent residence in the Islands furnished Melville the materials for "Typee" and "Omoo," both delightful tales of South Sea life. But fine as these works are, they are completely overshadowed by "Moby-Dick." The story of Captain Ahab's relentless pursuit of the white whale is an epic of man's struggle against nature—one of the world's great classics.

With the completion of "Moby-Dick," Melville's powers declined. The Transcendentalism which had its first glimmering in "Typee" and confessed its defeat in "Mardi" and "Moby-Dick" became despair. "Pierre" is a welter of extraordinary conjecture and save for a few war verses his subsequent work is almost unreadable.

TYPEE: A PEEP AT POLYNESIAN LIFE, DURING A FOUR MONTHS' RESIDENCE IN A VALLEY OF THE MARQUESAS. Map. 2 volumes in one in cloth, or 2 volumes in wrappers. New York & London, 1846.

OMOO: A NARRATIVE OF ADVENTURES IN THE SOUTH SEAS. One volume cloth, or 2 parts in wrappers. New York, 1847.

Copies with the gilt stamped ship ornament on the covers are preferred.

MARDI: AND A VOYAGE THITHER. 2 volumes. New York, 1849.

Copies with yellow end papers are preferred.

REDBURN; HIS FIRST VOYAGE; BEING THE SAILOR-BOY. Confessions and Reminiscences of the Son-of-a-Gentleman in the Merchant Service. New York, 1849.

WHITE-JACKET; OR THE WORLD IN A MAN-OF-WAR. New York, 1850.

Copies with yellow end papers are preferred.

MOBY-DICK, OR, THE WHALE. New York, 1851.

This was previously published the same year in England, in three volumes, under the title "The Whale." Copies with orange end papers are preferred.

Note: Melville possibly owed the idea of "Moby-Dick" to J. C. Reynolds, whose "Mocha Dick" was previously published in a Portland (Me.) newspaper.

PIERRE; OR, THE AMBIGUITIES. New York, 1852.

BATTLE-PIECES AND ASPECTS OF THE WAR. New York, 1866.

Copies bound in blue cloth, with brown end papers are preferred.

Note: The bibliographical differences in Melville's works above noted are treated as matters of preference rather than as mandatory requirements for the reason that the processes of assembly for binding were easily open to variation, and, meanwhile, such errors in text, etc., as would clearly establish priority seem, so far as observed, to be common to all right-dated copies.

MILLER, "JOAQUIN" (CINCINNATUS HEINE)
1841–1913

MILLER was born in a covered wagon, and journeyed to Oregon with his parents in 1852. Two years later he ran away to the California gold mines, but returned home shortly and graduated from Columbia College at the age of seventeen. He spent the next twelve years in varied activities,—riding express, editing a newspaper and acting as a Federal Judge. Meanwhile, he published his first book "Joaquin et Al," in 1866.

In 1870 Miller went to California, confident of a friendly greeting from its literary group. But being met with jeers he turned to the East, encountered a second cool reception and proceeded to England. The British received him more kindly, and with the publication of his "Songs of the Sierras," he found himself famous almost overnight. He returned to California in 1887 and resided there until his death.

Miller is neither subtle nor profound. He is the poet of rugged men and "wide open spaces." Much of his work is worthless. Yet the surge and sweep of poems like "Columbus," "The Missouri" and a few others have seldom been equaled in American literature.

SONGS OF THE SIERRAS. New York, 1871.

Printed for the author. This edition seems to be prior to the Boston, Roberts Brothers, 1871 edition. It does not contain "Kit Carson's Ride," which first appeared in the latter. The Roberts Brothers edition must have R. B. instead of the full name at the base of the backstrip. (Also London, 1871.)

SONGS OF THE MEXICAN SEAS. Boston, 1887.

SONGS OF THE SOUL. San Francisco, 1896.

MITCHELL, DONALD GRANT
(Ik Marvel)
1822—1908

ONE of the small group of masculine writers who, borne along by the current of reaction against the sensational novel of adventure, drifted into the sentimental field during the eighteen-fifties was D. G. Mitchell, better known by his pen name, "Ik Marvel." He was born in Norwich, Conn., and spent much of his time as a boy on his grandfather's farm, where he developed the love of nature so apparent in his later work. Following his graduation from Yale in 1841, and a course of law in New York City, he traveled extensively in Europe, and later settled in New Haven.

Of Mitchell's many graceful books two have come down to us as among the somewhat outmoded but charming bits of our literature, "Reveries of a Bachelor" and "Dream Life." Their names describe them aptly,—genteel, Irvingsque essays, in a slightly narrative vein. To them may be added the less known, but equally delightful "Wet Days at Edgewood."

REVERIES OF A BACHELOR: OR, A BOOK OF THE HEART. New York, 1850.

DREAM LIFE. A Fable of the Seasons. New York, 1851.

This appears both with and without the stereotyper's name at the foot of the copyright page. No priority has been established.

WET DAYS AT EDGEWOOD; WITH OLD FARMERS, OLD GARDENERS AND OLD PASTORALS. New York, 1865.

MITCHELL, ISAAC
?—1812

MITCHELL, a native journalist of Poughkeepsie, N. Y., was the author of "Alonzo and Melissa," one of the most popular novels ever written in America. An impossible romance of the Gothic type, it was for a long time the only novel which appealed to the romantic taste of a certain element of the fiction reading public, and it ran into an unrecorded number of editions.

Shortly after the story was published it was revised and reprinted by Daniel Jackson, Jr., under whose name most of the later editions appeared. After a long and involved controversy the question of authorship was settled by the discovery of the original Mitchell version in a Poughkeepsie paper published when Jackson was only fifteen.

THE ASYLUM, OR, ALONZO AND MELISSA. An American Tale, Founded on Fact. 2 volumes. Poughkeepsie, 1811.

(Abridged and pirated as) ALONZO AND MELISSA. . . . By Daniel Jackson, Jr. (1 volume). Plattsburg, 1811.

There is also an anonymous 1811 Plattsburg edition.

MITCHELL, S(ILAS) WEIR
1829–1914

MITCHELL was a native of Philadelphia and a neurologist of international reputation. After graduating from the Jefferson Medical School he spent several years of further study in Europe. During the Civil War he contributed numerous articles to the *Atlantic Monthly,* but until several years later wrote solely by way of avocation.

He turned seriously to fiction writing when he was over fifty, and under the circumstances his success was unusual. His style is graceful and cultured, and he tells his story admirably. In "Hugh Wynne" he gives an intimate, vivid and historically accurate account of the Philadelphia Quakers during the Revolution. "The Adventures of François," which he personally considered his best novel, lacks the power of "Hugh Wynne," but is an entertaining romance of the French Revolution. "The Red City" (1908) is usually considered his best work subsequent to 1900.

HUGH WYNNE, FREE QUAKER. 2 volumes. New York, 1897.

The color design and fleurs-de-lis on the cover and backstrip must be in red. Volume 2, page 260, line 16, must read "before us." Also 60 copies on large paper.

THE ADVENTURES OF FRANÇOIS, FOUNDLING, AND THIEF, JUGGLER, AND FENCING MASTER DURING THE FRENCH REVOLUTION. New York, 1898.

MOORE, CLEMENT CLARKE
1779–1863

MOORE was a native of New York. After graduating from Columbia he devoted the better part of his life to the ministry. In 1821 he became Professor of Biblical Literature at the New York General Theological Seminary. His writings were for the most part on religious subjects, but he also dabbled in verse.

Moore was not a great nor even a good poet, but he had the honor, or fortune, to write perhaps the best known of all American poems for the very young—"A Visit from St. Nicholas" or, to give it its more popular but incorrect title, " 'Twas the Night Before Christmas." This poem first appeared in a newspaper. While it is generally considered to have been first published in book form in the "New York

Book of Poetry" (1837), it is quite possible that prior printings exist. It was first collected in "Poems" (1844).

POEMS. New York, 1844.

MORRIS, GEORGE POPE
1802–1864

GENERAL MORRIS, ranked by contemporary opinion as one of the brilliant and versatile literary figures of his day, was born in Philadelphia, but moved to New York in early manhood. With Samuel Woodworth he began the publication of the *New York Mirror* in 1823. Later, progressively, he became associated with the foremost writers of the period in the publication of *The New Mirror, The Evening Mirror, The National Press,* etc., to all of which he contributed humor, drama and poetry. On one occasion he wrote the libretto of an opera.

Of all Morris' poems, widely popular in their day, only "Woodman, Spare that Tree" is remembered. His prose work, "The Little Frenchman and His Water Lots," a sketch of an unfortunate foreigner in the clutches of a slick New York real estate promoter, has to a degree failed of deserved recognition as an early example of genuine, native humor.

THE DESERTED BRIDE AND OTHER POEMS. New York, 1838.
Contains "Woodman, Spare that Tree."

THE LITTLE FRENCHMAN AND HIS WATER LOTS, WITH OTHER SKETCHES OF THE TIMES. Philadelphia, 1839.

MORTON, SARAH WENTWORTH
1759–1846

AFTER a girlhood spent in Braintree, Mass., Mrs. Morton returned to her native Boston as the wife of the eminent barrister, Perez Morton. For a time a well publicized "affair" between her husband and her sister threatened to wreck her domestic happiness. That crisis passed, she turned her attention assiduously to poetry and shortly, through her contributions to various periodicals, gained contemporary fame as the "American Sappho." To say that she was the best feminine poet of the period is more accurate; the famous Lesbian still retains her laurels.

For a discussion of the "Power of Sympathy," commonly attributed to Mrs. Morton, see William Hill Brown under addendum.

OUÂBI: OR THE VIRTUES OF NATURE AN INDIAN TALE. In Four Cantos. By Philenia, a Lady of Boston. Boston, 1790.

MOTLEY, JOHN LOTHROP
1814–1877

MOTLEY was born in Boston and was graduated from Harvard with Phi Beta Kappa honors at the early age of seventeen. He then spent two years in foreign travel, after which he returned to study law.

His first two works, published anonymously in 1839 and 1849 respectively, were novels. Subsequently, he conceived the idea of a history of the Netherlands, which, after several years of European residence spent in preparation, took final shape in his masterpiece, "The Rise of the Dutch Republic" (1856). He later added to his reputation with the publication of "John of Barnevelt" (1874). Meanwhile, in 1861 and

1869, he was appointed U. S. Minister to Austria and Great Britain respectively.

Motley's reputation rests secure upon his achievement as one of America's greatest historians. Of his two novels, "Merry Mount," a melodramatic tale of Massachusetts Bay Colony in 1628, is definitely the better, yet, save for its masterly handling of the historical aspects of the story, it cannot be counted a first class piece of work.

(Anonymous) MERRY MOUNT; A ROMANCE OF THE MASSACHUSETTS COLONY. 2 volumes. Boston, 1849.
Also two volumes in one.

MOULTON, (ELLEN) LOUISE (CHANDLER)
1835—1908

MRS. MOULTON, the social genius of the middle nineteenth century American literati, was born in Pomfret, Conn., and was educated in Troy, N. Y. Before she was twenty she had edited the *Waverly Garland* and had written her first book. In 1855 she married a Boston journalist and publisher, and her home thereafter became a favorite resort of the literary set. Repeated residence in England after 1876 but broadened the circle of her acquaintance, and, by the same token, the hospitality of her Boston literary salon.

Mrs. Moulton was the author of several books of tales and poems. Her lyrics and sonnets possess an undeniable grace, but her talent is not marked nor her inspiration great.

POEMS. Boston, 1878.

IN THE GARDEN OF DREAMS: LYRICS AND SONNETS. Boston, 1890.
Later editions are so marked on the copyright page.

MUNROE, KIRK
1850–

MUNROE was born in Prairie du Chien, Wisc., was educated at Harvard and later became editor of *Harper's Round Table* and *Eminent Men of Our Times.* His literary output, consisting chiefly of juveniles, covers a broad range of subjects, and is in the main carefully composed and of high quality. Perhaps the best of his novels are the story of the young Parisian, who, coming to Canada in the early days of the French occupancy, joined the Indians, and the more modern tale of a boy railroader, both listed below.

THE FLAMINGO FEATHER. New York, 1887.

CAB AND CABOOSE: THE STORY OF A RAILROAD BOY. New York, 1892.

MURFREE, MARY NOAILLES
(Charles Egbert Craddock)
1850–1922

MISS MURFREE was a frail child, early stricken with paralysis, and being denied the more boisterous sports of other children was restricted largely to reading for her amusement. She grew up in Murfreesboro, Tenn., the home of her ancestors, but vicissitudes of fortune consequent upon the Civil War forced her parents to abandon their family home and seek a simpler existence in the Tennessee mountains. To her impressionable nature here was a new world, rich in scenic background and peopled by an extraordinary species of mankind. She made the most of it.

In 1878 there came out in the *Atlantic* a story of the Tennessee mountains by Charles Egbert Craddock. In 1884 a book of "his" appeared. Later, the author, on walking into

Howells' sanctum, was discovered to be a woman,—and one of the literary sensations of the decade ensued.

Miss Murfree is usually judged by her first book. The pitiful, uncouth people who walk her pages, the desolate settings —almost characters themselves—are etched with a bold hand. The dictum that she failed as a novelist may bear revision, for "The Despot of Broomsedge Cove" will stand comparison with many better known books.

IN THE TENNESSEE MOUNTAINS. Boston, 1884.
The figures 283 in the list of illustrations must be in perfect type.

THE PROPHET OF THE GREAT SMOKY MOUNTAINS. Boston, 1885.

THE DESPOT OF BROOMSEDGE COVE. Boston, 1889.

MYERS, PETER HAMILTON
1812—1878

MYERS, a native of Herkimer, N. Y., and a self-educated Brooklyn lawyer, had a knack of winning prize story contests. This ability, however, was not synonymous with literary greatness. His historical novel "The First of the Knickerbockers," is occasionally remarked by the historian of American letters, but it is only of minor note.

(Anonymous) THE FIRST OF THE KNICKERBOCKERS: A TALE OF 1673. New York, 1848.

NEAL, JOHN
1793—1876

NEAL, a man of indomitable energy, was born in Portland, Me. He received only a common school education before going to work in a shop in Baltimore. Presently he began to study law, and eventually was admitted to the bar. Meanwhile he had written several poems and novels, and, despite its contemporary hazards, had determined upon a literary career.

Neal is reported to have been an extraordinarily rapid writer. It is perhaps this characteristic, plus his lack of a liberal education, which gives his work at times a looseness and incoherence but for which he might have been one of the permanently great. Be that as it may, his work shows more than traces of real strength, entitling him to rank as one of our better early novelists.

He published his first book, "Keep Cool," at the age of twenty-four. "Rachel Dyer," an extraordinarily powerful story of Salem witchcraft, and perhaps his masterpiece, appeared six years later. One of his last literary acts was to publish an autobiography of his picturesque career.

KEEP COOL, A NOVEL. Written in hot weather. By Somebody, M.D.C. etc., etc. . . . 2 volumes. Baltimore, 1817.

(Anonymous) LOGAN. A FAMILY HISTORY. 2 volumes. Philadelphia, 1822.

Has a leaf of errata at the end of Volume 2.

SEVENTY-SIX. 2 volumes. Baltimore, 1823.

RANDOLPH. A Novel. 2 volumes. (Philadelphia), 1823.

The figure 4 on page 4 is printed upside down.

RACHEL DYER: A NORTH AMERICAN STORY. Portland, 1828.

THE DOWN EASTERS, &c., &c., &c. 2 volumes. New York, 1833.

WANDERING RECOLLECTIONS OF A SOMEWHAT BUSY LIFE. An Autobiography. Boston, 1869.

NEAL, JOSEPH CLAY
1807–1847

NEAL, a native of Greenland, N. H., first became prominent as a journalist in Philadelphia, but later established himself in New York, where he conducted the *Saturday Gazette*. He was the author of a popular series of eccentric, local burlesques, "Charcoal Sketches," much admired at the time, notably by Dickens, who saw the English edition through the press. Time has sapped much of the flavor from these quasi-tales, though their monotony is occasionally relieved by a fair bit of characterization.

CHARCOAL SKETCHES; OR, SCENES IN A METROPOLIS. Philadelphia, 1838.

NEWELL, ROBERT HENRY
(Orpheus C. Kerr)
1836–1891

NEWELL, a native and lifelong resident of New York, entered the journalistic field as literary editor of the *New York Mercury*. Later he became editor-in-chief of *Hearth and Home*. He was the author of various novels and poems and of many humorous comments on politics and military affairs—the last immensely popular. Lincoln is reputed to have followed them with pleasure, and on one or two occasions to have read parts of them aloud to a disgruntled cabinet. Nevertheless, they were of ephemeral type and cannot be classed with the greater work of Derby, Shaw and Browne.

THE ORPHEUS C. KERR PAPERS. New York, 1862.

Later series were published in 1863 and 1865.

NORRIS, FRANK
1870–1902

NORRIS, who is regarded as one of the most important originators of the "modern" realistic movement, was born in Chicago, was educated at the University of California and Harvard, and, after spending three years as an art student in Paris, became a correspondent of the *San Francisco Chronicle* during the Boer War. In 1896 and 1897 he was editor of *The Wave,* and in 1898 covered the war in Cuba for *McClure's.*

Though Norris' literary artistry may be questioned, there is no denying his virility. He believed so intensely in realistic portrayal that at times his work is almost brutal. "Moran of the Lady Letty" and "McTeague" are important blazes on the trail towards the newer naturalism. He reached his heights, however, in "The Octopus" (1901)—one of the best of American novels—an epic of the age-old struggle between industry and agriculture—and in the only slightly less effective "The Pit" (1903). The third novel of this trilogy, "The Wolf," was still unfinished when he died.

MORAN OF THE LADY LETTY. A Story of Adventure off the California Coast. New York, 1898.

MCTEAGUE. A Story of San Francisco. New York, 1899.

The last word on page 106 is "moment."

NOTT, HENRY JUNIUS
1799–1837

NOTT was a South Carolina lawyer, born in Pacolet River, S. C., who later became a college professor. He was the author of a number of sketches of little merit, but rather widely popular, which he incorporated in a volume called "Novellettes of a Traveller."

NOVELLETTES OF A TRAVELLER; OR, ODDS AND ENDS FROM THE KNAPSACK OF THOMAS SINGULARITY, JOURNEYMAN PRINTER. 2 volumes. New York, 1834.

NYE, (EDGAR WATSON) BILL
1850–1896

NYE, though born in Shirley, Me., went with his parents to Wisconsin at an early age. After reaching maturity he tried law for a time in Wyoming, but soon abandoned it to accept a position on the *Denver Tribune*. Later he moved to Laramie, Wyo., where he established *The Boomerang* and became a sort of one man local government, acting as justice of the peace, U. S. Commissioner, postmaster and superintendent of schools. The increasing demand for his services as a lecturer finally brought him East, where he settled in New York.

Nye possessed a talent for the incongruous and a real gift for idiotic anecdote. The "gentle" mule, Boomerang, became for a time a famous national character.

BILL NYE AND BOOMERANG; OR, A TALE OF A MEEK-EYED MULE, AND SOME OTHER LITERARY GEMS. Chicago, 1881.

O'BRIEN, FITZ-JAMES
1828–1862

O'Brien, one of the most brilliant, if erratic figures of our literature, was born in County Limerick, Ireland, graduated from Trinity College, Dublin, and lived for the next two years in London, where he devoted most of his time to the spending of a very comfortable fortune of ten thousand pounds. That accomplished, he emigrated to New York in 1852, entered zestfully into its Bohemian life, and soon became recognized as one of the choice spirits of his particular coterie. Following the outbreak of the Civil War, with characteristic impulsiveness, he enlisted in the Union army, and after a period of creditable service died in great suffering as the result of wounds received at Cumberland.

O'Brien's work was done spasmodically, in the intervals between his Bohemian revels. It suffered in consequence to some extent from hasty composition, yet in sheer brilliance of imagination it has rarely been equaled by an American. He was a student of Poe, and was at all times deliberately sensational. Yet his rationalization of his sensationalism was more modern than Poe's.

Unfortunately O'Brien died before he fully realized his fine powers. Even so, he had earned for himself a place among the constructive forces of American literature. His collected works were first published in book form twenty years after his death.

The Poems and Stories of Fitz-James O'Brien. Edited by William Winter. Boston, 1881.

Some copies have a publisher's announcement slip tipped in between the front end papers. There is no present reason, however, for assigning priority to these. The second printing did not appear until 1885.

O'REILLY, JOHN BOYLE
1844–1890

O'Reilly was born in Ireland. At eighteen, after a period of attendance at Dublin University, he became an agent of the Fenian Society and a reporter for a London newspaper. At twenty-one he enlisted in the British army. Almost immediately thereafter he was detected plotting revolution, and was sentenced by court martial to be shot. His sentence, however, was eventually commuted to twenty years' servitude in the Australian penal colony. Following a short period of imprisonment he escaped in a small boat, and after suffering serious privations, was picked up on the open sea by the captain of a Yankee whaler, who brought him to the United States. Shortly after taking up his residence in Boston, he assisted in founding the Papyrus Club, a distinguished group of Boston literati, and presently established *The Pilot* with which he remained associated as editor and part proprietor until his death.

O'Reilly's antipodean experiences furnished him materials, refined by his rich nature, into a group of excellent South Sea lyrics and his novel "Moondyne," a story of penal colony life. He is superb at times, but his brilliance is that of inspirational flashes rather than of fundamental genius.

Songs from the Southern Seas, and other Poems. Boston, 1873.

Moondyne: A Story from the Underworld. Boston, 1879.
Later editions are so marked.

(d'OSSOLI) FULLER, (SARAH) MARGARET
1810–1850

Intellectually Miss Fuller was perhaps the most brilliant American woman of the first half of the nineteenth century.

From her earliest childhood, her father, a member of Congress from Cambridge, Mass., drove her relentlessly, at times beyond her strength. An early maturity found her, in consequence, possessed of an imperious desire for intellectual accomplishment, if superficially of a somewhat unlovely character. A mastery of the classics and modern languages, gained meanwhile, led to her appointment as teacher of Latin and French at Mr. Alcott's famous school in Boston, and later to a short teaching engagement in Providence, R. I.

When *The Dial,* the leading organ of Transcendentalism, was established in 1840, she was chosen as its editor, but resigned after two years' service to travel West. Upon her return, she settled in New York as literary editor of the *Tribune.* In 1847 she went to Italy, where she met and secretly married the Marquis d'Ossoli. While returning to New York with her husband and son in 1850, their ship sank just off Fire Island and she and her family, with nearly all on board, were lost.

Miss Fuller's range of interest was catholic, and her knowledge of literature remarkable. She was one of the important figures of the Transcendentalist movement, was one of the first to demand Women's Rights, and, with the exception of Poe, was undoubtedly the best American literary critic before Lowell.

THE DIAL. . . . 4 volumes or 16 numbers. July 1840 to April 1844, inclusive. Boston, 1840–1844.

WOMAN IN THE NINETEENTH CENTURY. New York, 1845.

PAPERS ON LITERATURE AND ART. 2 volumes, wrappers, or 2 volumes in one, cloth. New York, 1846.

PAGE, THOMAS NELSON
1853–1922

PAGE came of a prominent family in Hanover County, Virginia, and as a boy saw the last days of the "Old South." After graduating from Washington and Lee he established himself in Richmond as a lawyer. In his later years he served with distinction as Ambassador to Italy.

Page began his literary career as a poet, but found his true medium of expression in his first and perhaps his best short story, "Marse Chan," which was published in 1887 in "In Ole Virginia," a book that ranks among the better works of American fiction. He was the most idealistic and at the same time the most artistic portrayer of the "Old Régime," and his kindly pictures are among the pleasantest in our literature. He was essentially a short story writer. His talents were hardly calculated to handle a larger canvas and he never succeeded fully as a novelist. Even "Red Rock," fine as it is in conception, is weak in constructive art.

IN OLE VIRGINIA; OR, MARSE CHAN AND OTHER STORIES. New York, 1887.

TWO LITTLE CONFEDERATES. New York, 1888.

RED ROCK. A Chronicle of Reconstruction. New York, 1898.

The word "Illustrated," only, appears on the title page—not "with illustrations by," etc. The imprint of "Trow Directory" must appear on the title page. The decorations on the front cover are in brown and gold.

PAINE, Jr., ROBERT TREAT
1773–1811

PAINE, widely acclaimed in New England as the leading American poet of his day,—chiefly, perhaps, because he had no notable competitor—was born in Taunton, Mass., was graduated at Harvard, and practiced law in a sort of desultory way, while devoting himself to poetry and the stage. Though estranged from his family because of his marriage to an actress, and thereafter something of a social vagabond, he was called upon as poet for all sorts of public occasions.

Paine first became a celebrity with the appearance of his "Adams and Liberty," a patriotic song which in its original broadside form is rarely found. His odes and heroic verses, though in reality essentially labored, pompous and quite lacking in spontaneity, true sentiment or imagination, were at the time universally accepted as the outpourings of native genius.

THE WORKS IN PROSE AND VERSE OF THE LATE ROBERT TREAT PAINE, JUN., ESQ., WITH NOTES. . . . Boston, 1812.
Has a leaf of errata at the end.

PARSONS, THOMAS WILLIAM
1819–1892

DR. PARSONS was born in Boston where he was eventually established as a dentist. In 1836 and 1837 and again in 1847 he traveled extensively abroad. While in Italy he conceived an intense admiration for Dante, which resulted in his admirable translation of ten cantos of the "Inferno," published in 1843, followed by the publication of seventeen more cantos in 1865. In the first volume, also, appears an almost perfect bit of English verse—"On a Bust of Dante." A few of his other poems reach almost equal heights. He is one of the true minor poets of America.

(Anonymous) THE FIRST TEN CANTOS OF THE INFERNO OF DANTE ALIGHIERI, NEWLY TRANSLATED INTO ENGLISH VERSE. (Privately printed) Boston, 1843.

POEMS. Boston, 1854.

SEVENTEEN CANTOS OF THE INFERNO OF DANTE ALIGHIERI. (Privately printed). Boston, 1865.

PARTON, JAMES
1822–1891

PARTON, a prolific biographer of eminent Americans, was born in England, but was brought to New York at the age of four. After finishing his education he taught school for a time in White Plains and Philadelphia, and later became assistant to Willis on *The Mirror*. Following his marriage to Willis' estranged sister (infra) he resigned from *The Mirror* and retired to Newburyport, Mass., to devote himself to literary work.

Parton's reputation as a biographer has obscured the pioneer work he did in the juvenile field. Yet his was the first successful attempt to present biography to children in an attractive and entertaining form.

CAPTAINS OF INDUSTRY; OR MEN OF BUSINESS WHO DID SOMETHING BESIDES MAKING MONEY. A Book for Young Americans. Boston, 1884.

A second series was published in 1891.

PARTON, SARAH WILLIS
(Fanny Fern)
1811–1872

MRS. PARTON, the sister of N. P. Willis, in later life the wife of James Parton (supra), and the "Columnist" of the sentimental fifties, was born in Portland, Me., and educated at Hartford, Conn. She married an extravagant Boston banker, and, left at his death with two small children to support, began contributing to Boston newspapers under the nom-deplume of "Fanny Fern."

Eventually, after many rebuffs, she effected the publication of a collected edition of these sketches under the title "Fern Leaves from Fanny's Portfolio." As might be expected from the mood of the period, these were pleasant, guileless, consciously-cheery anecdotes, lacking of course any jarring profundity, and by the same token immensely popular.

FERN LEAVES FROM FANNY'S PORTFOLIO. By Fanny Fern. Auburn, 1853.
Later printings state the number of thousands on the title page.

PAULDING, JAMES KIRKE
1779–1860

THOUGH there were greater American authors no one writing before 1830 was more representative of the spirit of the new republic than Paulding. He was born and educated in Pawling, N. Y., so named in honor of one of his early ancestors. Later he moved to New York City, where for a time he lived with his brother-in-law, William Irving. It was there that he first met Irving's younger brother, Washington, and that the three collaborated in writing the then popular and now famous "Salmagundi" papers. Later still he was appointed Secretary of the Board of Naval Commissioners, and from that time on was prominent in public affairs, eventually serving as Secretary of the Navy from 1837 to 1841.

Most of Paulding's best known earlier writings were satirical essays in semi-narrative form—"John Bull and Brother Jonathan," his first book, and "John Bull in America" directed against Great Britain, and "Merry Tales of the Three Wise Men of Gotham" and "Chronicles of the City of Gotham," somewhat after the manner of Irving's "Knickerbocker History," playing up the city's public foibles and officials. Though at times heavy-handed, they display a ready wit and sound Americanism.

Paulding's most enduring works are probably his novels, notably his "Koningsmarke," a tale of the Swedish colonies, "Westward Ho!" a story of frontier Kentucky and "The Dutchman's Fireside," a picture of Colonial, up-state Dutch New York,—generally considered his masterpiece. Of his poetry not much that is favorable may be said. His best known poem is "The Backwoodsman," a long, narrative picture of life on the frontier. Beyond a few really fine descriptive passages, it has little to recommend it.

THE DIVERTING HISTORY OF JOHN BULL AND BROTHER JONATHAN. By Hector Bull-us. New York, 1812.

THE BACKWOODSMAN. A Poem. Philadelphia, 1818.

(Anonymous) KONINGSMARKE, THE LONG FINNE, A STORY OF THE NEW WORLD. 2 volumes. New York, 1823.

(Anonymous) JOHN BULL IN AMERICA; OR, THE NEW MUNCHAUSEN. New York, 1825.

THE MERRY TALES OF THE THREE WISE MEN OF GOTHAM. New York, 1826.

CHRONICLES OF THE CITY OF GOTHAM, FROM

THE PAPERS OF A RETIRED COMMON COUNCILMAN. . . . New York, 1830.

THE DUTCHMAN'S FIRESIDE. A Tale. 2 volumes. New York, 1831.

Later editions are so marked at the top of the title page.

WESTWARD HO! A Tale. 2 volumes. New York, 1832.

PAYNE, JOHN HOWARD
1792–1852

PAYNE, one of the best known dramatists of his day, was born in New York City, and early evidenced marked literary tendencies. His course at Union College was interrupted by his father's bankruptcy, and he was forced to turn to the stage. He toured the United States triumphantly, and, elated by his success, determined to go to England. Contrary to his expectation, the trip proved disastrous. Nevertheless, it was then that he composed the opera "Clari," in which his immortal song, "Home Sweet Home," first appeared.

CLARI; OR, THE MAID OF MILAN. An Opera in Three Acts. New York, 1823.

Also London, 1823, probably prior.

PECK, GEORGE WILBUR
1840–1916

PECK was born in Henderson, N. Y., but became a resident of Wisconsin at the age of three. As a young man he learned the printer's trade, and later became half owner of a newspaper, *The Jefferson County Republican.* He served during the Civil War as a private, after its close returned to journalism, and presently became owner of *Peck's Sun.* He was mayor of Milwaukee in 1890 and 1891, and governor of Wisconsin from 1891 to 1895.

"Peck's Bad Boy," reprinted from the files of the *Sun,* is straightforward slap-stick comedy. It is, and perhaps should be, remembered with affection by a host of former boys, now grown; but it is not literature.

PECK'S BAD BOY. Chicago, 1883.
The first edition bears the imprint of Belford, Clark & Co., and has thirty-six chapters only.

PECK, SAMUEL MINTURN
1854–

PECK was born in Tuscaloosa, Ala., and educated at the University of his native state. Following a classic precedent, at the age of twenty-five he determined to devote himself exclusively to farming and to literature. Though he has written nothing of great consequence, much of his light verse is polished, melodious and charming.

CAP AND BELLS. New York, 1886.

PERCIVAL, JAMES GATES
1795–1856

EVEN a partial list of Percival's varied accomplishments must include poetry, medicine, geology, botany, language and music. He was born in Berlin (?), Conn., and after graduation from Yale began the practice of medicine. Later he was for a time professor of chemistry at West Point, assisted Noah Webster in the preparation of his dictionary and did notable geological work in various places. The practice of his varied professions led him in due course to residence in Boston, Philadelphia, Charleston, S. C. and Wisconsin, as well as in his native Connecticut.

Percival's versatility seems clearly to have militated against the full development of his poetic gifts; but for his lack of concentration he would have attained high rank. He wrote fluently, but haste and diffuseness too often marred his work. Yet on a few occasions, as in "Seneca Lake" and "The Coral Grove," he struck a note of rare brilliance.

POEMS. New Haven, 1821.

CLIO NO. I. Charleston, 1822.

CLIO NO. II. New Haven, 1822.

CLIO NO. III. New Haven, 1827.

"The Coral Grove" appears in No. II.

THE DREAM OF A DAY AND OTHER POEMS. New Haven, 1843.

PHELPS, ELIZABETH STUART
1815–1852

ELIZABETH STUART (Phelps), a native of Andover, Mass., was the mother of Elizabeth Stuart Phelps Ward, the author of "The Gates Ajar." She was, in a very limited sense, a pioneer, and her "Sunnyside," though not a great work, was a slight improvement upon the average weepy fiction of her feminine contemporaries.

THE SUNNYSIDE; OR THE COUNTRY MINISTER'S WIFE. Philadelphia, The American Sunday School Union, (1851). Frontispiece.

142 pages. All copies so far observed bear a

note opposite the copyright page in which it is stated that "The present edition has been revised and enlarged by the author."

PIATT, JOHN JAMES
1835–1917

PIATT, a native of Dearborn County, Ind., and a well-known Mid-Western journalist and poet, was at one time associated with Louisville and Cincinnati papers, and later served as United States consul at Dublin, Ireland.

It is a matter of bibliographical interest that he collaborated with Howells in "Poems of Two Friends" (1860), which is commonly accepted as the latter's first literary effort. In his own work Piatt turned to America for his inspiration. His poems are for the most part descriptive of familiar scenes and incidents. There is art in them, but there is little fire. He was too much under the influence of the classicists to have attained the heights of which he appears to have been capable.

POEMS IN SUNSHINE AND FIRELIGHT. Cincinnati, 1866.

The copyright entry date of 1863 is probably an error; the preface is dated 1865.

PIERPONT, JOHN
1785–1866

THOUGH never rising to great heights, Pierpont may be regarded as one of the true poets of the early nineteenth century. He was born in Litchfield, Conn., entered Yale and after graduation tried his hand at tutoring, law and business.

Abandoning these in quick succession, he was ordained in the ministry in 1819, and for twenty-six years thereafter resided in Boston. During the Civil War he served in the Department of the Treasury at Washington.

Pierpont's literary work consisted of contributions to magazines and annuals, several Sunday School books, and various discourses. His poetic output was small. His first work, "Airs of Palestine," appeared in 1816 and proved popular enough to call for several reprintings, but it is interesting now chiefly as clearly marking the breaking away from the imitative school of Dwight and his followers. One or two of the forceful "Other Poems," for example, "Warren's Address," which appeared in the 1840 "Airs of Palestine," display his talents to better advantage.

Airs of Palestine; A Poem. Baltimore, 1816.

Airs of Palestine, and other Poems. Boston, 1840.

Two variations have been noted, one with an extra engraved title, untrimmed edges and reading "Pierpont's Poetical Works" on the backstrip, one without the engraved title, trimmed edges stained red and reading "Pierpont's Poems" on the backstrip.

PIKE, ALBERT
1809–1891

General Pike was a Bostonian, who, after a short student experience at Harvard and as a school teacher, traveled extensively in the South and West, and finally settled in Arkansas. He was prominently identified both as a journalist and lawyer with the development of his adopted state, and was a leading spirit in the establishment of Masonry in the South. His earlier military experience as a captain of cavalry during the Mexican War was supplemented by a more distinguished service as a general in the Confederate army.

Pike was the most important early literary representative of his immediate section. He was the author not only of the well known poems, "Hymns to the Gods," "To a Mocking Bird" and "Dixie," * but also of a series of fine sketches and tales, which are among the most valuable records of Southwestern life written in the early days.

PROSE SKETCHES AND POEMS WRITTEN IN THE WESTERN COUNTRY. Boston, 1834.

NUGAE. Philadelphia, 1854.
Printed for private circulation.

HYMNS TO THE GODS AND OTHER POEMS. No place, 1873.
Privately printed.
There is also a privately printed edition of the title poem, no place, no date. Such presentation copies of this as have been observed bear a presentation dating later than 1873.

PINCKNEY, EDWARD COOTE
1802–1828

PINCKNEY, a man of great native talent and distinguished lineage, was born in London at the time when his father was serving as ambassador to Great Britain. He received his early schooling in Baltimore. In 1816 he was appointed a midshipman in the Navy. He subsequently studied law, was admitted to the bar in 1824 and two years later became

* Pike's version differs considerably from Dan Emmett's. Of the two it is the better, but it has never equaled Emmett's in popularity.

editor of *The Maryland.* He died the following year, at the age of twenty-six.

Pinckney's literary reputation rests upon a single volume of "Poems" and on the ephemeral "Rodolph," published originally in 1823 for his intimates. Yet, meager as his output was, it stamped him as a poet of real power. The beauty of such songs as "Serenade" and "A Health" is undeniable.

POEMS. Baltimore, 1825.

POE, EDGAR ALLAN

1809–1849

WHEN Poe was born his parents, second rate actors, were playing at a Boston theatre. At the age of three he was left an orphan, and was adopted by John Allan, a tobacco merchant of Richmond, Va. He received his early schooling in England, and when barely seventeen entered the University of Virginia. Heavy gambling debts which he contracted at college led to a quarrel with his foster father, and Poe, in high dudgeon ran away to Boston, where, after arranging for the publication of his immature "Tamerlane," he enlisted in the Army. A letter written to Mr. Allan, following Mrs. Allan's death in 1829, led to a temporary reconciliation, during which Mr. Allan secured him an appointment to West Point. But his cadetship was short-lived. He was presently dismissed under conditions which resulted in a complete estrangement.

From West Point Poe went to New York, where he published his "Poems" (1831), and presently to Baltimore, where he lived with his kindly aunt, Mrs. Clemm, while engaged in literary hack work. Subsequently, having won a prize for his "M.S. Found in a Bottle," through the good offices of J. P. Kennedy he secured an important position on the *Southern Literary Messenger,* which prospered under his direction. The loss of this position through dissipation, following his marriage to his cousin Virginia

Clemm, drove him to New York, where he published "The Narrative of Arthur Gordon Pym." The following six years found him in Philadelphia, again, for the most part, engaged in hack work, interspersed with editorial work on *Burton's* and *Graham's* magazines, from both of which he was dismissed.

In 1844 he returned to New York, where Willis made a place for him on *The Mirror*. In 1845 he became the editor and proprietor of *The Broadway Journal* but the publication shortly failed, leaving him in debt, and he spent the next two years in destitution. His wife's death followed in 1847, and after a short interval he went desperately to work to mend his fortunes. The next two years were years of hectic effort, interrupted by a series of courtships and periods of dissipation. On October 3, 1849, he was found in serious condition in the rear of a barroom in Baltimore, and was taken to a hospital. Four days later he died.

The controversy waged over Poe's character has elicited all shades of opinion. Suffice it to say that, despite his undeniable dissipations, he sincerely loved his wife and was held in high esteem by Mrs. Clemm.

Poe was the first of our writers to lay down rules for the short story, which he considered the typical American literary form, the first to apply scientific methods to literary criticism, the first fully to develop the theory that poetry is in itself a thing of beauty. His great appeal lies in his imaginative quality—his power to hold his reader in suspense. The perfection of his tales and the almost uncanny melody of his best lyrics are due to his habit of constant and merciless revision. Few, if any, dispute his eminence in the world of letters.

TAMERLANE AND OTHER POEMS. By a Bostonian. Boston, 1827.

AL AARAAF TAMERLANE AND MINOR POEMS. Baltimore, 1829.

A very few copies were printed misdated 1820 on the title page.

POEMS. . . . Second Edition. New York, 1831.

THE NARRATIVE OF ARTHUR GORDON PYM OF NANTUCKET. . . . New York, 1838.

TALES OF THE GROTESQUE AND ARABESQUE. 2 volumes. Philadelphia, 1840.

Only seven hundred and fifty copies in all were originally printed. There is one known copy in which page 213 in Volume 2 is misnumbered 231.

THE PROSE ROMANCES OF EDGAR A. POE. . . . No. 1 Containing The Murders in the Rue Morgue and The Man that was used up. Philadelphia, 1843.

Though numbered 1, this is the only number that was published.

THE RAVEN AND OTHER POEMS. New York, 1845.

TALES. New York, 1845.

This is sometimes bound together, in cloth, with "The Raven."

EUREKA: A PROSE POEM. New York, 1848.

PRENTICE, GEORGE DENISON
1802–1870

PRENTICE was born in Providence and educated at Brown University. For several years after his graduation he was editor of the *New England Weekly Review*. He later moved to Louisville, Ky., where he edited the *Louisville Journal*.

It was from the files of the latter that the widely quoted

quips, later collected as "Prenticeana," were taken. Largely political in their nature, these sallies and bons-mots have lost much of their original zest. Yet they well reflect the viewpoint and spirit of their times.

PRENTICEANA, OR WIT AND HUMOR IN PARAGRAPHS. By the Editor of the Louisville Journal. New York, 1860.

PRESTON, MARGARET JUNKIN
1825–1897

MRS. PRESTON, the daughter of the Rev. George Junkin, founder of Lafayette College and later President of Washington College, though born in Philadelphia, was a true Southerner. She was a sister-in-law of Stonewall Jackson, herself a friend of Lee, and the wife of one of the most prominent members of the latter's staff. Her husband was at one time a professor at the Virginia Military Institute.

Mrs. Preston had made her first appeal and gained some recognition as a fiction writer prior to her marriage in 1857. But a greater popularity came to her through the poetry which she published during the Civil War. "Beechenbrook," to some extent a work of spiritual intensity but of conventional outlook, was hailed as a classic in the South. It warrants no such praise, however, even though it once caused her to be styled the "Greatest Southern Poetess."

BEECHENBROOK; A RHYME OF THE WAR. Richmond, 1865.

This is one of the very few works of belles-lettres bearing a Confederate imprint.

CARTOONS. Boston, 1875.

PYLE, HOWARD
1853—1911

Pyle was born in Wilmington, Del., was educated privately, and later studied art at the Philadelphia Art School and the Art Students' League of New York. He subsequently entered business, devoting his evenings to drawing. Success attained, after several years of New York residence, he returned to Wilmington.

His recognized ability as an illustrator has obscured his real distinction as an author. His writings furnish a pleasing background for his artistic work and at least once he wrote a children's classic, "The Merry Adventures of Robin Hood."

The Merry Adventures of Robin Hood. New York, 1883.

Within the Capes. New York, 1885.

Men of Iron. New York, 1892.
Measures 1-1/16 inches across the top of covers.

RANDALL, JAMES RYDER
1839—1903

Randall was born in Baltimore, and entered Georgetown University at the age of ten. He left college in his senior year, and went to Louisiana as professor of English in Poydras College. He enlisted in the Confederate army at the outbreak of the Civil War, but was discharged as unfit. In 1865 he joined the staff of the *Atlanta Constitution,* and eventually became its editor-in-chief.

His poem "Maryland, My Maryland" has been called the "Marseillaise" of the Confederacy. When first sung after the battle of Bull Run, it took its audience by storm, and from that time it was one of the great war songs of the South. Though not published in a collected edition until shortly after Randall's death, it may properly be classed as pre-1900 and included here as one of the most important martial poems in American literature.

Maryland, My Maryland and Other Poems. Baltimore, J. Murphy, (1908).
The title poem was first published as a song by Blackmar, in New Orleans, in 1862.

READ, OPIE
1852–

Read was born in Nashville, Tenn., and began his career as a newspaper man in Franklin, Ky. He was engaged in journalistic work until 1891, when he moved to Chicago and devoted himself exclusively to writing. Read is in some respects a later Roe, a popularizer of the novel, but an author of no great distinction—unless it be that of furnishing best sellers to the railroad trains.

A Kentucky Colonel. Chicago, 1890.

READ, THOMAS BUCHANAN
1822–1872

Read was born in Chester, Pa. He began his career in a tailor shop, ran away to Philadelphia, became a sign painter, drifted to Cincinnati and eventually made an enviable reputation as a portrait painter and writer. His work is of second rank, spirited only on occasion, and seldom well sustained. He is remembered chiefly for his Civil War verses, especially "Sheridan's Ride," and for his epic of the Revolutionary period, "The Wagoner of the Alleghanies."

THE WAGONER OF THE ALLEGHANIES, A POEM OF THE DAYS OF SEVENTY-SIX. Philadelphia, 1862.

A SUMMER STORY, SHERIDAN'S RIDE, AND OTHER POEMS. Philadelphia, 1865.

Page 75, line 2 must read "Bringing from;" later corrected to "Bringing to."

REMINGTON, FREDERIC
1861–1909

REMINGTON, the foremost depicter with brush and chisel of the cowboy and the Indian, and an author of ability, was born in Canton, N. Y. He attended Yale for a time, but left college following his father's death and went to work as a clerk in a country store. Finding a mercantile career too tame he went West, became in turn a cowboy, sheep rancher and scout, and wandered over the entire western half of the continent. Before he was thirty, he had gained wide recognition for his pictures of the rancher, fur trader and Indian, and his exhibitions were favorably received both here and abroad. He later turned to sculpture, and won an equal reputation in that field.

Though other men have done more notable and important literary work in his chosen field than Remington, his studies of the West are illuminating and in combination with his art entitle him to a distinctive place.

PONY TRACKS. New York, 1895.

REPPLIER, AGNES
1855–

Miss Repplier was born and educated in Philadelphia, and has been a frequent contributor to the *Saturday Evening Post* and other periodicals. She is an essayist and critic of real attainment. Her work is characterized by a light touch, keen humor and occasional biting irony.

Books and Men. Boston, 1888.

RICHARDS, LAURA E(LIZABETH) HOWE
1850–

Mrs. Richards is the daughter of Julia Ward Howe. In 1871 she married Mr. Henry Richards of Gardiner, Me., where she now resides. She is the author of a number of pleasing juveniles—the best known of them her "Captain January."

The Joyous Story of Toto. Boston, 1885.
Captain January. Boston, 1891.

RILEY, JAMES WHITCOMB
1849–1916

Riley has been called the "People's Laureate," and in a measure he deserves the title. He was a native of Greenfield, Ind., the son of a lawyer, and himself dedicated to law by parental decree. After leaving school he ran away and became in turn a sign painter, patent medicine vendor and actor. Before long he began contributing to the *Indianapolis Journal* and his dialect poems quickly brought him national recognition.

If one is to accept unqualifiedly the opinion of the critics, Riley is neither a great nor a good poet. He is accused of having prostituted real powers, abetted by a facile sense of rhythm, to the pleasing of the multitude. Possibly he did. But no contemporary equaled the popularity he attained through such poems as "The Old Swimmin' Hole," "When the Frost is on the Punkin," "The Elf Child" ("Little Orphan Annie") and "A Life-Lesson." Despite the critics, he seems destined to retain his place as a favorite of the people.

THE OLD SWIMMIN' HOLE AND 'LEVEN MORE POEMS. By Benj. F. Johnson, of Boone. Indianapolis, 1883.
  The facsimile (1909) edition lacks the "W" in "William" on page 41.

CHARACTER SKETCHES, THE BOSS GIRL, A CHRISTMAS STORY, AND OTHER SKETCHES. Indianapolis, 1886.
  A few advance copies were bound in dark brown wrappers. The regular issue is in light brown wrappers, with a design by Booth Tarkington. Cloth copies are later.

AFTERWHILES. Indianapolis, 1888.

RHYMES OF CHILDHOOD. Indianapolis, 1891.

POEMS HERE AT HOME. New York, 1893.

ROBINSON, EDWIN ARLINGTON
1869– 1935

ROBINSON, whom many consider the leading present-day American poet, was born in Gardiner, Me., and educated at Harvard. He is conceded to have grown steadily in poetic power with maturing years, and by the same token to have reached his heights after 1900. Even so, his first two books are a distinguished contribution to our literature.

THE TORRENT AND THE NIGHT BEFORE. Riverside Press. Gardiner, Maine, 1896.

Printed for the author; reprinted in New York in 1928.

THE CHILDREN OF THE NIGHT. Boston, 1897.

Five hundred copies on Batchworth laid paper, and fifty copies on Japan vellum represent the entire edition.

ROBINSON, ROWLAND EVANS
1833–1900

VERMONT in particular and the United States in general are indebted to Rowland E. Robinson for admirable pictures of his native state. His tales are told with a minute attention to the details of life in a past era, and abound in touches of typical Yankee humor and homely Vermont philosophy. "Uncle 'Lisha's Shop," in particular, merits far more attention than it has yet received.

UNCLE 'LISHA'S SHOP. Life in a Corner of Yankeeland. New York, 1887.

ROE, EDWARD PAYSON
1838–1888

DR. ROE, perhaps the most widely read fiction writer of his day, was born in New York. He was educated at Williams and served as a chaplain in the Northern army during the Civil War. Following its close, he devoted himself for a few years to the ministry, but, owing to serious illness, was presently obliged to give up his profession. He spent the latter part of his life at Cornwall-on-Hudson, where he devoted himself to farming and novel writing.

Despite the extreme contemporary popularity of Dr. Roe's novels, they cannot be called real literature. They are too much of the same pattern, too deficient in construction and imagination. Yet it stands to his credit that he did his work conscientiously, and that he stuck to the humble, fundamental facts of life. This, and his carefully disguised sensationalism, are the explanation of his popularity. There is little choice between his "Barriers Burned Away," "Opening a Chestnut Burr" and "Without a Home," though the first is probably the best known.

BARRIERS BURNED AWAY. New York, 1872.

OPENING A CHESTNUT BURR. New York, Dodd & Mead, (1874).

Five hundred and sixty-one pages.

WITHOUT A HOME. New York, 1881.

(ROHLFS) GREEN, ANNA KATHARINE
1846–

MRS. ROHLFS was born in Brooklyn, but after her marriage to Charles Rohlfs of New York City took up her residence in Buffalo. She was the first American to write a "modern" detective novel. "The Leavenworth Case" appeared in 1878. It was a work of genuine pioneering, and for lack of any model failed of complete structural excellence. Yet, though Mrs. Rohlfs herself improved upon it later, nothing can deprive it of the honor of being the forerunner of the endless stream of imitations which have since flooded the country.

THE LEAVENWORTH CASE; A LAWYER'S STORY. New York, 1878.

ROOSEVELT, THEODORE
1858–1919

ROOSEVELT's dramatic and strenuous career from cowpuncher to President is too well known to call for even outline here. His literary activities are much less widely recognized; yet he wrote in all over five thousand books and pamphlets, indicating a remarkable catholicity of interest and a prodigious intellectual energy.

Even before 1900 he had made notable contributions to American history with his "Naval War of 1812" and his "Winning of the West," and to the literature of the "strenuous life" with his "Ranch Life and the Hunting Trail." His charming and intensely human "Letters to His Children," revealing yet another side of his rich nature, was published almost immediately following his death.

RANCH LIFE AND THE HUNTING TRAIL. Illustrated by Remington. New York, (1888).
Correct copies have gilt edges, and are bound in light tan buckram, stamped with green and gold.

AMERICAN IDEALS AND OTHER ESSAYS. New York, 1897.

ROOT, GEORGE FREDERICK
1820–1895

ROOT, the most popular song writer of the Civil War period, was born in Springfield, Mass. He was interested in music from his early boyhood days and, after teaching for a few years in his native city, became prominent in his profession in New York City. In 1860 he moved to Chicago, where he subsequently lived. He received the degree of Doctor of Music from Chicago University.

WAR SONGS. Words and Music by George F. Root, Henry C. Work, and Walter Kittredge. . . . Boston, J. Knight Company, (1890).

Contains "Tramp, Tramp, Tramp," "Marching Through Georgia," etc.

ROWSON, SUSANNAH
1762–1824

MRS. ROWSON was born in England, but at the age of seven accompanied her father to America, where she remained until the outbreak of the Revolution. Returning to England, she married a bandmaster of the Royal Guards in 1786, and six years later emigrated with him to the United States. For three years following her arrival she played at a theatre in Philadelphia, but eventually she settled near Boston, where she taught school until her death in 1824.

Mrs. Rowson was the author of several novels, only two of which, "Charlotte" and "Reuben and Rachel," command attention. Though inevitably smacking of the stilted manner of the period, they are comparatively simple and direct. The former, the story of an English girl lured to New York by a British officer and abandoned, largely because of its sensational nature, and partially perhaps because of its seeming realism, became immensely popular under its later title, "Charlotte Temple." It was reprinted in endless editions, and can justly be called the first "best seller" published in America.

CHARLOTTE: A TALE OF TRUTH. 2 volumes. Philadelphia, MDCCXCIV.

The second American edition appeared in the same year as the first American, 1794, but has the words "Second Edition" on the title page, and the dating is Philadelphia, 1794 (Arabic numerals). A London, 1791, edition was unquestionably published, but no copy has ever been located.

REUBEN AND RACHEL; OR, TALES OF OLD TIMES. A Novel. Boston, 1798.

RUSH, REBECCA
(Dates unknown)

MISS RUSH, a native and resident of Philadelphia, was the author of "Kelroy," one of the first novels of social manners written in America. Though not devoid of the moralizing tendencies of its predecessors, it is a definite advance over the extreme didacticism of the earlier feminine literature.

KELROY, A NOVEL; BY A LADY OF PENNSYLVANIA. Philadelphia, 1812.

RUSSELL, IRWIN
1853–1879

RUSSELL, a native of Gibson, Miss., after a short and pathetic life, due, as Joel Chandler Harris feelingly says, to "the waywardness of genius," died in New Orleans at the age of twenty-six. With his passing America lost a poet of great promise.

"He was among the first—if not the very first—", as Harris notes, . . . "to appreciate the literary possibilities of the

Negro character" and to treat it with fidelity and understanding. Such stanzas as "Precepts at Parting" are genuine contributions to native American letters, and "Christmas Night in the Quarters" is one of our very few great poems of humble life. It is one of the ironies of authorship that a book like Russell's "Poems," so well entitled to stand upon its own merits, should be frequently exploited as among the minor works of a distinguished author, who, in deep appreciation of it, wrote its preface.

Poems. New York, The Century Co., (1888).
The first edition measures 7/16 inches, scant, across the top of covers, has gilt figured end papers, and is 7-5/16 inches tall.

RYAN, ABRAM JOSEPH
1839–1886

Abram Joseph Ryan, a Catholic priest, immediately following the Civil War, and in a measure by reason of its inspiration, became one of the most popular of the Southern poets. He was born in Norfolk, Virginia, and was educated in St. Louis and at the ecclesiastical seminary at Niagara, N. Y. Following the Civil War, in which he performed heroic service as a chaplain in the Confederate army, he resided temporarily in Tennessee and Georgia, but finally settled in Mobile, Ala., where he remained until failing health obliged him to spend his last three years in a monastery.

Poetry, with Father Ryan, was a matter of inspiration and not of studied effort, as witness the fact that his "Conquered Banner"—the greatest poem of the Lost Cause, composed immediately after Lee's surrender—was finished in one hour. Had he written nothing but this and "The Sword of Robert Lee," his fame would be secure.

Father Ryan's Poems. Mobile, 1879.

SALTUS, EDGAR EVERTSON
1858–1921

SALTUS, a native of New York, was educated at Heidelberg, Munich, the Sorbonne and the Columbia Law School. He began writing in 1884, and the next year brought out the first of two popular expositions of Schopenhauer's teachings, "The Philosophy of Disenchantment." The second, "The Anatomy of Negation," appeared in 1886.

Saltus' reputation as a novelist exceeds his fame as a philosopher. His fiction, dealing for the most part with high society and its manners, justifies his placement among the constructive forces of the new realism, though it hardly entitles him to a major rating. "Mr. Incoul's Misadventure" is generally conceded to be his best work.

MR. INCOUL'S MISADVENTURE. A Novel. New York, 1887.

It is said that copics of thc first cdition havc green end papers, but some copies lack them that have all the other indications of priority. The verso of the leaf of publisher's advertisements is blank, the advertisements themselves containing no mention of "Sea Spray."

MARY MAGDALEN A CHRONICLE. New York, Belford, (1891).

IMPERIAL PURPLE. Chicago, 1892.

SANDS, ROBERT C(HARLES)
1799–1832

A NATIVE New Yorker, a man of brilliant promise and a close friend of Bryant, Sands graduated from Columbia in 1815, immediately took up the study of law, and was admitted to the bar in 1820. Meanwhile, he published several poems and contributed variously to current magazines. After 1820 he engaged in editorial work, working with Bryant on the *New York Review, The Talisman* and "Tales of Glauber Spa," and assisting on the *New York Commercial Advertiser.*

There is no denying Sands' real talent, though its expression was limited by his narrow environment. His verse is not important, but his well-handled short stories and sketches like "A Simple Tale" and "Scenes at Washington" reveal him as a writer of real accomplishment.

THE WRITINGS OF ROBERT C. SANDS, IN PROSE AND VERSE. With a Memoir of the Author. 2 volumes. Portrait. New York, 1834.

SANTAYANA, GEORGE
1863–

SANTAYANA, one of the leading minds of present-day philosophy, is a Spaniard by birth, but came to the United States at the age of nine. He was graduated at Harvard in 1886, and, after a period of further study in Europe, taught philosophy at his Alma Mater until 1912, when he resigned to devote himself to literature.

From the beginning Santayana's work has been progressively distinguished, culminating since 1900 in some of the finest thinking yet done in America. Noted as he is as a philosopher, he is only less finished as a poet. His "Sonnets" are among the best in our literature.

SONNETS AND OTHER VERSES. Cambridge, 1894.

SARGENT, EPES
1813–1880

Sargent, a man of indefatigable energy, was a native of Gloucester, Mass. He entered Harvard, but left before his junior year to become associated with S. G. Goodrich on *The Token* and *Peter Parley's Magazine.* From these he graduated, progressively, to the editorship of several newspapers, among them the *Boston Advertiser* and *Boston Transcript.* He was a profound student, a sometime brilliant editor, the compiler of a vast number of readers, spellers and other school books, the author of several unimportant novels, dramas, and books of verse and of one famous poem, "A Life on the Ocean Wave."

Songs of the Sea, with Other Poems. Boston, 1847.

SAXE, JOHN GODFREY
1816–1887

Saxe, an author who has sunk into undeserved obscurity, was born in Highgate, a country hamlet of Vermont. He was educated in the district schools and in St. Albans, and graduated from Middlebury College at the age of twenty-three. He was admitted to the St. Albans bar in 1843, and four years later was elected Superintendent of Schools. In 1850 he entered journalism through the purchase of the *Burlington Sentinel,* which he continued to edit until 1872, when he joined the editorial staff of the *Albany Evening Journal.* His last years were passed in almost complete seclusion—a victim of distressing periods of melancholia, occasioned by the death of his wife, three daughters and a son.

Saxe came into prominence as a writer during the forties, through his contributions to various magazines and his own separate publications—most notably, perhaps, with the publication of his poem, "The Proud Miss McBride," ("Poems," 1850). He wrote with a deft and skillful touch, and next to Holmes was the best and most popular writer of humorous (and satirical) verse of his day.

POEMS. Boston, 1850.

THE MONEY-KING AND OTHER POEMS. Boston, 1860.

THE MASQUERADE AND OTHER POEMS. Boston, 1866.

SCOLLARD, CLINTON
1866–

SCOLLARD was born in Clinton, N. Y., was educated at Hamilton and Harvard, traveled extensively in Europe, and later became Professor of English and Rhetoric at Hamilton College. He is a poet of some pretensions, a pleasing writer of light verse, and, though lacking depth, has been justly praised for his lyric ability and his real mastery of technique.

WITH REED AND LYRE. Boston, D. Lothrop & Company, (1886).

SEDGWICK, CATHARINE MARIA
1789–1867

PERHAPS the best of the early feminine American novelists was Catharine Maria Sedgwick, of Stockbridge, Mass. She received an excellent education, and after her father's death opened a girls' school in her native town. For the next half century she gave her best energies to the cause of feminine education, finding time, however, for a vast amount of literary work in contributing to and editing a number of publications and annuals, and writing several novels, juveniles and travel sketches.

She commenced her literary career, under the stimulus of her brother's encouragement, with the publication of "A New England Tale," in 1822. Its favorable reception led her on to "Redwood"—contemporarily her most popular but not her finest novel. "Hope Leslie" followed, without doubt the best tale of early Massachusetts which had yet appeared. By common consent, however, she is conceded to have reached her heights in 1835, with the appearance of "The Linwoods," a Revolutionary story which Poe pronounced the best novel written by an American "female."

The conventional feminine point of view of her day is present in all of Miss Sedgwick's work, but her skill at depicting men and manners and her dramatic powers are undeniable. She can by no means be compared to Cooper. Nevertheless her position among the women writers of America is analogous to his among the men.

(Anonymous) A NEW-ENGLAND TALE; OR, SKETCHES OF NEW-ENGLAND CHARACTER AND MANNERS. New York, 1822.

(Anonymous) REDWOOD; A TALE. 2 volumes. New York, 1824.

An errata note appears at the end of Volume 2.

HOPE LESLIE; OR EARLY TIMES IN THE MASSACHUSETTS. 2 volumes. New York, 1827.

In the fourth and fifth lines on page 232 of Volume 1 the word "to" is repeated; in the second line of page 86 in Volume 2 the word "it" is repeated.

THE LINWOODS; OR, "SIXTY YEARS SINCE" IN AMERICA. 2 volumes. New York, 1835.

SEDGWICK, SUSAN (RIDLEY)
1789–1867

MRS. SEDGWICK, the wife of a prominent Stockbridge, Mass., lawyer and the sister-in-law of Catharine Maria Sedgwick, was the author of several books for young people, among them "The Young Emigrants," the story of the adventures of a New York family which emigrated to Ohio. Mrs. Sedgwick could not at times refrain from preaching a bit of a sermon. Nevertheless, "The Young Emigrants" stands in solitary state as, up to the time of its appearance, the only American story written for the young which by any stretch of the imagination could have given them pleasure. The well-thumbed appearance of copies of the scarce original edition attest its popularity.

(Anonymous) THE YOUNG EMIGRANTS. A Tale Designed for Young People. Boston, 1830.

SETON, ERNEST THOMPSON
1860–

ERNEST THOMPSON SETON, originally Ernest Seton Thompson, was born in Durham, England, and was educated at the Royal Academy in London. He emigrated to Manitoba, Canada, and eventually became official naturalist for that province. He is now a resident of the United States.

Seton is a good story teller, but, in his more popular studies, has a tendency to humanize his animals beyond the bounds of natural history. Nevertheless, his sympathetic treatment has done much to foster a kindlier feeling toward dumb life, and in so doing it has performed a universal service.

WILD ANIMALS . . . I HAVE KNOWN. . . . New York, 1898.

The words "And the Angel said, 'Don't go'!" must not be present in the last paragraph on page 265.

SEWALL, JONATHAN MITCHELL
1748–1808

Sewall, a nephew and adopted son of Chief Justice Sewall of Massachusetts and himself a lawyer, was born in Salem, Mass., but later moved to Portsmouth, N. H. He left but one work of literary interest, his "Miscellaneous Poems," which, with its renditions of Ossian, evidences the author's scholarly proclivities. His other published verse concerns itself with the character or public acts of Washington.

Miscellaneous Poems, with Several Specimens from the Author's Manuscript Version of the Poems of Ossian. . . . Portsmouth: Printed for the Author, 1801.

SHAW, HENRY WHEELER
(Josh Billings)
1818–1885

Shaw was born in Lanesborough, Mass., but went West when he was fourteen and for years led an irregular life as a deck hand, school teacher, storekeeper and auctioneer. His writings passed unnoticed until the "Essa on the Mule" appeared in 1860. In 1865 he became editor of a Poughkeepsie, N. Y., paper, to which he contributed articles signed "Josh Billings." Thereafter his fame spread rapidly, and he soon gained national recognition as a witty lecturer and writer.

Shaw used the common trick of his trade, misspelling—perfected by Artemus Ward. He lacked the latter's subtlety; but he possessed sufficient talent to rank as one of the few American humorists having a genuine claim upon posterity.

JOSH BILLINGS: HIS SAYINGS. With Comic Illustrations. New York, 1866.

The backstrip reads "Josh Billings his Book."

JOSH BILLINGS' FARMERS' ALLMINAX. Published annually, New York, 1870–1879, inclusive.

SHERMAN, FRANK DEMPSTER
1860–1916

SHERMAN was a native of Poughkeepsie, a graduate of the Columbia School of Architecture, and later a professor of Graphics. He lacked imagination, yet measurably supplied its place with technical skill.

MADRIGALS AND CATCHES. New York, 1887.

LYRICS FOR A LUTE. Boston, 1890.

SHILLABER, BENJAMIN PENHALLOW
(Mrs. Partington)
1814–1890

SHILLABER, an editor for ten years of the *Boston Post,* and later the owner of the comic *Carpet Bag,* was born in Portsmouth, N. H. He was widely popular in his day as a humorist, but his wit is rather crude and his writings cannot qualify as literature. He does, however, display a knowledge of small town society.

Life and Sayings of Mrs. Partington and Others of the Family. New York, 1854.

SIGOURNEY, LYDIA (HUNTLEY)
1791–1865

Mrs. Sigourney, one of the first protagonists of higher education for women in America, shared honors with Mrs. Willard as a pioneer in that field, yet she stopped short of the latter in believing that women should be properly trained to take their independent place in the world only in case of adversity —maintaining stoutly that a woman's true mission was to rear her children, rather than to "thunder in Senates."

Mrs. Sigourney was born in Norwich, Conn. She was a precocious child, learning to read at the age of three and writing verse at eight. She taught school in Norwich for a time, and later, with an intimate girl friend, in Hartford. She was married in Hartford in 1819, and resided there until her death.

She was the author of over fifty books and at least two thousand magazine articles—poetry, juveniles, sketches and essays—and the editor of various religious and juvenile publications. She was the most popular feminine poet of her generation, and perhaps the best. Her verse was typical of the sentimentality of the times—its piety and pathos the qualities most responsible for its former host of admirers both here and abroad.

Poems. Philadelphia, 1834.
Has a preliminary leaf of errata.

SILL, EDWARD ROWLAND
1841–1887

Though Sill is regarded as a Western poet, he was born and educated in Windsor, Conn., and went to the Coast only when failing health necessitated a change of climate. His continued residence there, however, was a matter of election, and the West was undeniably the inspiration of much of his best work.

Sill was introspective and remote—his chief literary limitation a tendency to didacticism. Yet enough of his verse has sufficient purity and spiritual beauty to entitle him to recognition as, next to Miller, the best of the nineteenth century Western poets.

THE HERMITAGE AND OTHER POEMS. San Francisco, 1868.
This was republished later the same year with a New York imprint.

POEMS. Boston, 1888.

SIMMS, WILLIAM GILMORE
1806–1870

SIMMS, unquestionably the leading novelist of the old South, was born in Charleston, S. C., and, after spending most of his boyhood in Missouri, returned to his native state to be admitted to the bar. His love of letters—he had already published two volumes of poems—led him speedily to an editorial connection with the *Charleston Gazette,* which was the real beginning of his literary career. Simms was a prolific novelist until the fifties, when his interest in the slavery question led largely to an abandonment of fiction and an active participation as pamphleteer and orator in the Southern cause. His fortunes were shattered by the Civil War; he died engaged in a valiant attempt to restore them, shortly after the conclusion of peace.

Simms' first novel, "Martin Faber," was published in 1833; his second, "Guy Rivers," an excellent story of the Georgia gold rush, in 1834. What is undoubtedly his best work of fiction, a story of the Yemassee Indian War, followed in 1835. In the same year, also, appeared "The Partisan," the first of his Revolutionary series, which further included "Mellichampe," "The Kinsman," "Katharine Walton," "The Sword and the Distaff," "The Forayers" and "Eutaw," and which are as a whole his most important novels. Simms wrote many other novels on varied subjects, the best of them his sensational frontier stories, "Richard Hurdis," "Border Beagles," "Beauchampe" and "Charlemont," and—certainly one of his finest works of fiction—"The Cassique of Kiawah," a splendid story of the early Charleston pirates. He published, also, in 1845, "The Wigwam and the Cabin," a book of short tales, one of which, "Grayling, or Murder Will Out," Poe declared to be the best story he had ever read.

Simms has sometimes been called the Southern Cooper, but the comparison is unjust. He is no mere follower; he is an important novelist in his own right—indeed, the most important Southern literary figure, Poe excepted, prior to the Civil War. Simms' work, like Cooper's, is occasionally careless and his writing forced, but he possesses equal power of giving life to men and events. His treatment of the single Indian lacks the dignity of Cooper's best portrayal, but his group treatment is more convincing and instructive.

Unquestionably Simms was the victim of his own over-production; yet, when the mass is sifted, not one, but several of his books remain which should endure. The present steadily increasing interest in his work bids fair to assure him a future recognition commensurate with his actual attainment and importance.

GUY RIVERS: A TALE OF GEORGIA. 2 volumes. New York, 1834.

THE YEMASSEE: A ROMANCE OF SOUTH CAROLINA. 2 volumes. New York, 1835.

In some copies the copyright notice is pasted in in Volume I and omitted entirely from

Volume II. Later the copyright notices were printed in.

THE PARTISAN: A TALE OF THE REVOLUTION. 2 volumes. New York, 1835.

MELLICHAMPE. A Legend of the Santee. 2 volumes. New York, 1836.

RICHARD HURDIS; OR, THE AVENGER OF BLOOD. A Tale of Alabama. 2 volumes. Philadelphia, 1838.

BORDER BEAGLES: A TALE OF MISSISSIPPI. 2 volumes. Philadelphia, 1840.

THE KINSMEN: OR, THE BLACK RIDERS OF CONGAREE. A Tale. 2 volumes. Philadelphia, 1841.

Later title, "The Scout."

BEAUCHAMPE; OR, THE KENTUCKY TRAGEDY.
A Tale of Passion. 2 volumes. Philadelphia, 1842.

THE WIGWAM AND THE CABIN. 2 volumes. New York, 1845.

(Anonymous) KATHARINE WALTON; OR, THE REBEL OF DORCHESTER. A Historic Romance of the Revolution in Carolina. Philadelphia, 1851.

THE SWORD AND THE DISTAFF, OR FAIR, FAT, AND FORTY. Charleston, 1852.

Later title, "Woodcraft."

THE FORAYERS; OR, THE RAID OF THE DOG-DAYS. New York, 1855.

CHARLEMONT; OR, THE PRIDE OF THE VILLAGE. A Tale of Kentucky. New York, 1856.

EUTAW; A SEQUEL TO THE FORAYERS. . . . A Tale of the Revolution. New York, 1856.

THE CASSIQUE OF KIAWAH. A Colonial Romance. New York, 1859.

SMITH, CHARLES HENRY
(Bill Arp)
1826–1903

SMITH was born in Lawrenceville, Ga., and graduated from Franklin College. For a time he practiced law in Rome, in his native state. During the Civil War he was a major in the Confederate army, and, when peace was declared, served for one term in the State Legislature. Shortly thereafter he began to contribute articles to the *Atlanta Constitution* over the signature of Bill Arp. These sketches did much to relieve tension in the South during the early Reconstruction Days.

BILL ARP, SO CALLED. A Side Show of the Southern Side of the War. . . . New York, 1866.

SMITH, FRANCIS HOPKINSON
1838–1915

SMITH, a descendant on the maternal side from Francis Hopkinson, the distinguished author of "A Pretty Story" (1774),—the first work of fiction written by an American and printed in America—was born in Baltimore. He was trained as an engineer, in which profession he attained high rank. An independent income permitted him to devote a large part of his time to his favorite avocations, art and literature, in which eventually he gained his chief repute.

Smith wrote numerous short stories and novels, some of which he illustrated, and nearly all of which are charming. His popularly accepted masterpiece, "Colonel Carter," is a wholesome, sympathetic story of a chivalrous, impractical, old Southern gentleman. Though at times a bit conventional, it reveals the heart of the South better, perhaps, than any other novel.

COLONEL CARTER OF CARTERSVILLE. Boston, 1891.

In the earliest printing the illustration of a flight of steps, which in later copies is on page 3, is on page 1. The page of advertisements at the front does not mention this book.

A DAY AT LAGUERRE'S AND OTHER DAYS. Boston, 1892.

There is a strong presumption that the earliest binding is in red cloth, paper label.

There were also two hundred and fifty copies on large paper.

TOM GROGAN. Boston, 1896.

CALEB WEST, MASTER DIVER. Boston, 1898.

A few advance copies were bound in plain cloth, paper label.

SMITH, SAMUEL FRANCIS
1808–1895

DR. SMITH was a Bostonian, a graduate of Harvard and during most of his later life an officiating clergyman in Maine and Massachusetts. He was the editor of several psalm books, hymnals and anthologies, and was a wide contributor to various religious magazines.

"America," his most famous hymn, was written in 1831 and may have first appeared in a program for the Children's Celebration of the Anniversary of American Independence at Park Street Church (Boston), July 4, 1831—although unrecorded, it seems probable that such a program existed. The poem was printed many times thereafter, in various publications. Its first separate printing would appear to have been in 1879.

THE CHOIR OR UNION COLLECTION OF CHURCH MUSIC. . . . By Lowell Mason. Boston, 1832. Contains "America."

SMITH, SEBA
1792–1868

SEBA SMITH, the Father of American Humor, was born in Portland, Me., was a graduate of Bowdoin and later became a journalist in his native city. In 1830, under the pen name of Major Jack Downing, he began the publication of a series of pseudo-political letters, the native humor of which gave them immediate vogue, not only in Portland but in other cities.

These "Writings" are the first clear examples of what has since come to be known as typical American political humor. The central figure, Jack Downing, is the first character in American letters to owe almost nothing to foreign models, and his creator must be accounted one of the most important figures in the emancipation of American literature.

THE LIFE AND WRITINGS OF MAJOR JACK DOWNING OF DOWNINGVILLE, AWAY DOWN EAST IN THE STATE OF MAINE. Written by Himself. Boston, 1833.

'Way Down East, or Portraitures of Yankee Life. New York, 1854.

SNELLING, WILLIAM JOSEPH
1804–1848

Snelling first attracted public attention in 1830 when he returned to his native Boston to pursue a literary career. Prior to that time he had led an adventurous existence, first as a fur trapper in the Missouri mountains while still a youth, and later as an under officer in the Army, stationed at various posts throughout the Northwest.

One of Snelling's earliest literary acts was to take his contemporaries to task for their lack of knowledge of the Indian character. "A man must live, emphatically live, with Indians," he said, to portray them veritably. In proof of this he wrote "Tales of the Northwest," in which he delineated the Red Man more faithfully than any of the early writers. Snelling's style is bold and rapid, his pictures are clearly etched. Only a lack of constructive art prevents his standing with the greater authors of the early nineteenth century.

Tales of the Northwest; or, Sketches of Indian Life and Character. By a Resident beyond the Frontier. Boston, 1830.

SOUTHWORTH, EMMA DOROTHY ELIZABETH NEVITTE
1819–1899

Mrs. Southworth was born in Washington, D. C., and was married there in 1841. Circumstances threw her upon her own resources in 1843, which experience appears to have been her primary urge to authorship. Her first novel in book form, "Retribution" (1845), was a story of negligible merit. Nor was her best work, "The Curse of Clifton," a product of the sentimental fifties, by any means the equal of three or four contemporary novels in similar vein; yet her books were as popular as they were numerous, at least twenty-nine appearing in approximately twenty years.

THE CURSE OF CLIFTON. (1853?).
First edition so far unidentified.

SPOFFORD, HARRIET (ELIZABETH) PRESCOTT
1835–1921

MRS. SPOFFORD was born in Calais, Me. During the gold rush she removed with her family to California, but returned when her father was stricken with paralysis. She completed her schooling at Pinkerton Academy in Derry, N. H., and shortly thereafter, encouraged by Thomas Wentworth Higginson, began writing for various magazines. For a time she contributed materially to her father's support. Following her marriage in 1865, she took up her residence in Newburyport.

Mrs. Spofford was not a constructive artist, but she combined a riotous imagination and a brilliant style to a degree theretofore unapproached by any American woman writer. When "The Amber Gods" appeared,—containing "Circumstance," one of Howells' list of great American short stories—it was hailed as a classic. Mrs. Spofford was soon outmoded by the newer local color school. Because of her later shortcomings, her earlier works have sunk into comparative obscurity.

(Anonymous) SIR ROHAN'S GHOST. A Romance. Boston, 1860.

THE AMBER GODS AND OTHER STORIES. Boston, 1863.

SPRAGUE, CHARLES
1791–1875

SPRAGUE, the son of one of the members of the famous "Boston Tea Party," was a Boston merchant and banker. Aside from a grace and skill in versification attained by few of his poetic predecessors or contemporaries, he showed at times fine flashes of a true inspiration, and must, therefore, be reckoned as one of the genuine minor poets of the early nineteenth century.

CURIOSITY: A POEM, DELIVERED AT CAMBRIDGE, BEFORE THE PHI BETA KAPPA SOCIETY, AUGUST 27, 1829. Boston, 1829.

WRITINGS, NOW FIRST COLLECTED. New York, 1841.

STANSBURY, JOSEPH, and ODELL, REV. JONATHAN
1750–1809 1737–1818

STANSBURY and Odell were by far the ablest and most prolific American loyalist poets of the Revolution. The former, a native of London and later a Philadelphia importer, was for a time imprisoned at Burlington, N. J., and after the war was an officer of several New York insurance companies; the latter led a less eventful life as a New Jersey clergyman.

Of the two, Stansbury was the better poet in breadth, power and humor, though not Odell's equal in satirical invective. It is customary to refer to these two satirists together, for with one exception none of their works were published in book form until a collected edition of their poems was issued in 1860.

THE LOYAL VERSES OF JOSEPH STANSBURY AND DOCTOR JONATHAN ODELL. . . . Edited by Winthrop Sargent. Albany, 1860.

This is No. 6 of "Munsell's Historical Series." Also issued on large paper in boards, half leather.

STEDMAN, EDMUND CLARENCE
1833–1908

STEDMAN was born in Hartford, Conn., and was educated at Yale. A subsequent experience in newspaper work led to his appointment as field correspondent of the *New York World* during the Civil War. Following the declaration of peace, he abandoned journalism to become a member of the New York Stock Exchange. A continuing interest in literature found expression in his lectures on poetry at Johns Hopkins, Columbia and the University of Pennsylvania, in the editing of certain more or less notable anthologies, and in frequent, if sporadic poems.

Despite a facile pen Stedman's earliest poems were colorless. The crisis of the Civil War inspired him temporarily to a series of flaming lyrics that caught the spirit of the nation, but peace left him sapped again, a graceful but dull poet, who only once or twice, as in his "Pan in Wall Street," felt a heart-deep inspiration. Stedman's best work probably was in the field of literary criticism, in which, had his sympathies been less generous, he might have attained a major ranking.

POEMS, LYRICAL AND IDYLLIC. New York, 1860.

ALICE OF MONMOUTH, AN IDYL OF THE GREAT WAR, WITH OTHER POEMS. New York, 1864.

THE BLAMELESS PRINCE, AND OTHER POEMS. Boston, 1869.

Contains "Pan in Wall Street."

POETICAL WORKS. Boston, 1873.

Contains "Wanted—A Man."

VICTORIAN POETS. Boston, 1876.

POETS OF AMERICA. Boston, 1885.

Also published in two volumes, on large paper—one hundred and fifty copies.

STIMSON, FREDERIC JESUP
(J. S. of Dale)
1855–

STIMSON was born in Dedham, Mass., where he continues to reside. His notable career as a public servant and lawyer began almost immediately after his graduation from Harvard Law School. He is a studious, graceful and vigorous writer, whose potential literary development has been to some extent affected by his other important interests. "King Noanett" is one of the better historical romances written in the nineties. Its movement is at times a little hesitant, but its portrayal of early colonial life and scenes is pleasing and historically reliable.

KING NOANETT. A Story of Old Virginia and the Massachusetts Bay. Boston, 1896.

It is reported that the large paper edition, bound in parchment, was the first published.

A map was added in the second edition, which is so marked.

STOCKTON, FRANK R.

1834–1902

FROM his early and precocious youth in Burks County, Pa., Stockton was marked for a literary career. He began writing at the age of ten, and at fourteen was contributing serials to various publications. In later years he was associated with the editorial staffs of *Scribner's* and *St. Nicholas*.

Stockton's books for adults are exaggerated fairy tales. His method consisted of telling the biggest possible lie in the gravest possible manner. When one has read "The Casting Away of Mrs. Lecks and Mrs. Aleshine" and its sequel, "The Dusantes," possibly "Rudder Grange" and certainly "The Lady or the Tiger?"—which, if not artistically the equal of "Mrs. Lecks" is at least his greatest gibe at humanity—he has run a reasonable gamut. Stockton's invention rarely failed him, but in fundamentals it varied little. His extraordinary whimsicality is delightful if taken in small quantities, but it palls in larger doses.

RUDDER GRANGE. New York, 1879.

The first page of advertisements does not mention this book.

THE LADY, OR THE TIGER? AND OTHER STORIES. New York, 1884.

THE CASTING AWAY OF MRS. LECKS AND MRS. ALESHINE. New York, The Century Co., (1886).

Cloth copies should measure only ½ inch across the top of covers.

THE DUSANTES; A SEQUEL TO THE CASTING AWAY OF MRS. LECKS AND MRS. ALESHINE. New York, The Century Co., (1888).

STODDARD, CHARLES WARREN
1843–1909

Stoddard was born in Rochester, N. Y., and spent his youth in business in San Francisco—a natural point of departure for his later journeyings to the Pacific Islands. He visited Hawaii in 1864, and from 1873 to 1878 traveled extensively over the world as correspondent of the *San Francisco Chronicle*. Eventually he gave up newspaper work to become Professor of English at Notre Dame College, Indiana. After another protracted period of foreign travel, he accepted appointment as Lecturer on English at the Catholic University in Washington, D. C.

Stoddard's "South Sea Idyls" are classics. Howells summed them up admirably—"the lightest, sweetest, wildest things that ever were written about the life of the summer ocean. . . . No one need ever write of the South Seas again."

South Sea Idyls. Boston, 1873.

STODDARD, ELIZABETH DREW BARSTOW
1823–1902

Mrs. Stoddard was a native of Mattapoisett, Mass., and the wife of Richard Henry Stoddard, the writer and lecturer. After her marriage she contributed verse and stories to a number of magazines. She was the author of three novels with a New England setting which evidence keen powers of observation and decided originality. Too "modern" for their day, they failed to gain popularity; yet paradoxically they now seem old fashioned. Of the three, the "Morgesons" is undoubtedly the best.

The Morgesons. A Novel. New York, 1862.

Two Men. A Novel. New York, 1865.

TEMPLE HOUSE. A NOVEL. New York, Carleton, (1867).

STODDARD, RICHARD HENRY
1825–1903

STODDARD was born in Hingham, Mass. As a boy he immersed himself in the English classics. Later, whether working as a lawyer's clerk, bookkeeper or iron molder, he devoted most of his spare time to writing lyrics; when subsequently he secured a position in the New York Customs House, he found more leisure for literary pursuits. Eventually he was appointed literary editor of the *New York World.*

Though Stoddard worshiped beauty, he was never a great poet. He excelled in imagery and rhythm, but lacked the inspiration of poetic genius. He must live, therefore, if at all, through his lyrics, where his lack of vision is powerless to mar the beauty of his lines.

SONGS OF SUMMER. Boston, 1857.

STODDARD, WILLIAM OSBORNE
1835–1925

STODDARD was born in Homer, N. Y., and educated at the University of Rochester. He served for three months in the Union army during the early part of the Civil War, and then, from 1861 to 1864, as Secretary to President Lincoln. He was appointed U. S. Marshal of Arkansas in 1864, and two years later entered business in New York City.

Stoddard wrote several juveniles of Indian life, of which he had made a careful study at various times during his career. Without prejudice to the narrative interest of these novels, he adhered closely to realities. His "Little Smoke," reaching its climax in Custer's Last Stand, is one of the most reliable and satisfactory stories of the Red Man that can be put into a boy's hands—as well as one of the most entertaining.

Little Smoke. A Tale of the Sioux. New York, 1891.

STORY, WILLIAM WETMORE
1819–1895

William Wetmore Story, one of the most versatile of nineteenth century artists, was born in Salem, Mass. He attended Harvard, and after graduation for some time practiced law. In 1848 he went to Italy, where he took up a permanent residence. Story's talents led him to law, literature and music, and in the end to sculpture, in which he attained distinction. His writings include legal and political treatises, poems, essays and plays. Probably his most valuable literary contributions are his sketches of Italian life.

Roba di Roma; or, Walks and Talks about Rome. 2 volumes. London, 1862.

The first American edition is in two volumes. New York, 1864.

Poems. 2 volumes. Boston, 1886.

Also 2 volumes, Edinburgh, 1885—clearly prior.

STOWE, HARRIET BEECHER
1811–1896

Mrs. Stowe, the author of the most popular single novel ever written in America, was born in Litchfield, Conn. She was the daughter of the famous theologian, Dr. Lyman Beecher, and the elder sister of the still more famous Henry Ward Beecher. When she was a young woman her family moved to Cincinnati, where she met and married Prof. Calvin E. Stowe, a member of the faculty of Lane Seminary, of which her father was then president. In 1850 Prof. Stowe was appointed to the faculty of Bowdoin, and in Maine Mrs. Stowe found leisure to begin the novel of slavery, which, as an observer of the "Underground Railway" in Cincinnati, she had decided to write.

"Uncle Tom's Cabin" is not a well constructed novel, but it is a great book. It has palpable faults of many descriptions. But its emotional fervor, its sensational exposure of the evils of slavery, and its political consequences lift it out of the realm of pure literature into that of constructive human endeavor. At least a million copies were sold within ten years. The story was dramatized, was translated in due course into forty languages, and is without a rival as the best known book ever written in America.

Mrs. Stowe was on surer ground when she turned to New England. Lowell praised "The Minister's Wooing" and Whittier thought highly of "The Pearl of Orr's Island." But her pedagogic tendencies failed to make either of these quite believable. "Oldtown Folks," on the other hand, though suffering from the same tendency, is still convincing realism, and "Oldtown Fireside Stories," while failing in constructive art, has given to American Letters in the figure of Sam Lawson, the narrator, one of its few autochthonous characters.

A New England Sketch. By Harriet Beecher. Lowell, 1834.

Uncle Tom's Cabin, or, Life among the Lowly. 2 volumes. Boston, 1852.

There is no mention of thousands on the title page. The stereotyper's imprint, only, is on the verso of the title page (without

George C. Rand and Avery). The bottom of the backstrip reads J. P. Jewett.

THE MINISTER'S WOOING. New York, 1859.

Also appears with a New York and Boston imprint. Priority undetermined.

THE PEARL OF ORR'S ISLAND: A STORY OF THE COAST OF MAINE. Boston, 1862.

OLDTOWN FOLKS. Boston, 1869.

"Oldtown Folks" is the last book listed on the leaf of advertisements opposite the title page.

OLDTOWN FIRESIDE STORIES. Boston, 1872.

STREET, ALFRED BILLINGS
1811–1881

STREET, the son of a Revolutionary general, was born in Poughkeepsie, N. Y., but moved to Albany in 1839. He was a historian of note, and was at one time Keeper of the State Historical Records. His verse is polished and good in description, but lacking in force.

FRONTENAC; OR, THE ATOTARHO OF THE IROQUOIS. A Metrical Romance. New York, 1849.

This is the first American edition. The English edition of the same date was published slightly earlier.

STUART, RUTH McENERY
1856–1917

MRS. STUART was born in Avoyelles Parish, La., and married a planter of her native state in 1879. Subsequently she took up her residence in New York. She is a writer of fair skill, and when dealing with the negro, of an understanding humor. "The Story of Babette" is her most popular work.

POEMS. (Baltimore, 1883).
Privately printed.

A GOLDEN WEDDING, AND OTHER TALES. New York, 1893.

THE STORY OF BABETTE, A LITTLE CREOLE GIRL. New York, 1894.

TABB, JOHN BANISTER
1845–1909

FATHER TABB was born in Richmond, Va., and when little more than a boy saw service in the Confederate army. Later he took orders as a Catholic priest and in due course became Professor of English at St. Charles College. Tabb's appeal is to the spiritual rather than to the mundane. His lyrics are exquisitely finished and his nature poems for the most part works of genuine beauty. He seldom enters the world of men, but within its limits his work is excellent.

LYRICS. Boston, 1897.
Five hundred and fifty copies only were printed, fifty of them on handmade paper.

CHILD VERSES. Boston, 1899.

TARKINGTON, (NEWTON) BOOTH
1869–

TARKINGTON is a native of Indianapolis and belongs quite definitely to the twentieth century. It is probable that at his best his contributions to American letters have permanence. Mr. Tarkington has published many other popular novels besides "The Gentleman from Indiana" which, because of the arbitrary date limitations set upon this work, do not come within its scope.

THE GENTLEMAN FROM INDIANA. New York, 1899.

Page 245, l. 15, must read "so pretty."

TAYLOR, (JAMES) BAYARD
1825–1878

TAYLOR, one of the commanding literary figures of his day—now dwarfed to somewhat less than his true proportions—was born of poor parents in Chester County, Pa. His father was unable to afford him a good education, but he grew up with a natural love of literature and travel.

At nineteen he made a trip to Europe, paying his way from the proceeds of his first book and from letters contributed to home papers. After his return, he taught school and edited a Pennsylvania country newspaper, until Horace Greeley made a place for him on the editorial staff of the *New York Tribune*. He then went to California and to the Orient, and joined the expedition of Commodore Perry to Japan. In 1857 he married Marie Hansen, daughter of a noted German astronomer. Returning home, he served for a time as correspondent for Northern papers during the Civil War, and later, from 1862 to 1863, as Secretary of Legation at St. Petersburg. In 1878 he was appointed Minister to Germany, but died in Berlin after a few months of service.

Taylor's contemporaries thought of him, first of all, as a traveler and lecturer; it was his own hope that he might be regarded as above all else a poet. Unfortunately he lacked the excellence necessary to the fulfillment of this wish, yet in "Poems of the Orient" and "The Picture of St. John" excellence is not far away. "Lars," too, displays a generous measure of sustained power and imagination, and his translation of "Faust" (1871) is accepted as one of the best English versions. Of his novels only one deserves mention—"The Story of Kennett," a tale of Pennsylvania at the beginning of the century, that leaves an impression of reality, but is markedly uneven.

VIEWS-A-FOOT; OR, EUROPE SEEN WITH KNAPSACK AND STAFF. . . . 2 volumes. New York, 1846.

ELDORADO; OR ADVENTURES IN THE PATH OF EMPIRE. 2 volumes. New York, 1850.

The one volume edition, which was later, had no plates.

POEMS OF THE ORIENT. Boston, 1855.

THE STORY OF KENNETT. New York, 1866.

THE PICTURE OF ST. JOHN. Boston, 1866.

LARS: A PASTORAL OF NORWAY. Boston, 1873.

THE NATIONAL ODE. July 4, 1876. (Boston, 1876).

This was a facsimile of the manuscript.

The first printed edition of this poem was published in Boston in 1877.

TENNY, TABITHA
1762–1837

MRS. TENNY, the wife of Dr. Samuel Tenny, member of Congress from New Hampshire, was the daughter of Samuel

Gilman, a distinguished citizen of Exeter. In obvious imitation of Mrs. Lennox, Mrs. Tenny satirized the didactic novel of her day in a romance which owed its name, "Female Quixotism," to Mrs. Lennox's earlier work. Mrs. Tenny's humor is crude, but she is to be commended as one woman who sensed the absurdity of contemporary feminine writing.

FEMALE QUIXOTISM: EXHIBITED IN THE ROMANTIC OPINIONS AND EXTRAVAGANCES OF DORCASINA SHELDON. . . . 2 volumes. Boston, 1801.

TERHUNE, MARY VIRGINIA (HAWES)
(Marion Harland)
1830–1922

MRS. TERHUNE was a literary prodigy. Born in Amelia County, Va., she began contributing to a Richmond, Va., weekly at the age of fourteen; two years later her first story was published in *Godey's Magazine*. Her first novel appeared in 1854. Subsequently she became widely known as the author of numerous essays and novels (and cook books) and as a staff contributor to *St. Nicholas, Wide Awake* and the *North American Review*. Mrs. Terhune did her best work in the romantic field. She was the author of several popular but hardly distinguished novels.

SUNNYBANK. New York, 1866.

THAXTER, CELIA LEIGHTON
1835–1894

MRS. THAXTER was the daughter of the lighthouse keeper on the Isles of Shoals. She was born in Portsmouth, N. H., and spent her girlhood among the rocks and sands and fisher folk of the New England coast. At sixteen she married Levi Lincoln Thaxter, but continued to spend much of her time at her girlhood home.

Mrs. Thaxter's poetry is generally of the sea, which she loved, particularly in its gentler moods. Her prose sketches are pleasant pictures of the brighter side of the life and scenes along her native coast.

POEMS. New York, 1872.

AMONG THE ISLES OF SHOALS. Boston, 1873.

THOMAS, EDITH MATILDA
1854–

MISS THOMAS, now a resident of New York, was born in Chatham, Ohio. She began her writing while a student at Geneva Normal School—contributing to local journals—and later, encouraged and favorably introduced by Helen Hunt Jackson, gained recognition in the pages of the *Atlantic Monthly* and *The Century*. Her first book of verse, "A New Year's Masque," was published in 1885. Painstaking workmanship, a gift for colorful phrasing and a fine lyric quality have won for her a small but faithful following.

IN SUNSHINE LAND. Boston, 1895.

A WINTER SWALLOW WITH OTHER VERSES. New YORK. 1896.

THOMAS, FREDERICK WILLIAM
1808 or 1810–1866

THOMAS, at different times a lawyer, minister, newspaper editor and professor of rhetoric, was born in Providence, R. I. His one novel of any distinction is interesting only because, departing from the usual method of contemporary writers, he chose to build it around conditions in which he was personally thoroughly experienced.

CLINTON BRADSHAW; OR THE ADVENTURES OF A LAWYER. 2 volumes. Philadelphia, 1835.

THOMPSON, DANIEL PIERCE
1795–1868

THOMPSON, a native of Charleston, Mass., a graduate of Middlebury College, sometime editor of the *Green Mountain Freeman* and later Secretary of State of Vermont, combined a real gift of story telling with an intimate knowledge of his subject and an instinct for realism, in a period when the followers of Cooper had degenerated into hurried tellers of "blood and thunder" tales. His first book, "May Martin," originally a prize story, gained him a certain popularity; but his great success was his "Green Mountain Boys," which has come down as a classic, though "Locke Amsden"—in part autobiographical—is perhaps its superior.

MAY MARTIN, OR, THE MONEY-DIGGERS, A GREEN MOUNTAIN TALE. Burlington, Vt., 1835.

THE GREEN MOUNTAIN BOYS: A HISTORICAL TALE OF THE EARLY SETTLEMENT OF VERMONT. 2 volumes. Montpelier, Vt., 1839.

LOCKE AMSDEN, OR, THE SCHOOL-MASTERS: A TALE. Boston, 1847.

LUCY HOSMER; OR THE GUARDIAN AND GHOST; A TALE OF AVARICE AND CRIME DEFEATED. Burlington, 1848.
Also Boston, 1848.

THE RANGERS; OR, THE TORY'S DAUGHTER. A TALE ILLUSTRATIVE OF THE REVOLUTIONARY

History of Vermont, and the Northern Campaign of 1777. 2 volumes in one. Boston, 1851.

THOMPSON, (J.) MAURICE
1844–1901

Thompson was born in Fairfield, Ind., but spent his youth and early manhood in the South. After the Civil War, in which he fought as a Confederate soldier, he returned to his native state to practice law. Save for a brief period of service as State Geologist, he continued in his profession until his death. Meanwhile he published several works of fiction, poetry and nature studies, and contributed to various magazines. In 1890 he became a member of the staff of the *New York Independent,* and eventually came to be recognized as one of the foremost American literary critics.

Thompson's best known work of fiction is his historical romance, "Alice of Old Vincennes" (1900). Though this is one of the better novels of its type, it is doubtful whether it is the equal either in force or enduring quality of the series of grim and truthful stories which he collected in his first book, "Hoosier Mosaics."

Hoosier Mosaics. New York, 1875.

(Anonymous) A Tallahassee Girl. Boston, 1882.

Published in the "Round Robin Series."

THOMPSON, WILLIAM TAPPAN
1812–1882

Thompson, one of the several pre-war Southern writers who left a fine product of local color humor, was born in Ravenna,

Ohio. He early moved to Philadelphia, then to Florida and finally to Georgia, serving progressively, meanwhile, on the staff of several weeklies. His Georgia classic, "Major Jones' Courtship," was first published in the columns of the *Madison Miscellany*. Later, in 1850, he established the *Savannah Morning News*.

MAJOR JONES' COURTSHIP; DETAILED WITH OTHER SCENES, INCIDENTS AND ADVENTURES, IN A SERIES OF LETTERS BY HIMSELF. To which is added, "The Great Attraction." Madison, Georgia, 1843.

CHRONICLES OF PINEVILLE: EMBRACING SKETCHES OF GEORGIA SCENES, INCIDENTS, AND CHARACTERS. Philadelphia, 1845.

THOMSON, MORTIMER M.
(Q. C. Philander Doesticks, P. B.)
1831–1865

THOMSON was born in Rega, N. Y., was educated at the University of Michigan, and later became in turn an actor, salesman, journalist and lecturer. He was a dabster at all sorts of "unpremeditated extravagances," using contempt, satire, exaggerated hyperbole—anything—to puncture every popular bubble of absurdity. His best known work was "Plu-Ri-Bus-Tah," written in the meter of "Hiawatha," a popular but clumsy burlesque on American spread-eagleism.

DOESTICKS: WHAT HE SAYS. New York, 1855.

PLU-RI-BUS-TAH: A SONG THAT'S-BY-NO-AUTHOR. New York, 1856.

THOREAU, HENRY DAVID
1817–1862

THOREAU, the most individualistic figure in American letters, was born in Concord, Mass., in a refined but simple home. He was educated at the village school and at Harvard, and later supported himself as best he could by random occupation as surveyor, school teacher, lecturer, or following his father's trade of pencil making.

Two years after graduation from college, Thoreau took a boating trip with his brother John, his impressions of which were later published in his first book, "A Week on the Concord and Merrimack Rivers." Despite its charm and originality, so generally recognized today, less than three hundred copies were sold.

In 1845, with the help of two friends, he built a tiny cottage on the shore of Walden Pond, where he spent the next two years alone, with the woods and waters and his furred and feathered friends as companions. His life during these two years is the theme of his famous "Walden," his masterpiece and one of America's greatest books.

Following the Walden experience, he roamed in Maine, Cape Cod and Canada, always carrying a journal in which he noted his impressions, and which later furnished the materials for his posthumously published "Maine Woods," "Cape Cod" and "A Yankee in Canada." He was later stricken with consumption, and after a painful period of confinement died at the age of forty-five.

From a purely scientific point of view Thoreau's observations as a naturalist are often open to question. It is rather his poetic prose and the originality of the philosophy which he derived from nature that stamp him as a master. In a way he defies analysis. As Professor Trent says in "American Literature to 1865"—"It seems best then merely to say that Thoreau was a prose writer of remarkable variety, power and charm, whose fame has been steadily growing, and in whose work sympathetic readers find much to delight and profit them."

A WEEK ON THE CONCORD AND MERRIMACK RIVERS. Boston, 1849.

A leaf announcing "Walden" follows page 413. All unsold copies were returned to Thoreau, and were later reissued with a new title page in 1862.

WALDEN; OR, LIFE IN THE WOODS. Map. Boston, 1854.

The dating of the advertisements varies from April to November. There is little, if any preference.

EXCURSIONS. (Edited, by R. W. Emerson). Boston, 1863.

THE MAINE WOODS. Boston, 1864.

Copies with the leaves of advertisements at the back headed, "The Thirteenth Volume," and dated January, 1864, are preferred, but there is no definite proof that they are prior.

CAPE COD. Boston, 1865.

LETTERS TO VARIOUS PERSONS. Boston, 1865.

A YANKEE IN CANADA, WITH ANTI-SLAVERY AND REFORM PAPERS. Boston, 1866.

THORPE, THOMAS BANGS
1815–1878

THORPE, one of the first democratizers of our literature and a true forerunner of the "Pike County School," was a native of Westfield, Mass. He drifted South after his graduation from Wesleyan in 1842, and settled in New Orleans, where he became assistant editor of a newspaper. Twelve years later he returned North, moved to New York, and became a regular contributor to the Metropolitan magazines. During the Civil War he served creditably as Surveyor of the Port of New Orleans, and in 1869 was appointed Chief Clerk of the New York Customs House.

Thorpe's unique contributions to our literature were his frontier sketches, like "Tom Owen, the Bee-Hunter" and "The Big Bear of Arkansaw,"—crude, picturesque tales of the earlier Southwest. Though his rough and boisterous humor jarred the sensibilities of the cultured Atlantic seaboard, he wrote understandingly, if extravagantly, in the spirit of the life of the contemporary backwoods.

THE BIG BEAR OF ARKANSAW, AND OTHER SKETCHES. Illustrative of Characters and Incidents in the South and Southwest. Edited by William T. Porter. Philadelphia, 1845.

THE MYSTERIES OF THE BACKWOODS; OR, SKETCHES OF THE SOUTHWEST. Philadelphia, 1846.

THE HIVE OF THE BEE HUNTER. A REPOSITORY OF SKETCHES. New York, 1854.

TICKNOR, FRANCIS ORRERY
1822–1874

TICKNOR was a native of Baldwin County, Ga., and for years a practicing physician in Columbia. Most of his verse is now forgotten, but his "Little Griffin of Tennessee" still lives—a touching lyric of simple heroism, inspired by the tragic scenes of the Civil War.

THE POEMS OF FRANK O. TICKNOR, M. D. Edited by K. M. R. Philadelphia, 1879.

TIERNAN, MARY SPEAR (NICHOLAS)
1836–1891

MRS. TIERNAN, a native of Baltimore and a sometime resident of the "Old Dominion," was the author of several novels of pre-war Virginia, which for a time led her admirers to proclaim her as the greatest delineator of the old régime. Though her work has been superseded by that of Thomas Nelson Page, it is not altogether negligible. She lacked Page's talent, but, being less of an idealist, she probably painted a more faithful picture of pre-war society. "Suzette" was her most popular book.

(Anonymous) HOMOSELLE. Boston, 1881.
Published in the "Round Robin Series."

SUZETTE; A NOVEL. New York, 1885.

TIMROD, HENRY
1829–1867

TIMROD, lifelong friend and associate of Paul Hamilton Hayne, was born in Charleston, S. C. At sixteen he entered the University of Georgia, but delicate health and straitened circumstances prevented his graduation. He then began to study law, which he abandoned to become a private tutor. During the Civil War he served as correspondent of the *Charleston Mercury,* until illness forced him to give up his position. He was married in 1864. The end of the War found him penniless and physically unable to cope with his difficulties. He died shortly thereafter.

A considerable amount of verse by Timrod had appeared

in *Russell's Magazine* and the *Southern Literary Messenger* prior to 1860. But though some of it attained real excellence, he was destined to wait for the Civil War to receive his greater inspiration. The volume of his poems collected and edited by his friend, Paul Hamilton Hayne, and published six years after his death, contains as a whole the best war poetry by a Southern author.

THE POEMS OF. . . . Edited, with a Sketch of the Poet's life, by Paul H. Hayne. New York, 1873.

Later printings have the words "New Revised Edition" on the title page. The "Ode . . . at Magnolia Cemetery" first appeared in the Revised Edition.

TOURGEE, ALBION WINEGAR
1838–1905

TOURGEE was born in Williamsfield, Ohio, and was educated at Kingsville Academy and Rochester, N. Y., University. In 1861 he left college to enlist in the Union army. He was twice wounded, once seriously at Bull Run, and again, after promotion to a lieutenancy, at Perryville. He also spent four months in a Southern prison. After the war, Tourgee settled in Greensboro, N. C., and engaged in agriculture and the practice of law. He published a paper from 1866 to 1867, was later one of the most influential members of the State Constitutional Convention and later still served as a Federal Judge.

Tourgee was intensely interested in the problem of Southern rehabilitation, and was grievously disappointed at the failure of the scheme for territorial Southern governments proposed by Thaddeus Stevens. Though he encountered bitter opposition, notably from the Ku-Klux-Klan which made several abortive attempts to capture him, his efforts were unquestionably disinterested and sincere. His novel, "A "Fool's Errand," which is based upon his own personal experience in an attempt to establish a Southern home, is essentially his credo in the matter, and an extremely interesting, if somewhat biased exposition of post-war Southern conditions.

A FOOL'S ERRAND. By One of the Fools. New York, 1879.

The copy filed for copyright measures 3/4 inch across the top of the sheets. Other copies measure 13/16 inch.

BRICKS WITHOUT STRAW. New York, Fords, Howard & Hulbert, (1880).

Page 343 reads "the poor man's war and the rich man's fight," later changed to "the rich man's war," etc. Some copies have an erratum slip, but this may not be necessary.

(TROUBETZKOY), AMELIE RIVES (CHANLER) 1863–

MISS RIVES (Princess Troubetzkoy) is a member of an old and well-known family of Richmond, Va. She began to write when she was only fifteen, and was still a girl when her first story was accepted by the *Atlantic Monthly*. In 1888 she married J. A. Chanler of New York, whom she later divorced. She subsequently married a Russian prince.

In 1888 Miss Rives rebelled against Victorian conventions and published a novel, "The Quick or the Dead?" which immediately raised a storm of protest from scandalized critics who attacked it as immoral—a protest immediately reflected in increased sales. Later and saner criticism has pronounced it harmless, and, in the light of time. its chief literary importance is historical, as a pioneer work making for greater intellectual freedom.

A Brother to the Dragons, and other Old-Time Tales. New York, 1888.

The Quick or the Dead? A Story. Philadelphia, J. P. Lippincott Company, (1888).

This is bibliographically an interesting book. It is one of the very few cases where the original magazine printing must be considered the first book form printing. Lippincott added a portrait and title page to the April 1888 number of their magazine, and issued it bound in marbled boards. This was later reprinted in the same form, but with an orange brown sheet added at the front advertising the forthcoming appearance of Miss Rives' "Herod and Mariamne," and with a note of such reprint at the bottom of the page. The advertisements at the back also vary markedly—for example, the lower right hand corner of the first page of advertisements in the first printing carries an advertisement of "Arnold's Writing Fluid," which in the reprint is replaced by a "Sheet Iron and Metal Ceilings" advertisement.

The first printing of this novel in ordinary book format is dated 1889.

TROWBRIDGE, JOHN TOWNSEND
1827–1916

Trowbridge, one of the great emancipators of the boys' juvenile, was born on a farm near Rochester, N. Y. He remained at home until he was sixteen, but following his father's death went to live with his sister. Later, encouraged in his aspirations by the occasional acceptance of his literary efforts, he went to New York, and after a hard struggle achieved marked success as a writer of boys' books.

Trowbridge's influence on the boys' book was profound. He was not the first to write a juvenile with the youthful point of view in mind, but he realized perhaps more than any of his near contemporaries the necessity of eliminating didacticism, and his position as editor of *Our Young Folks* gave him a singular opportunity to enforce his precepts.

His own juveniles are delightful, particularly his story of slavery, "Cudjo's Cave." He also wrote some good light verse, a few examples of which, like his "Darius Green and His Flying Machine," became deservedly popular, and some quite amusing sketches of rural New England.

Cudjo's Cave. Boston, 1864.
It seems probable that copies measuring 1½ inches plus across the top of covers were the first printed.

Coupon Bonds. Boston, 1866.
Later reprinted with other stories.

The Vagabonds and Other Poems. Boston, 1869.

TRUMBULL, JOHN
1750–1831

Trumbull, one of the "Hartford Wits," was born in Waterbury, Conn. He passed his entrance examinations for Yale at the age of seven, but did not enter until he was thirteen. Following his graduation he studied law in the office of John Adams, afterwards returning to New Haven, Conn., where he composed "McFingal," the most popular of the Revolutionary satires.

"McFingal" was overrated in its day. Yet, despite its extravagant absurdity, and its obvious debt to Butler, it is one of the rare early poems which contain a generous savoring of contemporary Americanism—as at least thirty editions attest. "McFingal" is Trumbull's bid for fame, but, in the opinion of some critics, the lesser known "Elegy on the Times" reveals him as a truer poet.

AN ELEGY ON THE TIMES: FIRST PRINTED AT BOSTON, SEPTEMBER 20TH, A. D. 1774, NEW HAVEN: Reprinted by Thomas and Samuel Green, 1775.

MCFINGAL: A MODERN EPIC POEM. Canto First, or The Town-Meeting. Philadelphia. . . . 1775.

Note: The first complete edition was published in Hartford in 1782, by Hudson and Goodwin. There was also a Hartford, Nathaniel Patten, 1782, imprint. An illustrated edition was published in New York in 1795.

TUCKER, GEORGE
1775–1861

TUCKER, a native of Bermuda, was educated at William and Mary College, practiced law for a time, served two terms in the Virginia State Legislature and in 1823 was elected to Congress. He later became Professor of Philosophy and

Economics at the University of Virginia. Tucker's writings took the form of essays, biographies, historical works, treatises on banking and novels. Among his works of fiction, "A Voyage to the Moon," a Jules Verne type of tale, contains some effective satire.

A Voyage to the Moon: with some account of the Manners and Customs, Science and Philosophy, of the People of Morosofia and other Lunarians. By Joseph Atterly. New York, 1827.

TUCKER, N(ATHANIEL) BEVERLY
1784–1851

Tucker's writing of fiction was incidental to his other and major activities. He was born in Matoax, Va., and was educated as a lawyer at William and Mary College. After completing his studies he moved to Missouri, where he served upon the bench from 1815 to 1830. He subsequently returned to his native state, and in 1834 was appointed Professor of Law and the Philosophy of Government in William and Mary College, which position he held until his death.

Tucker wrote several pamphlets of scholarly or professional interest, and contributed certain minor fiction to the *Southern Literary Messenger.* His literary reputation, however, rests upon "George Balcombe," for the time a realistic picture of contemporary Virginia and Missouri, which Poe considered "upon the whole, as the best American novel," and "The Partisan Leader," printed in 1836, with a fictitious dating of 1856, a bit of violent propaganda for disunion, that despite its defects and its author's prejudices remains an interesting document in the history of secession.

(Anonymous) George Balcombe. A Novel. 2 volumes. New York, 1836.

THE PARTISAN LEADER. A Tale of the Future. By Edward William Sidney. No place, 1856. This book was later printed in facsimile, with an added title.

TUCKERMAN, HENRY THEODORE
1813–1871

TUCKERMAN'S life through early manhood was divided between his native Boston and his beloved Italy. In 1845 he settled in New York, where he quickly became an intimate of leading literary circles. His writings ranged over a wide field, but he nowhere achieved distinction. His poetry is never well sustained; his graceful criticism, though unquestionably his most important work, is pleasant pedantry, not vital comment. He aided in the diffusion of a wider American culture, but little more than that can be said.

CHARACTERISTICS OF LITERATURE. Illustrations by The Genius of Distinguished Men. Philadelphia, 1849.
Second Series, 1851.

POEMS. Boston, 1851.

TYLER, ROYALL
1757–1826

TYLER, a native Bostonian, a jurist of distinction, and a man of marked public and literary attainment, received his legal training in the office of John Adams. Subsequently he served for a time on the staff of Gen. Lincoln. He began to practice law in 1790 at Guilford, Vt., and later, from 1800 to 1806, served as Chief Justice of the State Supreme Court. Meanwhile, he had earned an enviable reputation as a critic and author, notably of "The Contrast," the first American play acted by a professional company—produced in 1789 and published in 1790—and of "The Algerine Captive," for the times a realistic novel of the Algerian slave trade, and one of the first works of American fiction treating a foreign theme. He was also a contributor to Joseph Dennie's *Farmer's Weekly Museum* along critical lines.

THE ALGERINE CAPTIVE: OR, THE LIFE AND ADVENTURES OF DOCTOR UPDIKE UNDERHILL: SIX YEARS A PRISONER AMONG THE ALGERINES. 2 volumes. Walpole, N. H., 1797.

VAN DYKE, HENRY

1852–

DR. VAN DYKE, widely known as a poet, story writer and essayist, was born at Germantown, Pa. After graduating from Princeton he studied for a time in Berlin, but returned to the United States to become pastor of a Congregationalist church in Newport, R. I. He was later called to a pastorate in New York City. He subsequently lectured at the Sorbonne, and from 1913 to 1917 was U. S. Minister to the Netherlands. He is a member of the Academy of Arts and Sciences and a Commander of the French Legion of Honor. His work is graceful and cultured, though not of great distinction.

THE FIRST CHRISTMAS TREE. New York, 1897.

FISHERMAN'S LUCK AND OTHER UNCERTAIN THINGS. New York, 1899.
Also 150 copies, large paper.

(von TEUFFEL), BLANCHE WILLIS HOWARD
1847–1898

MISS HOWARD was born in Bangor, Me. After several years of schooling in New York, she went to Stuttgart, Germany, to complete her education. There she met and married the court physician of Württemburg. She later became prominent in European society.

Miss Howard is a one book author. She displayed a charming manner in her first work, "One Summer," but "Guenn" is so far superior to her other novels that she must be judged by it alone. It is the story of an amiable but self-centered American artist, a volatile Breton peasant maiden and an upstanding priest, and it moves like a prose lyric to its logical and inevitable end—the egocentric survival of Hamor, the suicide of Guenn and the spiritual exhaustion of Father Thymert. No romance written by an American woman during the nineteenth century is molded with a surer hand or defter touch.

(Anonymous) ONE SUMMER. Boston, 1875.

GUENN A WAVE ON THE BRETON COAST. Boston, 1884.

On page 340 in the third from the last line, "ought to be—is Victor" was later omitted. "Soyez gentille," in the next to the last line on page 283 was later changed to "Voyons, voyons." The advertisement in the front mentions "Aunt Serena" only. The text follows immediately after the copyright page.

WALLACE, LEW
1827–1905

GENERAL WALLACE was born in Brookville, Ind. As a boy he detested study, yet was devoted to art and reading. When the Mexican War broke out, though only eighteen years old, he entered the army, and during the following campaigns gained the inspiration for his first book, "The Fair God," which, however, was not completed for over twenty years. Later he served with distinction during the Civil War, retiring with the rank of Major General. He was subsequently Governor of the Territory of New Mexico under President Hayes, and completed his public service as Minister to Turkey during the Garfield administration.

Wallace's second and best known book, "Ben-Hur," a careful study of early Christianity, loses nothing in being a thrilling tale of adventure. Next to "Uncle Tom's Cabin" it is the most popular American novel. Its greatness is debatable, but its importance is not open to question. By presenting to the "hinterland" of culture a book of which it could thoroughly approve, it did more than any other single work to break down what Carl Van Doren has so aptly called the "village opposition" to the novel.

THE FAIR GOD; OR, THE LAST OF THE 'TZINS; A TALE OF THE CONQUEST OF MEXICO. Boston, 1873.

Measures 1⅛ inches across the top of the covers.

BEN-HUR. A Tale of the Christ. New York, 1880.

Must be dated on the title page. The binding is in light blue, decorated cloth.

(WARD), ELIZABETH STUART PHELPS
1844–1911

MISS PHELPS was the daughter of a distinguished professor at the Andover Theological Seminary. At the age of sixteen she had written and published her first story, and her first and best novel, "The Gates Ajar," appeared in 1869. Later she became a lecturer at Boston University, and in 1886 was married to the Rev. Herbert D. Ward, of Newton, Mass.

"The Gates Ajar" was the most popular book produced as a direct result of the Civil War, and ran into at least nine editions during its first year. As a portrayal of a woman's agony over the loss of a loved one in battle it brought spiritual comfort to thousands of bereaved women throughout the nation. Mrs. Ward was the most powerful feminine writer of her generation. Her emotionalism is undeniable. It is, however, the emotionalism of an intense soul.

MEN, WOMEN, AND GHOSTS. Boston, 1869.

THE GATES AJAR. Boston, 1869.

Reads "nears" instead of "approaches" at the end of the second line of the dedication. Some copies have an apostrophe present in the word "slickin' " in the first line of page 60.

THE STORY OF AVIS. Boston, 1877.

WARE, EUGENE FITCH
1841–

WARE, a native of Hartford, Conn., like many another ex-soldier, went West immediately after the Civil War. He subsequently became one of the leading citizens of Kansas, and served as U. S. Senator during two terms. Ware made his literary reputation under the pseudonym of Ironquill, and his poems of the West were at one time very popular. "Quivera," a poem of the Spanish Conquistadores, is probably the best single example of his work.

RHYMES BY IRONQUILL. Topeka, Kansas, 1885.

WARE, WILLIAM
1797–1852

DR. WARE was born in Hingham, Mass., and graduated from Harvard in 1816. He first entered the ministry in New York City, but was soon recalled to his native state, where later he became editor of *The Christian.*

His novels on the struggles of early Christianity form a trilogy, though "Julian," the scene of which is laid in Judea during the time of Christ, stands chronologically somewhat apart. Their scholarship is undeniable, and though written in the form of letters their narrative is for the most part well sustained. For grace of diction and for the clarity with which they portray the social and political struggle between Christianity and the dominant hierarchies of the age, they are the equal of any later novel of their type. "Julian" is a striking portrayal of the viewpoint of the orthodox Jew and the considerations which prevented his full acceptance of the "Man of Nazareth" as the Messiah.

Though "Letters . . . from Palmyra" (Zenobia) is the best known and most popular of the trilogy, they should be considered as a whole, as the first important American work dealing with this theme.

(Anonymous) LETTERS OF LUCIUS M. PISO, FROM PALMYRA, TO HIS FRIEND MARCUS CURTIUS AT ROME. Now first translated and published. 2 volumes. New York, 1837.

The title of later editions of this work was "Zenobia," etc.

(Anonymous) PROBUS; OR ROME IN THE THIRD CENTURY. In Letters of Lucius M. Piso from Rome. . . . 2 volumes. New York, 1838.

An errata slip for both volumes is at the bottom of the first page of Volume I.

The later title was "Aurelian," etc.

JULIAN; OR SCENES IN JUDEA. By the Author of Letters from Palmyra and Rome. 2 volumes. New York, 1841.

The copyright notice is pasted in in Volume I.

WARNER, CHARLES DUDLEY
1829–1900

AT THE age of thirteen Warner left Plainfield, Mass., his birthplace, to attend school in New York, and following his graduation from Hamilton College spent a short time on the western frontier. Upon his return to the East, he entered the University of Pennsylvania Law School, and later practiced in Chicago until 1860, when he accepted a position on the *Hartford Press*. In 1884 he joined the staff of *Harper's Magazine,* and in 1892 succeeded Howells as editor of *The Easy Chair*. His travels in Europe and North America were extensive.

Warner was an intimate friend of Twain, a philanthropist, a kindly critic and a helpful friend to budding authors. An occasional novelist and poet, he was more effective as a writer of sketches, which his warm humor and ingenious originality invariably made pleasant reading. Three books of his deserve especial mention—his graceful and genial "Backlog Studies" and "My Summer in a Garden," and his pleasant reminiscences of adolescence, "Being a Boy."

MY SUMMER IN A GARDEN. Boston, 1871.

The first issue has the Fields Osgood imprint and their monogram on the backstrip; later issues, similarly, have James R. Osgood & Co.

BACKLOG STUDIES. Boston, 1873.

The back of the "Contents" leaf is blank. The "List of Illustrations" is on the following leaf. In later issues the "List of Illustrations" is on the verso of the "Contents" leaf.

BEING A BOY. Boston, 1878.

The advertisements facing the title list this book as "just ready."

WARREN, CAROLINE MATILDA

(Dates unknown)

LIKE many other novels of the early nineteenth century Mrs. Warren's "Gamesters" is of interest only as illustrating a trend in the development of American fiction. When it appeared, extreme didacticism was on the wane, though still a powerful influence, and her work in consequence shows a slight tendency toward a more liberal treatment. Yet save for a few innovations, she too wrote "to regale the imagination and reform the heart."

THE GAMESTERS; OR, RUINS OF INNOCENCE. An Original novel, founded in Truth. Boston, 1805.

WEBBER, CHARLES WILKINS
1819–1856

CHARLES WILKINS WEBBER was born in Russellville, Ky. His was an adventurous spirit, and 1838 found him in Texas, a member of the Rangers. After several thrilling years on the border he returned home, and took up in sequence the studies of medicine and of theology. Finding these too dull he went to New York, secured a position on *The World,* and later became half owner of the *Whig Review.* Shortly thereafter he joined the Walker filibustering expedition to Nicaragua and was killed at the Battle of Rivas. Webber's stories, though crude, are spirited and picturesque. They have, moreover, the advantage of an entirely new scene of action. Though the school of "Wild West" fiction later established by Alfred Henry Lewis owed little or nothing to him, he was its true pioneer.

OLD HICKS, THE GUIDE; OR, ADVENTURES IN THE CAMANCHE COUNTRY IN SEARCH OF A GOLD MINE. New York, 1848.

TALES OF THE SOUTHERN BORDER. 3 parts. New York, 1852.

In a sense the existence of Part I is assumed, as the compilers have not as yet located a copy. The title pages of Parts II and III read respectively, "Tales of the Southern Border. Part II," "Tales of the Southern Border, Part III"—their wrappers, similarly, read, "The Texan Virago; or, the Tailor of Gotham; and other Tales" and "The Wild Girl of the Nebraska." There is reason to think that the title given on the wrapper of Part I reads, "Jack Tier; or, Shot in the Eye."

Also issued in one volume, New York, 1853.

WEBSTER, NOAH

1758–1843

WEBSTER, a man of such ceaseless and prodigious energy that even a partial list of his activities must of necessity be given in skeleton, was born in Hartford, Conn. He entered Yale before the Revolution, served during its first two years as a militia captain, returned to college in 1777, was graduated in 1778, and subsequently taught school for two years, during which he studied law. He was admitted to the bar in 1781, but abandoned practice to establish a classical school at Goshen, N. Y.

In 1783–85 he published his "Grammatical Institute of the English Language" in three parts. The revenues from the sale of part one—something like 62,000,000 copies of it were disposed of under the name of "Webster's Spelling Book" during the next one hundred years—were practically the sole means of support for his family during the twenty years in which he was compiling his "American Dictionary."

Having completed his "Grammatical Institute," he taught for a time in Philadelphia, established a paper in New York, and subsequently returned to Hartford to practice law. His consuming interest in language led to the publication, in 1806, of his "Compendious Dictionary," which he immediately determined to enlarge. After ten years' labor to that end he destroyed all that he had done and began anew.

From 1812 to 1822 he resided at Amherst, Mass., where he took an active part in the establishment of the new college. He spent the years 1824 and 1825 in England completing his great work, which appeared in two volumes in 1828, under the title of "An American Dictionary of the

English Language." It contained twelve thousand more words and forty thousand more definitions than had been compiled before, and was at once accepted as authoritative —the lineal ancestor of the "Webster's Dictionary" of today.

COMPENDIOUS DICTIONARY OF THE ENGLISH LANGUAGE. Hartford and New Haven, 1806. New Haven, 1806.

AMERICAN DICTIONARY OF THE ENGLISH LANGUAGE. 2 volumes. New York, 1828.

WELBY, AMELIA B. (COPPUCK)
1821—1852

MRS. WELBY, a native of St. Michael's, Md., married a Kentucky merchant and shortly after settling in Louisville began to contribute verse to the *Journal*. Her poems gained her an enviable contemporary reputation. They showed some genuine feeling, but they veered little from the conventional; and her eminent ranking as the best woman poet of the West was due in large part to the absence of other feminine versifiers whose work rose above mediocrity.

POEMS BY AMELIA. Boston, 1845.

WESTCOTT, EDWARD NOYES
1847—1898

WESTCOTT was born in Syracuse, N. Y., in 1847. After a successful career as a banker in his native town, he retired from active business, to spend two years in Italy, in search of health. While there he began a novel based upon his own previous experiences and observation, and having a sketchy background of local history. The book was rejected by several publishers, but, when it appeared, its sales exceeded four hundred thousand copies within a year. The encroachment of Westcott's disease denied him the privilege of seeing its complete success.

The strength of "David Harum" lies not so much in the story as in the original character Westcott has created. The shrewd, up-state, New York country banker is one of those rarities of American literature, a genuine type of American —as typical as Uncle Remus or Huck Finn.

DAVID HARUM. A Story of American Life. New York, 1898.

WETHERELL, ELIZABETH
(Susan Warner)
1819–1885

MISS WARNER, one of the leading exponents of sentimental fiction, was born and educated in New York City. Following the death of her father, she and her sister, Amy Lothrop, moved to West Point, where they remained in uneventful residence until Miss Warner's death. In 1851 she published "The Wide, Wide World," the novel which ushered in the sentimental era. Its success was instantaneous. Like "Uncle Tom's Cabin" it was promptly translated into several foreign languages, and save for the latter it became the "best seller" of the decade.

Without challenging the critic's distaste for this tearful type of girl's story, the fact remains that the emotional quality in the best of the sentimental novels still appeals to a vast audience. Their importance as factors in the development of feminine letters cannot be ignored. If this type of novel has any masterpieces, "The Wide, Wide World" is one of them. Miss Warner's next book, "Queechy," was only slightly less successful.

THE WIDE, WIDE WORLD. 2 volumes. New York, 1851.

There must be no indication of later printings on the title page. Previous bibliographies list this book as 1850, but careful search indicates the above date as almost certainly correct.

QUEECHY. 2 volumes. New York, 1852.

WHIPPLE, EDWIN PERCY
1819–1886

WHIPPLE, with the exception of Lowell the best American critic after Poe and Margaret Fuller, was born in Gloucester, Mass. He began contributing articles to the Salem newspapers at fourteen, and subsequently wrote for numerous periodicals. In 1837 he became associated with the Merchants' Exchange. His literary reputation is attributable to his essays, published in the *North American Review,* and to the lectures which he delivered at various leading colleges, etc. In 1872 he was appointed literary editor of the *Globe.*

Whipple wrote unhurriedly, with painstaking analysis, a fine insight and a refreshing wit—his faults, if any, lie in a too great emphasis on favored authors and an occasionally grating style. His work is still of value.

ESSAYS AND REVIEWS. 2 volumes. New York, 1848–49.

LECTURES ON SUBJECTS CONNECTED WITH LITERATURE AND LIFE. Boston, 1849.

The title of this book was later shortened to "Literature and Life."

CHARACTER AND CHARACTERISTIC MEN. Boston, 1866.

THE LITERATURE OF THE AGE OF ELIZABETH. BOSTON, 1869.

WHISTLER, JAMES ABBOTT McNEILL
1834–1903

WHISTLER was born in Lowell, Mass., and went from there as a cadet to West Point. He left before completing his course, and for a year or so worked in the Coast Geodetic Service. He then went to Europe to study art, took up permanent residence in London, and as his reputation grew became an exhibitor at all of the leading European galleries. Eventually he was recognized as one of the foremost etchers and artists of his day.

In addition to his artistic gifts, Whistler had a caustic pen. Probably no controversy has interested the entire artistic world more than his quarrel with Ruskin, which ended in a lawsuit. "The Gentle Art of Making Enemies," in part Whistler's trenchant reply to Ruskin's published views, is a classic of satirical wit.

THE GENTLE ART OF MAKING ENEMIES. New York, 1890.
Must bear the imprint of Frederick Stokes and Brother.

WHITCHER, FRANCES MIRIAM BERRY
1811–1852

MRS. WHITCHER, the wife of an Episcopal clergyman, was born in Whitesborough, N. Y. She was a contributor of humorous sketches to *Godey's*, the *Philadelphia Gazette* and numerous other periodicals. After her death her papers were collected into several books. They were popular in their day, the first volume running into twenty-three editions during its first two years; but their wit is clumsy and obvious.

THE WIDOW BEDOTT PAPERS, WITH AN INTRODUCTION BY ALICE B. NEAL. New York, J. C. Derby, 1856.

The Derby & Jackson imprint is later.

WHITMAN, WALT(ER)

1819–1892

WHITMAN was the second child of a Long Island carpenter, and received his early education in the Brooklyn public schools. At the age of thirteen he found intermittent employment in a printer's office, which left him time to read and to roam about the island, talking to all sorts of chance acquaintances. At seventeen he was teaching school and at twenty had started a paper. In 1847 he was made editor of the *Brooklyn Eagle*. Meanwhile, he mingled freely with the people—on the ferryboat or on The Bowery—gleaning all sorts of human impressions in his own way. The next year he took to the open road, visited the Middle States, and eventually journeyed down the Mississippi to New Orleans, where he found employment on a newspaper. He returned by way of the Great Lakes.

In the meantime Whitman had been a contributor to various publications, and in 1842 had published his first book, "Franklin Evans, or the Inebriate"—interesting because so markedly in contrast to any of his later work. In 1855 he published his *magnum opus*, "Leaves of Grass." Its appearance immediately raised a tempest of comment, and, though a few critics like Emerson acknowledged his genius, let loose a flood of personal abuse. In 1856, again in 1860 and several times later, he amplified and reissued it, but after the latter date he added little of importance.

During the Civil War Whitman served conspicuously as an Army nurse, and thereafter held a clerkship in the Department of the Interior. Meanwhile, in 1865, he published a series of war poems entitled "Drum Taps," quite out of key with his earlier work, and including some of his finest compositions, notably his poem on Lincoln, "O Captain! My Captain!" and "When Lilacs Last in the Door-yard Bloom'd." In 1873 he suffered a stroke of paralysis, and retired to Camden, N. J., where he continued to live in comparative poverty, the Mecca of the spiritual and reverent pilgrimage of an increasing number of converts to his greatness.

Whitman's two important prose works, "Democratic Vistas" and "Specimen Days," were issued respectively in 1871 and 1882. Both bear evidence of his range of vision and of profound emotional depths. His last poems were collected in "Good-bye My Fancy."

The controversy over Whitman still rages. By some he is reviled as a grossly vulgar egoist, a violator of all rules of poetic expression, a proponent of literary affectations; by others lauded as the great prophet of Democracy, the great exponent of a manly, vigorous Americanism. Each side has real basis for its contentions. There is much that is coarse and crude in Whitman, much that is incoherent; but there is also a strength, a sincerity, an untrammeled majesty and a knowledge of men and nature, and—in his descriptive poems which age has mellowed—a genuine beauty, which even his detractors are compelled to admit.

LEAVES OF GRASS. Brooklyn, N. Y., 1855.

The first issue has the portrait frontispiece on plain paper, gilt bands on the covers, gilt edges, marbled end papers, and lacks the eight pages of "Press Notices" at the end. Whitman's name is in the copyright notice. Line twenty, page 23, reads "abode" for "adobe." The portrait is on plain paper.

The second issue lacks the gilt cover bands and edges, and also the marbled end papers. The portrait is on plain paper.

LEAVES OF GRASS. Brooklyn, 1856.

Contains thirty-two more poems than the 1855 edition.

LEAVES OF GRASS. Boston, Thayer and Eldridge, 1860–61.

It has been claimed that the portrait must be on a buff tinted background, and vice versa, etc. It is probable, however, that all copies reading, "Printed by George C. Rand & Avery" on the verso of the title page are correct.

DRUM-TAPS. New York, 1865.

The first issue does not include the supplementary twenty-four pages with a separate title page—"Sequel to Drum-Taps," etc., containing, among other poems, "When Lilacs Last in the Door-yard Bloom'd" and "O Captain! My Captain!"

DEMOCRATIC VISTAS. Washington, 1871.

Whitman's name appears only in the copyright notice on the verso of the title page.

SPECIMEN DAYS & COLLECT. Philadelphia, 1882–83.

The first issue has the imprint of Rees, Welch & Co.

NOVEMBER BOUGHS. Philadelphia, 1888.

There is also a large paper edition.

WHITNEY, ADELINE DUTTON TRAIN
1824–1906

MRS. WHITNEY, the daughter of a Boston merchant and a resident of Milton, Mass., began her career as a novelist in 1857. Though by no means emancipated from the prevalent pedagogic tendencies, she was the first feminine author to abandon the extremes which had characterized girls' books of the "Lamplighter," "Wide, Wide World" era. She wrote with a real knowledge of feminine character, which she did not always insist upon idealizing, and with a sympathetic understanding of the juvenile point of view. Her books, in consequence, deserved their popularity. "Faith Gartney's Girlhood," her best known story, ran into at least eighteen editions within six years.

(Anonymous) FAITH GARTNEY'S GIRLHOOD. Boston, 1863.

WHITTIER, JOHN GREENLEAF
1807–1892

WHITTIER was born of Quaker ancestry in the town of East Haverhill, Mass. His education was of the most meager sort—the Bible and a few religious tracts to read at home, and two terms at the Academy, paid for out of his scant earnings as a shoemaker.

When a young man some of his verse attracted the attention of William Lloyd Garrison, then editor of the Newburyport *Free Press,* and with Garrison's assistance he secured a position on the *American Manufacturer,* a Boston paper. Following his father's illness, which called him home, he went to Hartford as editor of the *New England Review,* in which position he developed a growing interest in politics. His active participation in the abolitionist cause began in

1833, when he published at his own expense a pamphlet entitled "Justice and Expediency" and was sent as a delegate to the first anti-slavery convention. In 1840 failing health forced him to return to Amesbury, but he continued his political writings until the Civil War. The struggle over, he became as much interested in reconciliation as he had once been in abolition. His last years were spent serenely, revered and beloved by all the nation, and happy in the companionship of intimate friends.

For a time it was the fashion to criticize Whittier adversely, but he seems now to have recovered the ranking which is his due. That he often wrote in slovenly fashion and rhymed badly, and that he had not "the power to show the secrets of the heart and mind" he himself admits. But that he lacked depth of feeling is refuted by such poems as "Ichabod" (in "Songs of Labor")—a superb rebuke to Webster,— "The Barefoot Boy" (in "The Panorama") and "Barbara Frietchie" (in "In War Time"). Nor can there be any doubt about "Snow-Bound," the greatest farm idyl ever written in America—one of the greatest poems of its kind in all literature.

Whittier's humanity, his simplicity and sympathy, his love of nature and his homely understanding more than atone for any artistic shortcomings. "Snow Bound" called for something deeper and greater than cultural background.

JUSTICE AND EXPEDIENCY; OR SLAVERY CONSIDERED WITH A VIEW TO ITS RIGHTFUL AND EFFECTUAL REMEDY, ABOLITION. Haverhill, 1833.

Only a very few copies of this are known. It was reprinted by the American Anti-Slavery Society in New York, the same year, in two forms, the first of which ends with the poem "Decision."

POEMS WRITTEN DURING THE PROGRESS OF THE

Abolition Question in the United States, between the Years 1830 and 1838. Boston, 1837.

The first issue contains ninety-six pages. The first line of the second stanza on page 66 ends with "warnin."

Poems. Philadelphia, 1838.

Lays of My Home. Boston, 1843.

Voices of Freedom. Fourth and Complete Edition. Philadelphia, 1846.

This is largely a reprint of previously published work. The "Proem" and a few other poems, however, appear here for the first time.

Songs of Labor and Other Poems. Boston, 1850.

The Panorama, and Other Poems. Boston, 1856.

Home Ballads, and Poems. Boston, 1860.

In War Time, and Other Poems. Boston, 1864.

Copies with gilt top are apparently preferred, though without any evidence of priority.

Snow-Bound. A Winter Idyl. Boston, 1866.

The numeral 52 must appear at the foot of the last page of the text.

The large paper edition bound in white cloth is definitely a later issue.

The Tent on the Beach and Other Poems. Boston, 1867.

In the first issue the first line of the second

stanza on page 46 reads, "With quick heart-glow as one might meet."

WIGGIN, KATE DOUGLAS
1859–

Miss Wiggin was born in Philadelphia and went to college at Bowdoin. She later established the first free kindergarten on the Pacific Coast and has devoted her active life to juvenile education. Her stories for the young display a variety of fancy and a nice appreciation of the youthful point of view. "Rebecca of Sunnybrook Farm" (1903), is probably her best known book.

The Birds' Christmas Carol. San Francisco, 1887.

Timothy's Quest; a Story for Anybody, Young or Old, Who Cares to Read It. Boston, 1891.

WILCOX, CARLOS
1794–1827

Wilcox was born in Newport, N. H. He was educated for the ministry at Middlebury, but ill health forced him to spend practically his entire active life in retirement. Unfortunately he did not live to fulfil the promise of his early work. "The Age of Benevolence," however, is a poem of quiet strength and dignity, evidencing a keen sense of discrimination and a fine appreciation of the beauties of nature.

Remains of the Rev. Carlos Wilcox, . . . with a Memoir of His Life. Hartford, 1828.

"The Age of Benevolence. Book I" was separately published in New Haven in 1822; it is found complete in the "Remains."

WILCOX, ELLA WHEELER
1855–1920

Mrs. Wilcox's parents, originally Vermonters, had settled in Johnstown Centre, Wisc., when the future poetess was born. Following her marriage in 1884 she took up her residence in New York City. Her first book appeared in 1872, but she failed to attract attention until 1883, when she published "Poems of Passion." Of these she says– "I wrote of human nature as I found it," and, to a degree, she spoke the truth. The poems were accounted greatly daring, were roundly criticized and were even more widely purchased; but they are marred by an excess of sentiment.

Poems of Passion. By Ella Wheeler. Chicago, 1883.

WILDE, RICHARD HENRY
1789–1847

Wilde, the first author to give Georgia a prominent place in Southern literature, was born in Ireland. He came to the United States when he was six, was educated here, and in 1809 was admitted to the Georgia bar. He later served as State's Attorney General and was a member of Congress for several terms. In 1835 he went to Italy, and began a biography of Dante, which with his "Research Concerning Tasso" and the posthumous "Hesperia" comprises the bulk of his literary work.

About 1815 Wilde wrote a poem which he called "The Lament of the Captive." He read the lines to his family and a few intimate friends. One of the latter begged a copy for a "lady in Baltimore," and Wilde agreed to furnish it on the condition that it should never be published. Fortunately, the lady to whom it was presented, without thought of violating her agreement, gave it to a composer and the latter printed it anonymously as a song. The poem was copied everywhere, in newspapers, magazines and gift books, and was promptly claimed by numerous authors. Later, for amusement, Anthony Barclay translated it into Greek. Wilde was accused of plagiarism when it was finally published under his name.

By far the most interesting appearance of this poem is in a pamphlet by Barclay, in which he gives the different versions and the details of the controversy over its authorship.

> WILDE'S SUMMER ROSE; OR THE LAMENT OF THE CAPTIVE; AN AUTHENTIC ACCOUNT OF THE ORIGIN, MYSTERY AND EXPLANATION OF HON. R. H. WILDE'S ALLEGED PLAGIARISM; BY ANTHONY BARCLAY, ESQ., AND WITH HIS PERMISSION PUBLISHED BY THE GEORGIA HISTORICAL SOCIETY. Savannah, 1871. 70 pp.

WILLARD, EMMA C. (HART)
1787–1870

MRS. WILLARD, a descendant of the famous Puritan Thomas Hooker, was a pioneer in the field of feminine education. She began her career as a teacher in her home town, Berlin, Conn., but after her first marriage in 1809 and a short period of teaching in Westfield, Mass., established a boarding school in Middlebury, Vt. Five years later she enlisted the active support of Governor Clinton, and through his good offices received a subsidy for a school in Waterford, N. Y. In 1823 she removed this school to Troy, where it became known as the Troy Female Seminary, subsequently the Emma Willard School. Mrs. Willard traveled extensively throughout the States as a sort of educational missionary. In 1833, aided by the revenue from her numerous school books, she endowed a woman's college in Athens, Greece. She remarried in 1838, but secured a divorce in 1843.

Mrs. Willard wrote voluminously on the subject of female education, and was the author of numerous geographies, histories and atlases—and, curiously enough, of treatises on the circulation of the blood and respiration. She is probably best known for her poem, "Rocked in the Cradle of the Deep."

THE FULFILMENT OF A PROMISE; BY WHICH POEMS, BY EMMA WILLARD ARE PUBLISHED, AND AFFECTIONATELY INSCRIBED TO HER PAST AND PRESENT PUPILS. New York, 1831.

Because of unauthorized alterations of her manuscript Mrs. Willard made a strenuous effort, after its publication, to suppress this book.

WILLIS, NATHANIEL PARKER
1806–1867

WILLIS, the son of the founder of the *Youth's Companion*, was born in Portland, Me. He was educated at Yale, and during his college days gave evidence of the affability and personal graces which made his later life a series of social triumphs. He served his literary apprenticeship in Boston, but was later an associate and eventually a partner of George Pope Morris on the *New York Evening Mirror*. He visited Europe, and after traveling through the Mediterranean countries, Turkey and Asia Minor, as attaché of Embassy at Paris, returned to England, where he married the daughter of Gen. Stace, Commandant of the Woolwich arsenal. Following Mrs. Willis's death, he made another trip to Europe, this time in search of health. On his return to the United States, he remarried and settled down on his estate, Idlewild, on the Hudson—harassed during his later years by his own poor health and by his partner's insanity.

There is no doubt that Willis prostituted real talents to the demands of his audience. Judged by modern standards and save for his lines on "Unseen Spirits," a few humorous poems and a book of travel sketches, "Pencillings by the Way," he was the author of second-rate lines and superficial phrases. It was perhaps in part the price he more or less unwittingly paid for his social triumphs.

Nevertheless, in one respect posterity has treated him unjustly. In his lighter moments, Willis wrote a series of unusual sketches, published as "Dashes of Life with a Free Pencil." Many of these tales bear an extraordinary resemblance to the work of O. Henry—the same gift of expression, the same brilliant turn of ending, sometimes, though more unconsciously, the same constructive craftsmanship. For these at least he should be spared oblivion.

PENCILLINGS BY THE WAY. 3 volumes. London, 1835.
The first American edition appeared in New York, in 1844.

POEMS OF PASSION. New York, 1844.
Published as the "New Mirror Extra—No. 2."*

THE LADY JANE AND OTHER HUMOROUS POEMS. New York, 1844.
Published as the "New Mirror Extra—No. 3."

* The title of the "New Mirror Extra—No. 1" is "Sacred Poems."

DASHES AT LIFE WITH A FREE PENCIL. New York, 1845.
One volume cloth, or three parts in wrappers.
Later (1853), republished as "Fun Jottings."

WILLSON, FORCEYTHE
1837–1867

WILLSON was born in New York, but went to Indiana when he was fifteen, and remained in the West for the next twelve years—a part of the time in association with the *Louisville Journal.* His poems were few in number, but as a whole fairly well written, and one at least, "The Old Sergeant," won high praise from Holmes. Altogether he was probably the best Western poet of the Civil War.

THE OLD SERGEANT AND OTHER POEMS. Boston, 1867.

WILSON, ALEXANDER
1766–1813

ALEXANDER WILSON, the father of American ornithology, was born in Paisley, Scotland, where he published a volume of poems while earning a living as a weaver and peddler. In 1794 he emigrated to Philadelphia, and, after a short experience in copper-plate printing, a fresh attempt at weaving and peddling and a period of school teaching, made the acquaintance of William Bartram, the traveler, who first aroused his interest in natural history. Thereafter he devoted himself assiduously to ornithological work.

Wilson's later poetry was the direct product of his scientific journeyings. He loved nature and had the feel of it. In picturing the American scene simply, in its true colors, he pointed the way to emancipation from English poetic models.

The Foresters: A Poem Descriptive of a Pedestrian Journey to the Falls of Niagara, in the Autumn of 1804. By the Author of American Ornithology. Portrait. Newtown, Penn. July . . . 1818.

(WILSON), AUGUSTA JANE EVANS
1835–1909

Mrs. Wilson, one of the most bizarre figures of our literature, was born in Columbus, Ga., but moved to San Antonio, Texas, when a girl. She wrote her first novel at fifteen. After the Civil War she married a Mr. Wilson of Mobile, Ala. Her subsequent literary output was limited, in keeping with her own delicate health and her husband's wish.

Despite the critical verdict already rendered against her, Mrs. Wilson will be remembered for her strange "St. Elmo" —an extraordinary medley of sentimentalism, melodrama, pedantry and mad imagination. From a psychological point of view this novel was, and will remain, one of the most interesting books in American literature—by its extravagancies a unique document in the history of feminine emancipation. Coming when it did, its almost incredible sales are quite understandable.

St. Elmo. New York, 1867.

WILSON, ROBERT BURNS
1850–1916

Wilson, painter and poet, was born in Washington County, Pa., but early moved to Virginia, and later took up his residence in Frankfort, Ky. In every respect his work is genuine. He wrote with the painter's delicate sense of shading, a fine restraint, instinctive melody and, at times, with a touch of gentle wistfulness. Judged purely by literary standards, his best poem, perhaps, is "When Evening Cometh On." He is best known nationally, however, for "Remember the Maine," printed and reprinted throughout the country during the Spanish War. His output was small, but distinguished.

THE SHADOWS OF THE TREES AND OTHER POEMS. New York, 1898.

WILSON, (THOMAS) WOODROW
1856–1924

IT IS quite unnecessary to sketch the career of Woodrow Wilson save in briefest outline. Born in Staunton, Va., educated at Princeton and Ph. D. at Johns Hopkins, for a time a practicing attorney, Professor at Bryn Mawr College, President of Princeton, Governor of New Jersey, President of the United States—such, in headline, is the personal history of one who in the end became a most distinguished international character.

In its mastery of English everything he wrote is literature. But in the sense of larger values, his most important and enduring work, including his excellent "History of the United States," was in the field of government and politics. It falls, therefore, outside the present scope.

MERE LITERATURE AND OTHER ESSAYS. Boston, 1896.

WINTER, WILLIAM
1836–1917

WINTER, in his later days the dean of American theatrical critics, was born in Gloucester, Mass., was educated at Harvard, and in 1858 moved to New York and began writing for *Vanity Fair* and other papers. Later he formed an association with the *New York Tribune,* as dramatic critic, which continued for forty years.

Winter's caustic comments were often of a sensational nature. He viewed the increasing commercialism of the theatre with aversion, and he was at no pains to hide his opinion of its effect on theatrical art. As an essayist he was reminiscent of the leisurely manner of an earlier school.

GRAY DAYS AND GOLD. New York, 1891.
SHADOWS OF THE STAGE. 3 volumes.
(First Series). New York, 1892.
Second Series. New York, 1893.
Third Series. New York, 1895.

WINTHROP, THEODORE
1828–1861

WINTHROP came of a distinguished family in New Haven, Conn. As a young man he traveled widely in Mexico and throughout the West, gaining first hand knowledge of regions which he later depicted in several vigorous and entertaining novels. At the outbreak of the Civil War he enlisted in the Northern army, and, like Fitz-James O'Brien, almost immediately met a tragic, but glorious death.

Winthrop was among the first, perhaps the first, strong writer to adopt a breezy style. He was a gifted story teller, and in "John Brent," an excellent tale of the Western plains, entered a field until then almost untouched in fiction.

All of Winthrop's novels were published during the War, and were to a degree obscured by the larger issues of that struggle. Had they appeared at a more favorable moment, the freshness of his manner and materials might easily have gained him a larger reputation.

CECIL DREEME. Boston, 1861.

This, as well as "John Brent," "Edwin Brothertoft," and "The Canoe and the Saddle," was published posthumously.

JOHN BRENT. Boston, 1862.

Later editions are so marked on the copyright page.

EDWIN BROTHERTOFT. Boston, 1862.

THE CANOE AND THE SADDLE. Adventures among the Northwestern Rivers and Forests; and Isthmiana. Boston, 1863.

WIRT, WILLIAM

1772–1834

WIRT, a noted lawyer and orator, and a man of eminent talents and of fine accomplishments, was born in Bladensburg, Md., became an orphan at the age of seven, and was educated at a private school. Following his admission to the bar in 1792, he moved to Virginia, where he began a distinguished public career. He was assistant counsel to the Government in the prosecution of Aaron Burr for high treason, a member of the Virginia House of Delegates and Attorney General of the United States from 1817 to 1828.

His first book, "Letters of a British Spy," was a series of essays in the manner of Addison, purporting to be the letters of an English traveler to a British M. P. Though falling far short of their model in literary excellence, they are important as touching the life and regions delineated, and as the best work of Southern literature published during the very early eighteen hundreds. Wirt also wrote a life of Patrick Henry, which, though criticized for its inaccuracy, was widely read.

LETTERS OF A BRITISH SPY. . . . Richmond, 1803.

The second edition is so marked, and has a December (1803) date after the publisher's name, on the title page.

WISE, HENRY AUGUSTUS
(Harry Gringo)
1819–1869

WISE spent practically all of his life in the Navy. He was born in Brooklyn, N. Y., and after graduation from the U. S. Naval Academy served in the Seminole War, in California, and in the Mexican and Civil Wars—in the latter earning the rank of captain. He was the author of various sea tales and stories of adventure, notably a series of unique sketches in which, with a good deal of exaggeration, he pictured the life of our overseas fighting forces.

TALES FOR THE MARINES. . . . Boston, 1855.

WOOD, SALLY SAYWARD BARRELL KEATING
1759–1855

MRS. WOOD had the distinction of being the author of the first novel written in what is now the State of Maine. She was the daughter of Nathaniel Barrell of York, and the wife of Gen. Abiel Wood of Kennebunk. The part Mrs. Wood played in the development of the didactic novel is important, despite the fact that her work lacked literary distinction. In her book, "Julia and the Illuminated Baron," a tale of the French Revolution, she made what seems to be the first attempt of an American woman to write a "thriller." That didacticism was still a force, however, is evident when the inevitable moral lesson crops out.

JULIA AND THE ILLUMINATED BARON. A Novel. Founded on Recent Facts which have transpired in the course of the late revolution of Moral Principals in France. By a Lady of Massachusetts. Portsmouth, N. H., 1800.

This is the first novel written within the present boundaries of Maine.

WOODBERRY, GEORGE EDWARD
1855–1930

PROF. WOODBERRY was born in Beverly, Mass., and educated at Harvard. During 1878 and 1879 he was Professor of English at the University of Nebraska, and for the two succeeding years served upon the editorial staff of *The Nation*. He was subsequently literary editor of the *Boston Post*. In 1891 he became Professor of English at Columbia.

Woodberry's contributions to American letters as a scholar and critic are uniformly admirable. His still standard life of Poe was published in 1885. With the exception of this and of "Studies in Letters and Life," the larger part of his most distinguished work was done after the turn of the century.

THE NORTH SHORE WATCH: A THRENODY. (Cambridge), 1883.

Privately printed. The first published edition was Boston, 1890.

STUDIES IN LETTERS AND LIFE. Boston, 1890.

WOODWORTH, SAMUEL
1785—1842

WOODWORTH, a native of Scituate, Mass., after a short sojourn in New Haven, settled permanently in New York, where he quickly became prominently identified with the journalistic world. He was at various times associated with a number of publications, notably with the *New York Mirror,* which he and George Pope Morris founded in 1823.

Woodworth's present fame rests almost wholly on his authorship of "The Old Oaken Bucket." "The Champions of Freedom," a weird novel of the War of 1812, with a ghost-like central character in deification of Washington, is interesting only as a literary curiosity, and his drama, "The Forest Rose," long popular, is of secondary importance.

THE CHAMPIONS OF FREEDOM, OR THE MYSTERIOUS CHIEF, A ROMANCE OF THE NINETEENTH CENTURY. . . . 2 volumes. New York, 1816.

MELODIES, DUETS, TRIOS, SONGS AND BALLADS. Pastoral, Amatory, Sentimental, Patriotic, Religious and Miscellaneous. New York, 1826.

WOOLSEY, SARAH CHAUNCEY
(Susan Coolidge)
1835—1905

MISS WOOLSEY was a niece of President Theodore Dwight Woolsey of Yale University, and a resident of Cleveland,

Ohio, her birthplace. She devoted her life to writing poetry and books for girls. Her verse, though tender in expression and musical in form, is not distinguished. But her juveniles are to a considerable degree a fulfillment of Louisa Alcott's wish for more "lively" and natural girls' stories. She was one of the first to rescue this type of juvenile from the moralizing bog in which it had been mired so long. Her books, once widely read and popular, have not entirely lost their charm.

WHAT KATY DID. A Story. Boston, 1873.

There is one leaf of advertisements at the back, the first of which is devoted to Miss Woolsey's earlier work, "The New Year's Bargain."

WOOLSON, CONSTANCE FENIMORE
1838–1894

MISS WOOLSON, a niece of James Fenimore Cooper and a worthy pioneer of realism, was a native of Claremont, N. H. In early girlhood she moved to Cleveland, Ohio, and thereafter spent her summers on the Great Lakes. Later, her mother's health compelled her to reside in Florida. Following Mrs. Woolson's death, she traveled extensively in Europe, dying suddenly in Venice.

Miss Woolson was a frank disciple of Bret Harte. In her first book, "Castle Nowhere," a collection of stories of the Great Lake region, she displayed a grasp of realities quite foreign to earlier feminine literature. Like Harte she was never satisfied with the commonplace—was always searching for the glamorous or bizarre. She was equally at home with the short story or the novel. Her best short story work, "Rodman the Keeper," gave the North a true picture of the war-torn South, and her novel, "East Angels," a story of Florida, gives ample evidence of her sure touch. Yet in both cases an insistence on too riotous coloring barred the way to true greatness.

Castle Nowhere: Lake-Country Sketches. Boston, 1875,

Rodman the Keeper: Southern Sketches. New York, 1880.

Anne. A Novel. New York, 1882.

East Angels. A Novel. New York, 1886.

Jupiter Lights. A Novel. New York, 1889.

Horace Chase. New York, 1894.

ADDENDUM

THE recent monograph on Sarah Wentworth Morton by Emily Pendleton and Milton Ellis (University of Maine Studies, Second Series, No. 20), has come into our hands too late to permit the inclusion of William Hill Brown in the body of this work. The conclusions of these students, however, make it impossible to deny him a place.

BROWN, WILLIAM HILL
1765–1793

BROWN was a native of Boston and a neighbor of Sarah Wentworth Morton and her husband, Perez. In 1789, inspired by the much advertised "affair" between Perez Morton and Mrs. Morton's unmarried sister, Frances Apthorp, he wrote "The Power of Sympathy." As a literary effort it has no merit. Its importance lies solely in the fact that, with the exception of Hopkinson's "Pretty Story" (1775), it is the first attempt at fiction and the first novel written and published in America.

On the strength of the unsupported statement of Francis S. Drake "The Power of Sympathy" has generally been attributed to Mrs. Morton. The fact that she and her husband attempted to buy and destroy the entire edition would appear to be ample refutation of Drake's claim.

(Anonymous) THE POWER OF SYMPATHY: OR, THE TRIUMPH OF NATURE. Founded in Truth. Plate. 2 volumes. Boston, 1789.

INDEX